Bahá'í Herit

Never Be Afraid to Dare

Bahá'í Heritage Series

Never Be Afraid to Dare

The Story of 'General Jack'

Marion Elizabeth Jack

1866–1954

by

Jan Teofil Jasion

George Ronald • Oxford

George Ronald, *Publisher*
46 High Street, Kidlington, Oxford OX5 2DN

*A catalogue record for this book is available
from the British Library*

ISBN 0–85398–449–2

Typeset by Stonehaven Press LLP, Knoxville, Tennessee
Printed and bound in Great Britain by Biddles Ltd
*www.*biddles.co.uk

Contents

Prologue

The Pioneer
– for all the lovely ladies –

Ye are . . . the soft-flowing waters upon which must depend the very life of all men . . . the breezes of spring that are wafted over the world . . . Through you the countenance of the world hath been wreathed in smiles, and the brightness of His light shone forth.

Bahá'u'lláh

I

You will meet her anywhere,
the river, market, roadside, bus,
in Carcross, Nairobi, Liverpool, Duluth,
and the old girl will be smiling: she knows.
The sincere costume, the workworn hands, say little.
Satin or leather, the good, earnest face
belongs on a chocolate box, affirms,
could endorse nutritional causes on billboards
or in glossy magazines;
but she has far greater power
than Westinghouse or General Mills.
I warn you, she is dangerous.
In her bag there is a weapon
more potent than a gun.
If her lips move noiselessly

she is not litanizing her grievances
nor reading subway signs.
She carries more than recipes in her head.

II

It is fatal to speak to her,
no comment so mundane
she cannot bend it to her own design.
Chance a remark about the weather
and she may tell you of The Tempest,
leave you re-examining the roots of social unrest
and worrying about the fate of the House of Hapsburg.
She is not dismayed by headlines, calls them as her
      witness,
carries answers like neat balls of coloured yarn,
familiarly handled, spun of truth.
The mysteries are few and lives with them com-
      panionably,
sibyl or saint, mystic or madwoman,
in ready-made dress and sensible shoes.

III

She has faced it, reconciled it all,
the whole human struggle,
the journey from the cave,
the love and the ashes,
the song and the blood,
the suffering, the stillborn, the greed,
ordered, forgiven, reconciled it all.
Her compassion spans eras and epochs,
finds room for Luther King, Lenin and Lao-tse,

all our lost leaders,
sorted, accommodated like the memory
of good or wayward children she has known; finds room
for the Aztec, Ibo, Tlingit, Vietnamese –
she might be one of them.
Fashions in indignation puzzle her.
It did not come as news that black is beautiful
(may be herself black);
knows Eskimos (or is one);
calls the Kalahari Bushmen brothers;
counts the Maoris as friends;
would have saved the hapless
of Nagasaki, Warsaw, Buchenwald,
with her own body, if she could.
Long ago she wept and worked for causes
not then named,
knows symptom from disease
and is not resigned to evil.

IV

No, you do not imagine her authority;
dynasties might dissolve before it
or her concern melt mountains.
She is dangerous: she cannot be dismissed.
Your eloquent despair does not dissuade her;
The future is inestimably glorious,
and when one considers the life to come . . .'
You will want to hurt her, destroy her dream,
but her words hang like heavy golden pears
and she knows your hunger.
Even as you strike she heals you
and in so doing heals herself.
You may crush her but she will not die –

she yields like grass
and is as indestructible.
She knows what you defend;
many times a midwife, she understands rebirth.
Your credentials don't impress her; she tinkers with
  souls.

V

Do not accept the invitation to her home
to meet her friend from Adelaide, Ṭihrán, Kaduna;
they are conspirators and drink from the same well.
Her own certitude is baked
into the cakes she serves with tea
tasting of her own contentment
that leaves you crazed,
thirsting forever for assurance.
Be warned, she is dangerous.

VI

The moment is selected.
You will not see all heaven's angels,
all ancient good,
the very weight of history
rush to her support as she gathers breath
(her smile never more gentle) –
Have you heard the Message of Bahá'u'lláh?'–
nor will you know that God Himself
throughout all worlds
gives ear to your reply.

I tell you, she is dangerous!

Roger White

Introduction

This is the story of one Marion Elizabeth Jack, 'Jacky' to her friends, called 'General Jack' by 'Abdu'l-Bahá and 'immortal heroine' by Shoghi Effendi. Painter by profession, a pioneer[1] in the Army of Light by vocation. The story begins in the Maritime Provinces of Canada, tours the capitals of Europe, touches the Middle East at least twice, crosses the Continental Divide, meanders up the Yukon River and ends in the Balkans. It is not a story of brave deeds or fearless actions; rather it is the story of the courage to be.

The story is not complete. The ravages of time, the frailty of yellowing paper and the caprices of the human ego have taken their toll. For many years we have nothing, for others only a headline and for others a postmark stating 'she was here'. However, now and then we are surprised by a rich tapestry of detail woven with mirth and pathos, pain and faith. Wherever possible, I have let her weave her own tale, aided by accounts written by her contemporaries and friends.

Acknowledgements

Over a score of years have passed since I first starting seeking traces of Marion Jack, during which time many people have assisted me in a variety of ways. Owing to many moves, changes of abode and other circumstances, not all of the records have been kept. Apologies to all those I have omitted. Those whom I would wish to thank for their encouragement, assistance and in providing information are the following, without order of merit or alphabet: Mehmet Niazi, R. Jackson Armstrong-Ingram, Don Morris, Roger White, Bonnie Ellis, Mariam Rabbani, John Taylor, David Rendell, Nooshfar Afnan, Albert Ouimet, Moojan Momen, Marion Hofman, Ann Wilson, Mrs Marion Logie, Jane Lodge Smith, Ruth Cunningham, Randall Speller, Nora Blair, Mabel Garis, Mrs W. A. Logie, Dan O. Clemmer, Morna Partridge, Gaby Pelletier, Vera D. Lindley, Martha Shipman Andrews, Lewis V. Walker, Beverley Rennie, David Rendell, Will C. van den Hoonard, Eleanor Hutchens, Sophie Loeding, Becky Murphy, Ann Dodd, David Witherly, Dr Iain Palin, Graham Hassall, John Taylor, Christian Cimpa, Kenneth B. Moore.

The following institutions provided me with both needed material and encouragement: The Universal House of Justice; Bahá'í World Centre Library; Bahá'í World Centre Research Department; Bahá'í World Centre Archives; Bahá'í World Centre Audio-Visual Department; Ralph Pickard Bell Library, Mount Allison University, Sackville, NB; The New Brunswick Museum, Saint John, NB; Art

ACKNOWLEDGEMENTS

Gallery of Ontario, Toronto; United States National Bahá'í Archives, Wilmette, Illinois; Vancouver Art Gallery, Vancouver, BC; Annapolis Valley Regional Library; National Spiritual Assembly of the Bahá'ís of Alaska; National Pioneer Committee of the National Spiritual Assembly of the Bahá'ís of Canada, Thornhill, Ontario; British Library, London; United States Department of State. Library, Washington DC; National Museum of American Art, Washington DC; Newfoundland and Labrador Provincial Archives, St John's Newfoundland; Harriet Irving Library, University of New Brunswick, Fredericton, NB; Saint John Art Club, Saint John, NB; Archives of the National Spiritual Assembly of the Bahá'ís of Germany, Hofheim-Langenhain.

And last but certainly not least, the publisher George Ronald and its wonderful staff for their constant encouragement.

Preface

Several years ago I had the good fortune of being able to visit Sofia, Bulgaria, on my way to Greece. While there I took the opportunity to pay my respects to a Canadian lady from Saint John, New Brunswick. With the aid of a crudely drawn sketch map, I made my way on a lurching, noisy streetcar across the Lions Bridge and into the grey, drab northern districts of Sofia. As instructed, I alighted near the terminus and crossed the busy road dodging huge Škoda trucks and tiny Polski Fiats. Among a ramshackle collection of booths, sheds and corrugated iron buildings I found the flower kiosk and the path next to it as indicated on my plan. Following this muddy path through knee-high weeds, I soon came to a hole in a fence where somebody had removed the entire gate and so I passed through the rear entrance to Bulgaria's largest cemetery. The path continued past piles of broken granite and marble from monument carvers and there were heaps of decomposing flowers and wreaths along the way until it joined a wide avenue. Taking the turning left as instructed, I walked a short distance until I came to a low wall with a simple gate surrounding the small Sofia War Cemetery. Inside were row upon row of well cared for graves of the British and Commonwealth military from both world wars who had died in Bulgaria. Near the gate were some civilian graves and among these lay the grave of the lady who had spent all her life promoting peace, brotherhood and the unity of humankind. On that simple granite monument these words were inscribed:

MARION JACK
1866 – 1954

IMMORTAL HEROINE . . .
GREATLY LOVED AND DEEPLY ADMIRED BY ABDU'L-BAHA.
A SHINING EXAMPLE TO PIONEERS . . .
HER UNREMITTING, HIGHLY MERITORIOUS ACTIVITIES . . .
SHED IMPERISHABLE SPLENDOUR
ON CONTEMPORARY BAHA'I HISTORY
SHOGHI

I bowed my head in silent prayer and wondered what prompted this lady to leave her comfortable middle-class, tranquil and well-ordered life in Saint John for a city in the heart of the Balkans, an area synonymous with violence and anarchy. The text on the monument spoke of heroic deeds, courage and struggles but who really was this 'immortal heroine' and what were those 'meritorious activities' for which she was so highly honoured?

This book is an exploration of this 'immortal heroine' and her 'meritorious activities'.

Part One

1

Marion

1866–1894

Marion Elizabeth Jack, a descendant of Scottish and Loyalist[2] immigrants, was born in Saint John, New Brunswick, Canada, on 1 December 1866. The history of the Scots in Canada goes back to 1613, when Captain Argyle seized Acadia from the French in the name of James VI of Scotland (James I of England). Settlement began after Sir William Alexander received a charter from the king in 1621. The history of the early Scottish migration is associated with the Scottish regiments serving in the British army. In 1761 a Highland regiment garrisoned at Fort Fredrick (today Saint John). Most of the members of the famous 'The King's First American Regiment', victors of the Battle of Brandywine, settled in New Brunswick after the American Revolution. The aftermath of the Revolution saw a large influx of Loyalists, many of whom were of Scottish ancestry, migrating into this province: by 1843 there were 30,000 Scots in New Brunswick. Among them were descendants of people from the Highlands and Islands, the Lowlands and from Ulster. Many took up leading business and political positions, positions that were denied to them in their homeland, especially after Culloden and the enclosures.

Marion, writing to a Bahá'í whose wife was from Scotland, recalled that 'My great-grandfather was mayor (for life) of

Cupar, Fife and my grandfather Johnston was from the border counties.'[3] In another letter she again stated that 'Our grandfather Jack was Lord Provost of Cupar, Fife – a sort of lifetime post like mayor.'[4] In this same letter Marion remarked that her grandfather on her mother's side, Hugh Johnston, was the Marquis of Bute and Annandale, a title he abandoned when he came to Canada.[5]

Marion's grandfather, David William Jack, who was born in Cupar, Fife, in 1785, came to Saint Andrews, New Brunswick from the West Indies around 1800 'to seek his fortune'. The records show that in this he succeeded. The American Revolution had greatly increased the commerce that came through the Maritime ports and both Saint Andrews and Saint John greatly prospered in the post-revolutionary years. David William Jack was able to obtain a clerical position with a local trading firm. He proved himself so capable that he was later taken into partnership. He became a respected and well-established citizen of Saint Andrews and held the following posts: Gauger of Dutiable Articles and Tide Surveyor of the Port of Saint Andrews; Deputy Provincial Treasurer; County Treasurer; Director of the Public Grammar School; Commissioner of the Marine Hospital; and Quartermaster, First Regiment Charlotte County Militia. In 1810 he married Rebecca Russell Wyer (1788–1828) and they had nine children. Tragically, Rebecca succumbed to illness and died at the age of 40. Two years after her death David William Jack married Rebecca's sister, Mary Wyer, and they had seven children. Only nine of the 16 children survived infancy, such was the state of medicine in those days.

Marion Jack's father, Henry, was born in 1824, the eighth child of David and Rebecca. The lack of opportunity in Saint Andrews forced Henry to move to Saint John,

4

where he studied law for several years before obtaining a position with the Bank of British North America. During his service with the bank he lived in Saint John's, Newfoundland, for five years. Later he left the bank and took the position of general agent for New Brunswick of the North British and Mercantile Insurance Company. Around 1862 he also became the agent for the Scottish Union and the National Insurance Companies. Soon after 1865 he was appointed vice-consul of Spain for the colony of New Brunswick. He held all these positions until his death in 1884 and was financially well-established:

> The Spanish Consulate, up to the year 1877, was a particularly lucrative office. The Consul being paid a proportion of the fees collected, over two-thousand dollars were received during the year 1876, when two hundred and eighty vessels were cleared for Cuba alone.
>
> Soon afterward the substitution of bags for boxes caused a decline in the demand for sugar-box shooks, much to the disadvantage of the shipping and lumber industry of New Brunswick and of the Spanish Consul.[6]

Henry Jack married Annie Carmichael Johnston in June 1862. Annie was born in 1840, the youngest daughter of the Hon. Hugh Johnston, a noted Loyalist settler, and Harriet Millidge. Her health was never very robust and during her later years she became a complete invalid. Her son describes her as:

> A woman of great fortitude and deep Christian character, she bore her suffering with a calm resignation, cheered by the constant companionship of a devoted husband.[7]

Marion remembered that 'my dear sick mother always had

the Bible in her hands, or on the night table beside her bed'.[8]

Henry and Annie had six children: David Russell (1864–1913), Marion Elizabeth (1866–1954), Henry Wyer (1870–3), Malcolm Millidge (1872–6, died of spinal meningitis), Helena Mary 'Nina' (1875, died aged eight weeks) and Louisa Millidge (1875–1951). The death in infancy of three of their children was a terrible blow to the Jacks. Marion Jack also suffered from this trauma, as she recorded many years later.

When your dear mother was born, and the other twin died, the children in school told me that Louisa was sure to die too, so my heart was full of fear. I remember often running through Queen's Square in my haste to find out about her, and asking first thing 'Is Louie living? Is she well?' Maybe I have told you this. She was always gay and laughing whereas poor little Nina was sad and sickly – she soon gave up struggling to keep alive, poor wee mite . . .[9]

The Jack family lived on fashionable Queen Square, in what Marion described as 'a large home, with a dining room, sitting room, kitchen & butler's pantry on the ground floor and the second and third floors each had five bedrooms'.[10] In that same letter Marion described some of the social activities organized by her mother when she was able to:

Dear Mother loved society too, but was not strong enough to do much at it. She was the first in St John to introduce big tea parties, then called kettle-drums, but like dear grandmama she loved the relations and after the fire she introduced many to Mrs Jarley's Wax-works, and what fun they had. She had a stage made for the actors in the big double or triple window in the drawing room.[11]

Henry Jack was a sensitive and generous man, well-liked in the community. He is described by his son as strong, 'rigorous of active habits' and with a fine physique.[12] He was religious by nature and attended the Presbyterian church until he married Annie Carmichael, after which he attended Trinity Church and later St James Church in Saint John. When a branch of the Reformed Episcopal church was established in Saint John, Henry and his wife were among the strongest supporters. However, the movement failed for a combination of reasons. The church, built largely with the assistance of Henry Jack, was sold after his death.

Marion Jack remembered her father as being talented musically:

> Dear papa loved music dearly. He had a fine voice and sang in the choir once or maybe oftener. He played the flute and cornet, but had to give up the latter, as the lips could not adjust themselves to both instruments.[13]

Over half a century later Marion Jack vividly recalled her parents' struggle with the family's poor health:

> It was dear papa's delight to have guests, and one of his favourite verses in the Bible was about being hospitable . . . Guest after guest came to our mid-day dinner when dear Mama was unable to be present, or was away because of her poor health. The dear one was forced away by the doctors so often, in the cold and dreary winters. Science was little understood in those days, and who knows whether the science of diagnosing was either? How sick and tired she got of having to leave us. The last time before she passed away, she took dear Russell – but as he was a lad of 17 or so, she said, 'I prefer to die than go off again' and sure enough she got rheumatic fever (in November I think). I don't think she had much of a time the year she

7

spent in England with Aunt Louisa Bayard either. She had to leave your dear Mother, then a wee baby, as dear Malcolm had spinal meningitis. The M.D. said they would both die if she stayed, she was so frail after the birth of Louie and Nina, her twins. Her passing just about broke dear papa's heart. How often I have heard him sigh heavily as he passed her room, or as he came up the stairs. God was good to take him only two years after. Strong affection is not to be found so very often.[14]

An earlier tragedy struck the Jack family on 20 June 1877 when a disastrous fire swept through Saint John destroying two-thirds of the city. Henry Jack and his wife lost most of their valuables when their home on Queen Square burned to the ground. An eyewitness described the ferocity of the fire about half an hour after it began:

> Lower Cove was on fire, and the dryness of the houses rendered them as useless to withstand the blaze as bits of paper would have been. The huge blazing brands were carried along in the air for miles around, and whenever they dropped a house went down. The engines were powerless, and the fire-men, though they worked like heroes, availed but little. The wild, mad flames, now in sheets, now with a million tongues of angry fork-like columns, dashed against the wharves, levelling them to the water's edge, ripping up the pavements of the streets, and crushing houses out of existence in a single swoop. Nothing could be done. The leaping demon swept all before him. Hare's Wharf with its buildings bowed before the destroyer, and with a roar which thrilled every heart, and unnerved every man who stood there, the whole force dashed into Smythe Street and shattered every building flat.[15]

The fire continued for nine and half hours and left in its wake 200 burnt acres; 1,612 buildings at the centre of the city were levelled. Fortunately, most of the Jack family along with their servants were at their summer retreat 'Roseneath' at Gagetown, about 40 miles north of Saint John, when the fire broke out and only Henry Jack and his eldest son David Russell were in the city. The firestorm together with a lack of water made any attempt to save the home futile. A few possessions were removed from the house into Queen Square but some of these were looted by thieves and the rest burned when the fire swept the square. Only a few family heirlooms of silver were recovered and later a couple of paintings. Besides losing his home, Henry Jack's office building on Canterbury Street was also destroyed. Henry immediately started to rebuild his house and the family was able to move into their new home in April 1878.

After the fire generous amounts of aid poured into the stricken city from many sources. The North British and Mercantile Insurance Company donated $2,333 to the general relief fund. Henry Jack, as general agent for New Brunswick, would have been instrumental in obtaining this money.

Many years later when writing to a friend who had lost her home in a bombing raid, Marion recalled her family's experience of the fire:

> I may have told you that as a child our town was half burned up. My dear little mother & brothers and sister & I were in the country for the summer. No telephone, no telegraph. The next day my brother arrived in shocking condition, his oldest clothes & so on. He told us we had lost our home, furniture and everything, my dear little mother simply asked, 'Is your father alive & well?' Not a murmur or complaint, no regret. The fact that we were

alive overpowered all loss. This example has stood me in good stead to this time.[16]

Marion Jack's mother died in 1882 and her father died two years later on 28 October 1884 after a comparatively short illness.[17] Fortunately, the three surviving children had aunts and uncles to look after them and a bequest from Henry Jack's estate.

Very little is known of Marion's aunts and uncles. Some of them lived in England and Scotland, others in various parts of eastern Canada and Newfoundland. Only two aunts are mentioned in Marion Jack's papers, Elizabeth Neville in Newfoundland and Louisa Bayard in England (or perhaps in Scotland).

Marion's father's sister, Elizabeth Jack, married John Thomas Neville, the superintendent of public buildings in Saint John's, Newfoundland. They had four children.[18] At some time Marion Jack visited her aunt and cousins, accompanying her father. It is likely that she also visited them after her return from Europe between 1908 and 1910 and again in 1917.

More is known about Marion's surviving sister and brother. Louisa Millidge Jack attended the Edgehill Church School for Girls at Windsor, Nova Scotia, from 1891, the year the school was founded, to 1894 and received the gold star in 1893. Later she married Wilmot Hubbard and the couple settled near Fredericton, New Brunswick. Louisa became a devout Christian Scientist and remained so until her death in 1951.

David Russell Jack, Marion's brother, followed his father into the insurance business and later expanded into real estate. In 1884 he was appointed honorary vice-consul for Spain. However, he is better known as a writer, local historian and genealogist. The historical journal *Acadiensis* was founded and edited by him for over eight years, from 1900 to 1908. He also contributed articles to many newspapers and journals in the United States and Canada and wrote several monographs on the history of Saint John. He was very active in local civic affairs, serving on local commissions and societies, and for several years he served as an alderman. Jack's civic work and historical research did not go unnoticed and he was inducted into the Saint John Heritage Hall of Fame in 1998. It is believed that he was responsible for one, if not both, of the biographical articles about his sister Marion that appeared in contemporary biographical dictionaries.[19] Like his sister, he was a supporter and member of the Saint John Arts Club. He died at Clifton Springs, New York, in 1913.[20]

Very little is known about Marion's early life. One reference work, *The Canadian Men and Women of the Times*[21] states erroneously that Marion was educated at Edgehill, Nova Scotia, obviously mistaking her for her sister. Marion was in fact educated in a private boarding school in Quebec, possibly in or near Trois Rivières. In a letter to her sister, Louisa recalled that they were once taken on a trip up the Saguenay River to Chicoutimi by their father on their way home from Mrs Machin's boarding school in Quebec.[22] Marion's brother wrote to her in October 1884 while she was in Quebec concerning her father's illness.[23]

Marion probably received the standard finishing school education for girls. Afterwards she attended art classes in Saint John. In later years she was able to put three of the subjects she studied to very good use: French, music, especially the piano, and, of course, painting.

2

The Artist
1884–1907

Information about Marion Jack's career as an artist is very sketchy and is based mostly upon secondary sources. It is reported that she first studied painting in her home town of Saint John under John Hammond, RCA (1843–1939), and at the St John Art School and the Women's Art Institute, both in Saint John, New Brunswick. However, at the age of 20 and while she was still at school in Quebec, Marion was able to participate successfully in an international exhibition. A report of the International Forestry Exhibition, Edinburgh, held in July 1884 states:

> The Chief Canadian features of the Exhibition are such as received the following awards at the hands of the International Jury: . . . Commendation was also awarded to . . . Miss E. M. Jack, of Quebec, for hand-painted flowers of forest trees.[24]

The Maritime provinces were in the backwater as far as art was concerned in Canada during the 1800s and early 1900s. There were few art schools or institutes and few noteworthy painters. The region was also rather isolated from the main art centres of Montreal, Toronto and Boston. However, there was a special quality about the region's natural features and a physical beauty that attracted a few well-known artists. The sea, with its rugged coastline, picturesque harbours and busy ports, acted as a magnet. John Hammond, adventurer, traveller and painter, arrived in Saint John in 1880 and worked for a while with the photographic firm of Wm. and J. Notman. From 1884 to 1888 he travelled in Europe and painted with the American painter James Whistler (1834–1903) and painters of the Barbizon school. He returned to Saint John in 1888 and in 1892 assumed the directorship of the Owen's Art Institution. The next year Hammond moved with the Institution to the small New Brunswick town of Sackville where the Institution later became part of Mount Allison University. Hammond was appointed director of the School of Art at the University in 1907, a post which he held until his retirement in 1919. Hammond is best known for his paintings of the Saint John fogs, in which the yellows, pinks, oranges and reds of the sunsets are reflected in the sails of the fishing boats as they appear out of the mist. A study of Marion Jack's early paintings which still exist show that she was considerably influenced by Hammond.[25]

The Owen's Art Institution, which Marion attended, was one of the earliest art schools in the Maritime provinces. It was founded by John Owen, a Saint John shipbuilder and merchant who bequeathed a sum of money for the establishment of an art school. It was incorporated in 1884 and opened its doors in 1885 to 20 students. The next year 144 students were enrolled.

Marion Jack left Canada around 1890 or perhaps a few years later to continue her art education in Europe. It has not been established exactly when she attended art classes in Canada or when she arrived in England. In London she attended the Lambeth School of Art for several years. The Lambeth School of Art, founded in 1854, is noted for its association with Henry Doulton's pottery company. Among its students were well-known sculptors and illustrators, including Arthur Rackham (1867–1939). At Lambeth, Marion was taught by the landscape painter Walter Donne (b. 1867).[26] She first participated in a major exhibition in 1898 at the 72nd autumn exhibition of the Royal Society of Artists in Birmingham. This was a jury exhibition and must have brought a great deal of joy to Marion. She had three paintings selected for the show: two showed scenes from Rye and the other was a Venetian scene. According to the information in the catalogue, Marion was living at Delaney, Rye. A charming walled town, Rye is one of the ancient Cinque Ports on the southeast coast of England. Since there are no records extant from this period other than the exhibition catalogue, we can only surmise that Marion also must have visited Venice, always a mecca for artists. Three of her exhibited paintings from the period 1898 to 1912 depict Venetian scenes.

In 1899 Marion had four paintings selected for the autumn exhibition, all of them scenes of the Suffolk coastal region. No trace of these paintings can be found. Her participation in the Royal Society of Artists autumn exhibition continued in 1901 and 1902. The subjects reflected her new home, France.

In the late 1890s and perhaps as late as 1900 Marion Jack was drawn to Paris. The art scene in Paris at the end of the century was a turbulent, vibrant, ever-changing kaleidoscope of styles, schools and movements. Impressionism, with its concentration on light and nature, had given way to post-Impressionism, which was infused with a greater degree of permanence, and to Expressionism. These in turn

14

were followed by Fauvism, with its emphasis on pure colour, and Cubism. Art historians have given more or less precise dates and descriptions for these periods and have combined and divided them in order to more precisely define styles and developments. In truth, the vibrancy of the individual personality of the artist makes this task difficult. Many painters taught a variety of styles and combined and experimented with both new and old styles in their own works. This was one of the features that made the Parisian scene so exciting. Then there was the very Parisian style of art nouveau, which had the greatest impact on the populace, especially those using the Metro, which was opened on 19 July 1900.

J. Russell Harper in his masterful study *Painting in Canada* writes:

> The Parisian academies and art schools during the late nineteenth century were the mecca of every enterprising young Canadian artist. They crossed the Atlantic to join other young people from the United States, England, every continental country, and even the Orient. The hoard of students lived in left bank tenement rooms reached by seemingly endless flights of stairs. Many lived a bohemian night life in the cafes. They congregated by day at the state-operated Ecole des Beaux-Arts, at Julian's, Colarossi's, or a dozen other private academies set up to accommodate the overflow. After drawing and painting for long hours, they had an occasional momentary criticism from celebrated painters of the world's art capital.[27]

In her letters to her friends and relatives written many decades later, Marion occasionally mentioned her bohemian life style and it seems that the description given us by Harper also applied to her. A contemporary reference work states that Marion studied at the Académie Delacluse-Colarossi (formerly the Académie Suisse) for a short period.[28] Many famous artists studied at Colarossi during the first decade of the century. It is impossible to say with whom Marion studied, who she met and who she admired and modelled her work after. The fragmentary correspondence left to us from that time reveals precious little. However, from other sources we know that the students at Colarossi at this time were a very diverse group of artists, including Max Weber (1881–1961) from the United States; Amedeo Modigliani (1884–1920), an Italian painter famous for his nudes; the British-born American illustrator and poet Mina Loy (1882–1966); and Julius Mordecai Pincas, better known as Pascin (1885–1930), the Bulgarian-born etcher, illustrator and painter of Montparnasse and Montmartre. Did Marion meet any of these or speak with them, have coffee with them? Perhaps through an introduction from one of her teachers she rubbed shoulders with them during one of the Paris salons, exchanging a few words or more. Parisian art circles were vibrant, colourful and ever-changing affairs.

It is known that while in Paris Marion studied under several expatriate painters, including the American painter Charles Augustus Lasar (or Lazar) (1856–1936) who, though he specialized in portrait paintings, is best known for his landscapes; the Canadian impressionist Ernest Percyval Tudor-Hart (1873–1954); and the American Impressionist landscape painter Max Bohm (1868–1923), who taught her composition.

Little is known of Lasar and even less of his work, except for a small volume of instructions entitled *Hints to Art Students* and a note in a contemporary journal.[29] His best-known students were the American miniaturist Minerva

16

Chapman (1858–1947) and portrait painter Cecilia Beaux (1855–1942). Marion studied alongside both of these painters and corresponded with Minerva Chapman well into the 1940s.

Tudor-Hart, who was from Montreal, had an art studio in Paris from 1903 to 1913 and another in Hampstead, England, from 1913 to 1916. Some of his students included C. Anthony Long (1916–96), Annie Hilda Carline (1889–1950) and Owen Heathcote Grierson Merton (1887–1931), the father of the Catholic mystic Thomas Merton.

Max Bohm of Cleveland, Ohio, studied at the Académie Julien and the Ecole des Beaux-Arts. After completing his studies he stayed on in Europe, primarily in Paris and London, for the next 12 years before returning to the United States.

Marion studied and worked in Paris for the next six or seven years. She exhibited at the Paris Salon (Salon des Artistes Indépendants) in 1905 and 1906. The Salon des Indépendants was the name given to the annual exhibitions held in Paris by the Société des Artistes Indépendants, an association formed in 1884 by Georges Seurat (1859–91), Paul Signac (1863–1935) and other artists in opposition to the official Salon. There was no selection committee and any artist could exhibit on payment of a fee. The Salon des Indépendants became the main showcase of the post-Impressionists and was a major art event in Paris up to the time of the Great War. Marion Jack exhibited eight works at these exhibitions. All were landscapes depicting rural and coastal scenes, including one showing the canals of Venice.

Marion also exhibited at the Salon des Humoristes (between 1905 and 1907) and the Paris Salon of the Société Nationale des Beaux-Arts in 1906 and 1907.[30] This annual

17

exhibition was founded in 1890 by a group of artists including Auguste Rodin (1840–1917) who, among others, seceded from the official Salon. The Salon of the Beaux-Arts was a jury exhibition and it was considered a sign of recognition and accomplishment to have one's art selected for it. A well-known reference work of the period, referring to Marion Jack exhibiting at the Paris Salon of the Société Nationale des Beaux-Arts in 1907, stated:

> . . . 4 decorated panels recently contributed to the 'Nationale' attracted much attention, being noticed in *The Strand* and other publications . . .[31]

For the 1906 Paris Salon the jury selected for exhibition one of Marion's landscapes, two decorative panels and two decorative designs.

Writing to her niece in 1951, Marion recalled those early days as a struggling art student in Paris and Canada:

> . . . I got what I wanted most, fine lessons, and at last pictures in the Paris Salon, ten of them, some 'on the line' – after being refused a few times. Then when I returned, the Canadian Academy also turned me down. I just gave them one chance then I decided not to bother playing that game all over again. The game was not worth the candle . . .[32]

It was while studying in Paris that Marion first encountered the Bahá'í Faith and although she continued to paint and exhibit, it was the Bahá'í Faith that became her first love. After Paris, she not only exhibited but was active in art societies in London, Montreal, Vancouver, Toronto, her beloved New Brunswick, Chicago and other cities both in the United States and Canada.[33]

18

3

The Seeker
1900–1907

Marion Jack grew up in a home where emphasis was placed on prayer and the Bible and living according to spiritual principles rather than religious dogmas and ritual. Her father and mother were religious free-thinkers and were not bound by inherited religious customs. The influence of the home environment coupled with her experiences in the international art circles of Paris and London prepared Marion to be open to new ideas and concepts.

It was in Paris that Marion first heard of the Bahá'í Faith. Many years later in a letter to a friend in Budapest she briefly related that experience:

> When I first heard of the Cause in Paris, I heard of it as something 'queer'. This thought made me curious & fortunately I was led to someone, Mr. Charles Remey, who explained things so beautifully & reverently, that I found the 'queer' was something great & precious.[34]

Charles Mason Remey, an American architect and early exponent of the Bahá'í teachings in America and Europe, wrote a lively account of his first meeting with Marion Jack:

> My first remembrance of Marion Jack was when we were students in the Latin Quarter in Paris. She was studying

painting, and I architecture, and I used to see her in the Quarter along the boulevard on Mount Parnasse. In the Quarter lived a Mme. Philippe who kept a Pension where a number of girl students lived. Mme. Philippe gave dancing parties at infrequent intervals. It was at one of these affairs, a fancy dress dance, that I met Marion. She was dressed in a fiery red costume that she had made herself of crinkled tissue paper topped by an enormous 'Merry Widow' hat decorated with large yellow paper flowers . . . It was as we danced and sat out between dances that I told Marion of the Bahá'í Faith. She was, as many were in those early days, afire with the Faith then and there, all at once. Marion met the Bahá'ís, came to meetings in my studio and elsewhere, and that was the beginning of her belief.[35]

Mason Remey also recalls that in those early days the Bahá'ís did not have much literature:

> All that the [early believers in Paris] knew of the Bahai Cause was what someone had heard from someone else, and thus the word was passed on . . . we had very little real information about the Teachings. We depended mostly upon our faith and on our feelings rather than on actual information. It was a time, however, of great spiritual romance and adventure. The great religious fire of the Cause was uppermost in our minds. We all sang, as it were, a lyric Spiritual Song, and like all youth the adventure and the new outlook created a tremendous enthusiasm in our hearts . . . having so little [written literature] we were obliged to dwell largely on the emotional plane. Dreams and visions frequently made up to us our lack of actual knowledge.[36]

The year was 1900[37] and Marion Jack was 34 years old. She lived in Paris for about eight years from sometime before

1900 to 1908. She also visited Paris for extended periods when she was living in London before the First World War. While in Paris Marion fully participated in Bahá'í activities and did what she could with her limited resources to help spread the Bahá'í teachings:

> When there seemed to be no home for the Cause in Paris, that is in the students' quarter, I was moved to offer my wee room, in a few years when the Cause grew, Bahá'u'lláh found me the ways & means to have a big studio, – a thing I never dreamed of when I began in my wee place so humble & modest.[38]

Mason Remey provides a glimpse into those meetings of 1907:

> Marion Jack was in Paris that summer and we held meetings in her studio. With her were two English sisters by the name of Febris. They had been through the siege of Peking and had returned to Paris with a cargo of Chinese loot which they displayed and sold in a tea shop and restaurant they were running in the rue du Bac opposite the Bon Marche. I don't think these girls ever became Bahá'ís but they were very much associated with the friends and were more or less conversant with the teachings.[39]

The Bahá'í community of Paris during the first decade of the 20th century was mostly composed of English and American Bahá'ís, with a few Persians, Germans, Swedes and Canadians but not many French people. Activities were centred mainly on the expatriate community. This is illustrated by Marion Jack's description of one of her friends, Miss Wyman, an American Bahá'í:

How she worked for the Cause in Paris with only one book
– Phelps.[40] One person per week. Her hunting ground was
the Girls Club (American). And she fairly haunted the tea-
rooms for recruits. She was keen as Alma Knobloch[41] in
Germany, but so many she taught went back to America
so she could not see results, as Alma could.[42]

Another believer in Paris at that time was Louisa Mathew,
a young music student who later married Louis Gregory.
Marion wrote about her when they were both in Bulgaria:

> Louise too is a regular brick, perhaps few know her as I
> do, & I was a sort of nurse maid to her when she was
> struggling to get into the Cause years ago in Paris.[43]

Years later, writing to her friends, Marion would recall
those early days in Paris. These excerpts from four letters
provide us with a brief pen sketch of the Paris community
and Marion's involvement with it.

> Please give my love to Mrs Dreyfus Barney,[44] Miss Sander-
> son,[45] Mrs Scott[46] & Mrs Stannard.[47] I have never forgotten
> my happy days spent with these beloved ones of Bahá'u-
> 'lláh – in fact the early days in the Cause stand out most
> vividly as the most vital period of my life, when first as the
> Songster puts it 'God was trying to speak to me and I was
> trying to hear'.[48]

> Painting was my profession, and God called me to Paris
> to study, for it was there I learned of His latest Message
> through our fine and outstanding believer – there a student
> of architecture (Charles Mason Remey of Washington).
> He certainly was a fine soul and it was because of his fine
> clean life that I was attracted to know about the Cause. He
> was such an unusual man.[49]

22

I know you have a difficult time in Paris as I began my career as a believer there & held meetings myself before I went to spend my wonderful six months with the Beloved Master. It was through Mr Remey that I heard of the Cause & the first meetings I attended were up six flights. There I first heard Mrs Lua Getsinger.[50] I also heard her at Mrs Sanderson's home. One of our best pioneer workers in the student quarter of Montparnasse was an artist who had only the Phelps book. She visited the tea of the American Club every day almost & used to loan this book a week at a time to friends. I had the joy of being in Paris the first time 'Abdu'l-Bahá was there, and in London. Those were indeed wonderful days.[51]

Before I left Paris for good just before the last war there was such a cool wind blowing over the Cause there that I was glad to escape. Maybe it was the unfortunate heart affairs of the friends or the greater spirit of conventionality or an outside influence, one knows not.[52]

Paris was the first Bahá'í community in Europe. The first Bahá'í to visit Paris was Lua Getsinger, in 1898 on her way to the Holy Land. She taught the Faith to May Bolles,[53] who was then living in Paris with her mother. Later May was to marry William Sutherland Maxwell and move to Montreal where she would become the Mother of the Canadian Bahá'í community. She remained a close friend of Marion throughout her life. Before leaving Paris in 1902 May managed to establish a small but highly spiritually motivated community of Bahá'ís. The list of the early believers associated with Paris reads like a who's who of some of the most outstanding Bahá'ís of the century:

The first to believe was Edith MacKay,[54] and by the New Year of 1900, Charles Mason Remey and Herbert Hopper were next to follow. Then came Marie Squires (Hopper), Helen Ellis Cole, Laura Barney, Mme. Jackson, Agnes Alexander, Thomas Breakwell, Edith Sanderson and Hippolyte Dreyfus, the first French Bahá'í. Emogene Hoagg and Mrs Conner had come to Paris in 1900 from America, Sigurd Russell at fifteen returned from 'Akká a believer, and in 1901, the group was further reinforced by Juliet Thompson, Lillian James and the frequent passing through Paris of pilgrims from America going to the Master.[55]

To this group of pioneer Bahá'ís, most of whom Marion Jack knew or met, must be added Miriam (Mary Virginia) Thornburgh-Cropper, the first Bahá'í in the British Isles; Ethel Rosenberg, first English Bahá'í in England; Sara Louisa, Lady Blomfield, 'Abdu'l-Bahá's hostess in London; Mírzá Abu'l-Faḍl, eminent Persian scholar; Edwin Scott, English artist; Mary Hanford Ford, American art critic; William Sutherland Maxwell, Canadian architect who designed the Shrine of the Báb; Dr Edward C. Getsinger, American physician; Alice Pike Barney, American painter and mother of Laura Clifford Barney; Louisa Gregory, English believer active in America and Europe; Mary Basil-Hall, daughter of Lady Blomfield; Henri Kunklust, Swedish writer, probably the first Swedish Bahá'í[56] and others.

Thus there were many artists, architects and writers in the Paris Bahá'í group. During the first decade of the century Marion Jack, Edwin Scott and perhaps others from the community exhibited in the various salons, yet there is nothing to suggest that the members of the group exchanged ideas or notions about art. It was as if their careers and their beliefs occupied two different spheres.

From Paris the Bahá'í Faith was taken to England, Germany, Sweden, America, Canada and a host of other countries. France was the 'mother community' of Europe. There were at this time very strong links between the Bahá'ís of Paris and London and many travelled back and forth, spending a considerable time in each city. Marion Jack was one of these, travelling to such an extent that it is difficult to know where and when she lived during that period. She also travelled to Canada on several occasions while living in Europe.

There is very little information about Marion's journeys to Canada or what she did there. A letter from Dorothy C. Cress written in 1969 gives some clues:

> Probably Marion Jack was the first person to introduce the Faith to St John & maybe to Fredericton as I think she had a sister living there. We met her in Paris about 1908 or 9 so it must have been before that she spoke of it in St J. I remember her saying that her family thought she was crazy. Did you know that Abdul Baha called her (Jacky) General Jack? I think she amused him. She was such a dedicated Bahai and her whole life was given over to teaching people mostly thru living the life. She did give 'chalk talks' – making sketches of the Holy Places & often another person would give the talk. She was living here in Eliot[57] when my family came after my father retired so we saw a lot of her and loved her very much. She also visited us in St John and gave her chalk talks there, I remember.[58]

4

The Teacher
1908

The dream and wish of every Bahá'í in those early days of
the 20th century was to go on pilgrimage to the Holy Land
and to visit the Master, 'Abdu'l-Bahá. The Holy Land was
at that time under the rule of the Ottoman Empire and
'Abdu'l-Bahá was still a prisoner and an exile, living under
what would be today termed house arrest. Enemies of the
Faith of Bahá'u'lláh abounded in the area. Pilgrims came
only at the special invitation of 'Abdu'l-Bahá.

In 1907 Mrs Edith Sanderson, an American living in Paris,
returned from a visit to Acca & the prison city & told us
that Abdul Baha's daughters were in need of an English
teacher. Miss Anna Watson[59] was first invited to go as such.
She was obliged to refuse as her sick mother needed her
in America. Then I was asked. I could not refuse because
I had long desired this visit but I did say that I would stand
aside if a real teacher could be found, for although I had
taught a little painting my experience in teaching English
was nil. No one who could teach was then free to go so it
fell to my lot to have this, the greatest & most blessed
experience of my life[60] and early in 1908[61] I landed on
the shores of Haifa in company with two lovely Bahai
friends[62] from California.[63]

Marion Jack seemed to fit into the routine of the household and became part of the family. Sometime during the first two weeks of her stay a special relationship developed between herself and 'Abdu'l-Bahá, a relationship greatly enhanced by their sense of humour and joviality and by Marion Jack's deep spiritual certitude.

> With a merry twinkle in His eye He would ask Miss Jack how she liked being on the roll of prisoners . . . When she answered that she would like to be written down as 'the woman who had just found her freedom', He laughed with the rest, and was highly pleased that she responded to Him in the same tone.[64]

Marion's duties as a teacher were not strenuous, the children coming to her only in the morning, so the afternoons she devoted to her painting.

> I so longed to paint the portrait of the Master, but at that time He seemed averse to any such proceedings, so dear Rhua Khanum[65] suggested that as I could not paint Him I could paint the places which He frequented. One day I saw Him at prayer in the little garden on the side of the house[66] away from the sea, so I did a little sketch of this spot including the little garden or summer house where He kept His prayer rug. On the wall in the room of the Greatest Holy Leaf[67] was a view of the sacred shrine of Baha'u'llah as seen from a distance under a pine grove. The Beloved suggested my painting this view, as He said it was the only view in the world that would help people to be spiritual. The first painting I did of it was given to Him at His request. I told Him all my sketches were His if He desired them, but He said He only wanted that scene. Later when dear Mrs Rosenberg of London, a devoted friend of the Cause, one of the most active and very first

27

of the pioneers there, sent us some Illustrated London News, I copied the portrait of the Shah of Persia from one of the numbers and the Beloved liked it and gave it to the Persian Consul. He was always so interested in my work, enquiring what I had done or was doing. This was gratifying since the family did not seem to care for it. Repeatedly He would say, 'Good Painter Jack, Good Painter Jack.' This seemed to put new life into my efforts. The family, however, encouraged me to do a painting of the Prison[68] which was very close to us so fortunately there was a good view of it from the window of Tuba Khanum's[69] room, as I never could have sat out on the ramparts just outside the window without exciting suspicion. In those days the prison was in a bad state of disrepair . . . I remember one day Him sitting at the window and taking off His fez rubbed His head. It was the first time I saw that splendid head without the turban and I was so struck with its beauty and symmetry that I breathed to myself a greater longing than ever to paint His portrait. He glanced up and though saying nothing I felt as if He were letting me know that He preferred me to think more of spiritual and less of material things. But how could I, a lover of the beautiful, help admiring that most superb head I had ever seen.[70]

Mason Remey states that on one occasion Marion Jack went to the House of 'Abbúd, where pilgrims sometimes lodged, to paint from there the lighthouse with Mount Carmel in the distance.[71] In that closely-watched society, Marion Jack could only paint landscapes from behind heavy latticed windows.

The household gravitated around 'Abdu'l-Bahá. His all-embracing personality endeared Him to everyone. Marion Jack speaks of Him with much devotion:

Such a saintly man I have never expected to meet. Such a kind loving unselfish being I had never expected to meet.

Words fail one in speaking of this Great One . . . Whenever
anyone heard His wonderful voice in the court or in the
garden there was a rush for the windows. It seems as if
the family, servants or guests could never see enough of
Him, and I was just as keen as anyone else. It was as if just
catching a glimpse of this heavenly being was like a
benediction.[72]

'Abdu'l-Bahá's generosity was, it seems, boundless and His
caring hands reached all who were in need, believer or non-
believer, rich or poor, friend or foe. The annals of His actions
are replete with such examples of His giving, His pure love
and His gentleness. Marion Jack wrote of one of her
experiences while living with the family of 'Abdu'l-Bahá.

They remind me of my happy days when in the holy
household at Akka, and the family were getting modest
garments for spring & the Blessed Master said I must also
have a garment or two, so the goods were brought around
from the store of His brother-in-law for our selection. He
always thought of everything for everybody, even sending
pocket money to the sister of Leticia, the little children's
governess who lived at home and could not earn for
herself.[73]

Abdul Baha's life as I saw it day in & day out for about six
months was one of absolute selfless beauty. He slept little,
he ate sparingly; he would not accept of a multiplicity of
garments. If his wardrobe contained more than one it was
immediately given to the poor. He loved them, as if they
were his flesh & blood children, and they adored him.
Every week on Friday morning they came to the gate and
he lovingly went out to talk to them and to help them
from his own little store which he and his family had
saved from their own frugal living. They were of a

princely family, but never allowed their tastes to become in any sense luxurious. Even when presents of silken material were brought to them as gifts they gave them away, lest their example would lead others to strive to assimilate what was beyond their means.

The Governor of Akka,[74] a very fine upright Mohammedan, was one of Abdul Baha's most ardent admirers. He called frequently & asked humbly for advice from the one whom he recognized as being infinitely his superior. His family too had great admiration for the family of Abdul Baha and came often to call, also we went to them to pass evenings being led through the dark and narrow streets by attendants carrying lanterns. Coming from the well lighted western world this was indeed symbolic of the state of the material degradation of this little prison city. The youngest daughter of the Governor sang and danced for us while the elder sister played a sort of guitar and others beat time on little drums of terracotta & parchment. The elder daughter was particularly enraptured with Abdul Baha's youngest daughter, and one day when Monever Khanum[75] appeared in a simple little grey cotton gown this young girl was so lost in admiration of it that upon our next visit, I saw a similar one hanging in the cupboard. One could not but feel that imitation is the sincerest flattery.

Many Syrian & Arab visitors to the family of Abdul Baha had all sorts of fantastic tea gowns which they displayed when removing the outer garment of black then almost universally worn by all but the peasant class in those days in the orient, and yet the Governor's daughter preferred to copy this little simple robe which was made of what we then used in America as lining cotton, black on one side and grey on the other, because she loved and admired the sweet & gracious young girl within the robe.

In Acca there were no hospitals, no soup kitchens, no charitable institutions. Abdul Baha was the one vitality interested in the needs & wants of this dreary unhealthy town. Then when people were consumptive the members of the family shrank back in fear from them. These were Abdul Baha's special care. He arose very early in the morning, and when the poor were sensitive about accepting his attention he quietly slipped a basket or bowl of food into their dwelling, for the doors were often not locked, in fact an Italian lady told me that the only time they locked their homes was when the European gypsies came to town. He also helped other missionaries, all were servants of God to him, whether in service as Protestants, Catholics or Mohammedans. So when they came to him he helped them. I saw a loving letter of a Protestant missionary who had been his neighbour. It was filled with loving gratitude for Abdul Baha's kindness & help. He said never in his life could he ever forget the days when they had lived side by side and that he would never cease to pray for his beloved friend.[76]

All of the men of the town or most of them adored the Beloved and every morning after prayers and meeting with the Persian and other believers in the men's quarters on the ground floor he came up to the side of the house, and there all were free to come to Him, rich and poor alike. The Governor of Akka, a good and devout Mohammedan, called frequently for he not only was very fond of the Master, but like others valued His advice on all matters. So often it was ten at night before the Beloved One had His little supper which the Greatest Holy Leaf his dear sister would try to keep warm on the brazier in her room, and by the way that room was open for all in the household. Guests were received in the tea room but all the family and servants of both sexes were free to come to this haven of refuge at any time. Part of the room was higher than the rest and the modest & humble generally sat on the step where the division came. All around the windows was a raised seat with cushions and the family usually sat there. At times the Beloved One came there too . . .

It was this room that the children flocked to. And I shall never forget our beloved Guardian[77] when as a little boy home for his holidays from the Monastery school on Mount Carmel[78] was graphically describing to her whom he so loved all his experiences during his absence from her, and she loving him equally seemed to hang onto his words. He stood on the bed and emphasized his tale with the gesticulations he had probably caught from the French in the monastery. It is a sweet picture often before me.

And speaking of the beloved Guardian I may tell you that these visits were the joy of all the young people as well as for the older members. For days before his coming there was an excitement in the air and great preparations. Then when he came he took hold of himself and with his splendid initiative kept the ball rolling and the household amused and entertained during his stay.

As there was a dramatic element at the Monastery School so he felt there should be in the holy household, and he drew up a poster which was placed in the hall. I never saw the theatricals but I can imagine that they were stage-managed. Then he held a banquet or feast rather in the servants quarters for all the young people, and I am told it was beautifully arranged with little paper napkins and flowers at each place. I wish I could remember more about those delightful but fleeting visits. I only know that they meant everything to the little people, and I am sure to his dear mother[79] and the Beloved and to the Greatest Holy Leaf.

One of his cousins and I hit it off very well though we could not then hold much converse. He was only about four years old. He would knock at the door and say 'Zelle Jack singlish? singlish?' He had learned this from the others, before that he had looked at me with disgust because I could not understand him. He and his little cousin Hassan[80] would hunt in pairs and often came in to see what I was up to. I could not understand why he seemed so happy to scuff around in grown folks rubbers. It seems he thought he was grown up with them on. Another cousin not more than two and a bit, but less than three was a great raconteur and the bigger children were very pleased to listen to her romancing. One day they said that she said 'and Abdul-Baha beat her and beat her', this was a great joke as of course the Beloved never beat anyone in His life except the slaps on the back to help dearest Monever Khanum to forget her sadness and fear for Him. Another time she was found washing Abdul Baha's shirt. She said when asked what she was doing, 'But he told me I might' – She loved to wash the glasses in the tea room too, a regular little house-keeper. I can see her now traipsing through the house calling in her husky baby voice, 'Aji Atoom Aji Atoom'.

The children were all sweet-natured, never once did I see any sign of teasing or quarrelling. The only time I ever saw anything but calm was once when one got his sister to hold a little cotton sunshade while he beat it to pieces, perhaps he had been provoked and took it out on the sunshade, who knows.[81]

Marion Jack was concerned about her ability to teach English properly to her charges:

> Those were glorious days for me but my dear pupils I fear did not profit much for I am certainly no born teacher and felt my want of capacity. But how I longed to have them progress so that they might be of more assistance to the dear Master in interpreting and in so many ways . . .[82]

One of Marion's students who did some translating for 'Abdu'l-Bahá was His daughter Munavvar Khánum. Marion and Munavvar Khánum became good friends and Marion later recalled several adventures they had together.

> Sometimes in the afternoon we drove to the Sacred Shrine.[83] On one of these drives dear Monaver Khanum told Isphendiar[84] to drive to the top of the mound where Napoleon had placed his guns to get a better shot at the fortress. It was a bit steep and the poor horses made a great fuss over the effort, neighing lustily. One moonlight evening dear Monaver Khanum said, 'Let us take a drive on the sands and see the moonlight.' This was a unique experience and was not repeated, probably because the carriage was stopped at the gates while the guards examined it thoroughly. Probably to see if we were trying to help Abdul Baha to escape. So the next moonlight evening we just sat on the wall.[85]

At this time the Ottoman Empire, known as the 'sick man of Europe', was crumbling. Deceit, treachery, lies, superstitions and self-aggrandizement were the hallmarks of the bureaucracy and government. In 1901, after a period of a more liberal regime, 'Abdu'l-Bahá was once again restricted in His activities owing to the machinations of the enemies of the Cause. In the winter of 1907 a second Commission of Inquiry arrived and stayed several months. It was there at the time of Marion Jack's visit, for she wrote about the effect that the Commission of Inquiry had on the Holy Household:

> . . . this too was the spot where later He received the beautifully clad deputy of the Governor General of Syria who offered him a much greater liberty than he had hitherto enjoyed in return for a big sum demanded of him. From the window of the room of the Greatest Holy Leaf we saw the Beloved gesticulating vehemently so when he came upstairs a little later we asked what had been the matter

since the Master was always so calm and poised. He told us saying, 'I told him the Governor could do as he liked with me, but that I never either gave or received bribes.' This took place near the end of my stay when the whole town was alive with drastic rumours as to what should be the fate of the Beloved. They said that he should be taken and hanged at the gates of the city or taken to sea and drowned or other horrible things should be done to him, least of which was a further exile, probably into Tripoli[86] where [we] should have to travel on the backs of camels. The Master who was even more gay than usual at this time asked me what I should do in such a case? I replied that I should go with them wherever they went. For some reason or other I never felt that anything dreadful could ever happen to these wonderful souls, but some of the family, particularly dear Monever Khanum the youngest daughter who looked after the Master was not so sanguine in fact the dear little soul looked so pale and sad that Abdul Baha used often to slap her on the back. His method of putting life into her. He used to frequently make jokes or tell funny stories at this time to cheer them up. He certainly was indifferent himself as to these threats. No doubt he longed to be free from this terrible imprisonment and deprivation which he had undergone since he was a little boy, but he could not bear to see others pass through the sufferings he had endured . . .

Once the sister of Zia Bagdadi's wife Zinat[87] said to me, 'Do pray Miss Jack that we shall never be separated from the Master', and Isphendiar the coachman had the same request. And you all know how hundreds and thousands felt about it when he passed. His great love for all humanity left love in their hearts for him.

To return to more prosaic things. I was told to put away all my letters and some I felt I wanted to keep I gave to one of the believers, whether they were buried or what I do not know but I never saw them again. But the new mails kept coming bringing requests begging for news of the Beloved and as time went by there was quite an accumulation on my writing table, when one day one of the little maids came running to me saying, 'A man has come to search the house.' I looked with dismay at my letter strewn table. I glanced at the window wondering if I could throw them out, but as soldiers from the barracks passed by that way en route for other quarters I knew that was worse than holding them there. It suddenly came to me that I could hide them on my person, and having on a double breasted sweater I opened it up and bundled all I could into that and putting a shawl over my head and body I went into another room and seated myself on a rocking chair bending over as if I were as old as I am now. It turned out later that my alarm was wasted as the man sent to look through the house was one who loved the Master and who barely came into the hall and humbly apologizing for his intrusion he said he just wanted to get an idea of the place in case he should ever think of taking it for a residence himself. This it seems the officials are free to do. Of course he had no such thought, but being sent he had at least to come in so anyone watching him could say he had been doing his duty.[88]

Marion also states that at this time an Italian official or consul placed a ship at 'Abdu'l-Bahá's disposal to carry Him to safety, which He refused.[89] Charles Mason Remey, who was briefly in Acre in 1908, relates that sentries were posted outside the House of 'Abbúd.[90] In July 1908 the Young Turks revolt resulted in the freeing of all political and religious prisoners, including 'Abdu'l-Bahá. Marion Jack, however, does not relate many of these events. She, like the other ladies of the household and perhaps most of the other Bahá'ís, had to stay indoors during the most troublesome periods and was not privy to all the information concerning the political motives and actions of the officials in Acre.

There were not many western pilgrims at this time. Mention has already been made of Helen S. Goodall, Ella Cooper and Charles Mason Remey. Marion Jack's notes reveal that Mrs Stannard also came to the Holy Land at this time. The Bahá'ís came from a wide variety of religious backgrounds and spiritual experiences, many unconventional, and as Marion Jack relates, Mrs Stannard was not an exception.

Not long after I got to Akka, but shortly after the authorities became more strict, one day a lady arrived without warning from Haifa. This was Mrs Stannard from England. The Beloved said she ought not to remain but he could not allow her to leave without an interview and a dinner as a nine mile drive is quite tiring so while the meal was preparing, with my youngest pupil Monever Khanum as interpreter Mrs Stannard and I had the joy of being with the Master over an hour. She told him that she had had such severe experiences in her search after Truth and in psychic matters that her faith had been sadly shaken, in fact she felt she had almost lost confidence in people because of these sad events. I took no notes but I can never forget the gentle loving treatment the Master gave her. He seemed then just like the All-Wise Physician dealing with a very sick patient. It was such a privilege to have been present that day that I cannot forget it. Then he told her to read the words of Baha'ul'llah, the Hidden Words.[91] She like a rebellious child said, 'I have read and read so much that I don't feel I can read any more.' He said, 'Just try, try for one month and see how you will be helped.' Also he said, 'I want you to return to the West.' Her idea had been to live in Eastern countries because of misunderstandings and false reports in the West. When he left the room she said to me, 'Abdul Baha advises me to return to the West but I am not going to do so.' After the meal she drove back to the German Hotel in Haifa and waited there for permission to return to Akka. About a month or more later the Master sent me to see her and to tell her to dress in the Persian covering of his niece when she came back with me. It was funny to see her, because she was so slim and her manner of walking was so different from the graceful but slow movements of the dear ladies of the holy household. Anyway she had a very lovely visit this time with Abdul Baha, but nevertheless she still remained obstinate & was just a little eager as before to return to the West. The next visit however was quite other. The Hidden Words had done their work and the dear dame was like a changed being. This time she stayed three days and had wonderful talks with the Master, sometimes he would pace up and down the room while answering her very pertinent questions. When she left he said something to me about having given her what she was asking for. I said, 'Oh Master she is a very changed woman from the one who had first come to you.' He said, 'Yes but I worked very hard over her, very hard.' Doubtless he had also prayed much, perhaps when he was pacing the floor. Dear Mrs Stannard is a very intelligent woman and later at the World Congress of Nations in London[92] which was attended by American friends and big meetings were held for the Bahai Cause it seemed to me that of the speakers she best set forth the real purport of the Cause and in the clearest manner. No doubt the Beloved foresaw this, and realized that this woman was a woman worthy of his effort. Although I am sure he would have done the same for a much humbler person so great was his loving heart.[93]

Of the Persian Bahá'ís who were at this time in Acre, other than the family and the servants of 'Abdu'l-Bahá's household, Marion Jack only mentions Ḥájí Mírzá Muḥammad-Taqí-i-

Afnán, the builder of the first Bahá'í House of Worship in Ashkabad, Turkmenistan, who came to the Holy Land in 1907, and Ḥájí Mírzá Haydar-'Alí, an early believer and companion of Bahá'u'lláh, known to western pilgrims as the 'Angel of Mount Carmel', of whom Marion was very fond. An isolated sentence reveals something about Marion's relationship to the Faith and to her beloved Master:

> I told the beloved I was like Diogenes with a lantern, and no doubt our steps were guided.[94]

Marion's departure from the Holy Land was a very painful experience which she always remembered. In a letter written in 1948 she described those moments.

> Did I tell you that when I first got to Akka, some dear Persian & other friends were leaving there. Their grief was severe. In the pride of my heart I said to myself 'Well that is something I certainly will not do. How could I grieve the Beloved with my sorrows.' Well, to make a long story short, when my turn came to leave Him, I started weeping so much that I was a perfect fountain of tears. Nor could I often keep them back. It was awful, but it taught me a lesson not to be so cock-sure of myself on what I could or could not be. I shall never forget the miserable show I made of myself in the presence of a whole room full of the Holy family and friends when He told me before them all how I must be a comfort for the sorrowing and all sorts of lovely things I must be. My own handkerchief was wringing wet, and I believe it was sweet Monaver Khanum who gave me hers to fill with tears too – finally I was forced to get up & run to my own room I was so overcome. Imagine how much of a ninny I made of myself! That condition went on for days. The day before I left He sent me to say good bye to the Governor's daughters, and how

they stared at my miserable blotched face, for I look awful when I cry. However, the blessed Master gave me some perfume to drink[95] from my hands so that at least I did not have to boo-hoo before them. One of those days He called me to dinner in the hall with the family. I had to excuse myself in order to spare them such a spectacle – for I was never sure of myself. After dinner He came with such lovely grapes in His beautiful hands. But alas as soon as I saw Him I at once began that awful circus once more. He said in English in His sweet sympathetic way, 'Not cry Jack, not cry Jack.' Can you imagine what a lesson all this was to me? I who gave up crying years before! And was so sure that, I at least, was going to spare the glorious one such scenes? How little worthy I was to be in that holy place & to be able to see Him almost daily! But how I envied the men believers who went to so many places with Him, and could sit & walk with Him in the garden. I said often 'Next time I come I shall come as a man.' Maybe they envied us sitting at prayers and at tea with Him upstairs.[96]

God gave me the great bounty of being in His home for about six months and I know the never-ending joy it was for every single member of that household to hear the beauty of His voice as He came joyously within ear shot – Servants and everyone rushed to the windows when He drew near. No Adelina Patti or Caruso ever could compare with His celestial tones heard in that old prison city. And I can never forget His loving words to me when my heart was overflowing as well as my eyes when my time was up. Just 'not cry Jack, not cry' as He came to my door with His beautiful hands full of grapes.[97]

During Marion's stay in Acre, 'Abdu'l-Bahá began calling her 'General Jack'. This is probably something to do with her work with the children, perhaps some game or activity. Marion Jack left Acre for Paris in July or August of 1908.

40

On her way to Paris she visited Alma Knobloch[98] in Stuttgart, Germany, probably at the request of 'Abdu'l-Bahá.

5

The Hostess
1908–1914

After landing in the south of Europe, Marion Jack travelled by train to Stuttgart, where she visited Alma Knobloch. This visit must have made a strong impression on Marion for she would often refer to Alma and her teaching methods in her later years. Marion also found time to do some painting of the historic buildings of Stuttgart.[99]

> Splendid Alma Knobloch taught me to seek contacts in restaurants . . . That is the way this modest and unassuming little Alma opened up Germany.[100]

Marion stayed only a few months in Paris and London before departing for Saint John, New Brunswick, arriving there in the early autumn of 1908. She stayed in New Brunswick until the end of 1910, when she returned to London. In Saint John, Marion immediately became involved in the art life of the city and became one of the charter members of the Saint John Art Club when it was founded on 12 November 1908. She proved to be a very active member of the club, forming an inner group, the Associated Artists Society, whose purpose was to contribute paintings to the club's spring exhibitions.

Even before she returned to Canada, two of her paintings

had already been selected for inclusion in two of Canada's most prestigious exhibitions, the Royal Canadian Academy of Arts Annual Exhibition, 24 April 1908 in Toronto, and the Spring Exhibition of the Art Association of Montreal. In the Toronto exhibition a set of 'Decorative panels' and the landscape *French Woodland Scene* were selected. The latter was also chosen for the Montreal exhibition. The early date indicates that Marion probably presented the paintings to the organizers during one of her trips to Canada before she went to the Holy Land. The paintings were definitely from her French period.[101]

During these two years Marion visited Montreal and Maine, as well as her beloved New Brunswick. In 1910 she stayed at the Green Acre Inn, Eliot, Maine. Eliot was the venue of the annual Green Acre School of Comparative Religions, a summer religious conference founded by Sarah J. Farmer in 1894. Farmer later helped to develop this into a permanent Bahá'í summer school. Among the Bahá'ís at Green Acre that summer were Mirza Sinore M. Raffie,[102] Mrs Aline S. Devin,[103] Mrs Stansell from New York, Miss Juliette Zimmerman of Washington DC, Kate C. Ives, Isabella Brittingham, Ella Robarts,[104] the Canadian painter Percy Woodcock[105] and his family, Charles Mason Remey and the first Canadian Bahá'ís, Mrs Esther Magee and her daughters Harriet and Edith, formerly of London, Ontario.[106]

In Montreal, Marion renewed her friendship with May Maxwell and her husband William Sutherland Maxwell and met other Bahá'ís of the Montreal community, such as Professor Henry F. Armstrong of McGill University and fellow artist Mary Pomeroy.

Before leaving Canada, Marion had four of her paintings displayed at the Dominion Exhibition in Saint John in

1910. These were cityscapes depicting the 13th-century Gothic cathedral of Bourges, France, the town hall and market place in Stuttgart and the Cluny Museum and Notre Dame, both in Paris. She also had a solo exhibition in October of that year at the Saint John Art Club.

When Marion Jack arrived in London late in 1910 or early 1911 she found that the British Bahá'í community only had about 50 members altogether. They were mostly in the London area but others were scattered across the British Isles in Bristol, St Ives, Liverpool, Manchester and Leeds in England and Belfast in Northern Ireland. They were in constant contact with their fellow believers in North America, Europe and the Middle East by way of the post, personal visits and the American Bahá'í magazine *Star of the West*, published in Chicago. Personal visits were very important in strengthening the Bahá'í community and giving the Bahá'ís the feeling of belonging to an international endeavour. In 1910, for example, the following visitors from America arrived in England: Charles Mason Remey, Louis Gregory, Julia Culver and Albert H. Hall, to name a few. Also visiting England at this time were Hippolyte Dreyfus-Barney from Paris and Khosroe Bohman from Burma.

However, the high points were visits from Bahá'ís who had just returned from pilgrimage to the Holy Land and who could relate firsthand the words and actions of 'Abdu'l-Bahá. The Bahá'ís of London had by 1910 organized themselves into a sort of local assembly, as was often reported in the *Star of the West* during that year. They held regular meetings every Friday at 10 Cheniston Gardens, Wright's Lane (137A Kensington High Street), which later became known as the Bahai Reading Room. Individual Bahá'ís also organized meetings up and down the country.

44

In London, Marion Jack shared a studio flat with Elizabeth Herrick,[107] at 13 Hanover Street, where she had meetings on Saturday afternoons. Later she moved to Stratford Place Mews, Oxford Street. Marion immediately started to help the other Bahá'ís in London to hold meetings about the Bahá'í Faith.

> How often I have thought of you and of our days in East Putney, and of the things you saw of a Sunday afternoon seated by the fire, as I did my best to tinkle the keys. Those dear days in London are very vivid in my mind, when you and I bussed from north to south, east to west to start new circles all over the place for those who could not afford the omnibus or other means of joining our circle . . . What lovely fireside Sunday meetings we had in East Putney. How poor Miss Walker wanted to have it nearly all Theosophists & yet would not bring her own friends to hear the Bahai Teachings!![108]

The first important meeting that the British Bahá'ís participated in was the First Universal Races Congress held from 26 to 29 July 1911 at the University of London. It was an international symposium on the theme of the brother-hood of humankind and attracted leading politicians, theologians and scholars from the whole of the British Empire and from Europe. During the Congress itself there were several Bahá'í presentations, including the reading of a letter sent by 'Abdu'l-Bahá, who was unable to attend in person. The Bahá'ís organized a series of four meetings to run in conjunction with the Congress. Marion Jack attended these meetings and was most impressed by the talk given by Jean E. Stannard on 'Awakening the East', held on 18 July.

An event of unprecedented importance occurred on

4 September 1911 with the arrival in England of 'Abdu'l-Bahá from the Holy Land by way of Egypt. After being imprisoned and exiled for most of His life, He had finally been allowed to leave the prison-city of St Jean d'Acre a few months previously. He stayed in England for what was for the Bahá'ís a most memorable 30 days. The Master, as He was called by the Bahá'ís, stayed mostly at the home of Lady Blomfield at 97 Cadogan Gardens but He also made trips to Clifton, a suburb of Bristol, and to the village of Byfleet in Surrey. He spoke at a variety of public and private meetings and had many private audiences with people from all walks of life. He addressed the congregations of two churches and had a private meeting with the Lord Mayor of London. The British Bahá'ís were drawn as if by a magnet to Him and most tried to attain His presence at every opportunity. Lady Blomfield paints this portrait of Him in London:

> A silence as of love and awe overcame us, as we looked at Him; the gracious figure, clothed in a simple white garment, over which was a light-coloured Persian 'abá; on His head He wore a low-crowned táj, round which was folded a small, fine-linen turban of purest white; His hair and short beard were of that snowy whiteness which had once been black; His eyes were large, blue-grey with long, black lashes and well-marked eyebrows; His face was a beautiful oval with warm, ivory-coloured skin, a straight finely-modelled nose, and firm, kind mouth. These are merely outside details by which an attempt is made to convey an idea of His arresting personality.
>
> His figure was of such perfect symmetry, and so full of dignity and grace, that the first impression was that of considerable height. He seemed an incarnation of loving understanding, of compassion and power, of wisdom and authority, of strength, and of a buoyant youthfulness,

which somehow defied the burden of His years; and such
years!

One saw, as in a clear vision, that He had so wrought
all good and mercy that the inner grace of Him had grown
greater than all outer sign, and the radiance of this inner
glory shone in every glance, and word, and movement as
He came with hands outstretched.[109]

On Friday, 22 September, Elizabeth Herrick and Marion
Jack had the rare distinction of hosting a public meeting
at which 'Abdu'l-Bahá spoke. The meeting was held at 10
Cheniston Gardens, Wright's Lane, sometimes given as
137A Kensington High Street. The composition of the
audience is not known. However, unlike many of 'Abdu'l-
Bahá's talks, this one was recorded stenographically and
subsequently published as 'Discourse by 'Abdu'l-Bahá given
at the Unity Meeting of Misses Jack and Herrick. September
22nd, 1911'.[110] His talk was very short, as was His custom,
and was about the spiritual teachings being brought to the
West from the East.

'Abdu'l-Bahá left London for Paris on 3 October 1911.
Marion Jack, like so many other Bahá'ís, went with Him
to Paris and attended many of the public meetings at which
He spoke.[111]

'Abdu'l-Bahá's second trip to Britain began on 13
December 1912 when He arrived in Liverpool from a very
successful journey to the United States and Canada. After
spending three days in Liverpool where He was met by
Bahá'ís from Manchester, London, Paris and other places,
He left for London. As on His previous visit, He spoke in
churches and before groups of Esperantists, Theosophists,
suffragettes and the poor and homeless and had private
audiences with people from all backgrounds. The Bahá'ís
considered themselves most fortunate when He spoke with

them personally and they felt especially honoured when He accepted an invitation from them.

We can comfortably assume that 'Abdu'l-Bahá had personal talks with Marion Jack during both visits to London. However, only the following fragment has been preserved by one of His translators:

> Speaking to Miss Jack, Abdul-Baha said: Those souls who consider themselves as imperfect, they are the people of the Kingdom. These persons who prefer themselves above others are egotists and worshippers of self; they are deprived of the graces of the Lord of mankind.[112]

Lady Blomfield was once more 'Abdu'l-Bahá's hostess when He stayed in London. During this period He also visited Bristol, Edinburgh, Oxford and Woking. He left London for Paris on 21 January 1913.[113]

'Abdu'l-Bahá visited Edinburgh between 6 and 10 January 1913. It is known that Marion Jack had relatives in Scotland and that she visited there several times. In a letter to her niece she stated that she had visited Edinburgh[114] and she no doubt visited the ancestral family seat in Cupar in Fife, which is north of Edinburgh. Bahá'í meetings began in Edinburgh in April 1913 and shortly afterwards

> . . . regular weekly meetings were held every Sunday afternoon at 3.30 p.m. at Woodburn, 54 Canaan Lane, hosted by Misses Marion Jack and Isabel Fraser.[115] Very little information exists concerning these meetings, though they were mentioned in the October 1913 edition of *Theosophy in Scotland*.[116]

Where Marion travelled in Scotland, how long she stayed and who she met are details lost in time. The only other evidence of her being in Scotland is a watercolour of Loch

Marion Jack in Saint John, circa *1880s*

*Marion and her sister
Louisa Millidge Jack,
Saint John, circa 1870s*

Marion, circa 1870s

David Russell Jack and Marion Jack, Saint John, circa 1880

Marion Jack, circa 1884

On The Dawson, *Alaska*

The Casca

Marion Jack, Elfie Lundberg and Mrs Lundberg at Rockford, Illinois, 1921

The Gift Shop of Marion Jack and Ivy Edwards, St Augustine, Florida, 1930

Martha Root

Marion in Varna, 1932

Louisa Gregory

George Benke

Bulgarian Bahá'ís, 1931

The Bahá'ís of Varna with Louisa Gregory

Esperanto class in Varna, 1932

Bahá'ís of Sofia, Naw-Rúz 1933

Lomond at the Bahá'í World Centre which probably dates from this period.

When a member of Britain's Bahá'í Youth Committee asked Marion about her experiences in London, she penned the following reply:

> . . . later I devoted about four years to the blessed work in London, and with Miss Gamble[117] helped to encourage those who opened their houses for meetings. Then the Glorious Master wrote me to institute a public meeting place so we hired the little hall in the public library in B___. It was there that dear Miss George[118] made her first maiden speech. I believe it was also Beatrice Irwin's first public appearance in that capacity, and maybe others, but my crowning glory as a humble worker was a visit to a meeting at my little studio in Oxford Street Stratford Mews of our Glorious Master. It is too bad that nothing was taken down of what He said there.
>
> Mr C.[119] with more money at his disposal, about this time hired another more central place for meetings, so I stepped out of the picture to give him full swing (in those days there was no Administration). And as I did not feel the need for the little help I could contribute I returned to America and Canada to work there early in 1914 . . .
>
> Miss Gamble's home was a really happy centre for enquirers and believers in those early days. Before taking my studio in the Mews I roomed with that dear soul and my work was to make sandwiches for the crowd. They came before four and many remained until ten or there abouts so needed two relays of tea and sandwiches so it took most of my evenings to prepare the little refreshment. Among those nearly always present were Mrs Moss and Mrs Young. She is a historic little woman for though humble and modest it was to her the heavenly Master gave the most profound of His teachings, Mr Dreyfus (Barney) told me. He said that to no one did the

49

Glorious One speak as to her, and since he was the inter-preter he ought to know. So dear friends include the name of this humble little woman, the wife of a daily labourer, with a few others in your early history. She always looked so neat and nicely dressed, and was always so quiet and dignified . . .

I forgot to mention our dear brother Mirza Hakim Lotfulla.[120] Now a doctor in Persia. He was such a comfort and such a stand by to us in those early days, one of those really reliable souls one can always count on. Another Persian was with him who always spoke in our little public meetings. Dear Miss Rosenberg was devoted to Lotfulla Hakim, and as an appreciation the family sent her one of the robes of the Blessed Perfection. A priceless gift, she used to show us this at meetings. In those days we had four meetings a week because of the great distances in London. A Mrs Crosby held one in the West Central district. I held mine in my little studio, the third was either at Miss Rosenberg's or Lady Blomfield's and the fourth at East Putney at Miss Gamble's. The latter and I tried to go to all four – and the hours we spent on busses![121]

In 1914 'Abdu'l-Bahá wrote to Luṭfu'lláh Ḥakím and, in part, told him

> . . . write to General Jack that she should not go back to Europe and instead leave for Toronto in Canada and St Johns and teach the Faith of God there . . .[122]

Thus early in 1914 Marion Jack set sail for New Brunswick. There is some reason to believe that she had paid at least one visit to North America during her four-year stay in England.

Of Marion's career as an artist during her stay in England little is known except that she participated in two major exhibitions of the London Salon in 1911 and 1912.[123]

The London Salon was organized by the Allied Artists Association. This was a group of British artists who banded together with the intention of creating a new exhibition society that would be non-jury. The leading artists of this group were Frederick Spencer Gore (1878–1914), Charles Isaac Ginner (1878–1952) and Harold John Wilde Gilman (1876–1919). It is quite possible that Marion continued her study of painting while living in London. The paintings included in the two salons were landscapes from New Brunswick, Ireland and Venice and a portrait. This means that Marion probably visited Venice and also Ireland, and in particular County Kerry, during this period.

Living in Ireland at this time was the family of Colonel Henry S. Culver and his wife Mary Culver, who were Bahá'ís. Their daughters Dorothy and Louise studied painting in Paris – where Dorothy first met Marion – and also became Bahá'ís there, around 1907.[124] It is quite probable that Marion Jack knew them in Ireland, since their home in Cork was not far from the places she sketched. Marion Jack and the Culvers were members together of the Saint John Art Club, later in New Brunswick.

6

The Suffragette
1910–1912

From 1905 to the beginning of the First World War, England and, in particular, the streets of London were the scenes of bitter and sometimes violent struggles by women for the right to vote. Many Bahá'ís of the time must have felt a great deal of sympathy for the suffragette cause and some were caught up in the militant struggle. The teaching of the equality of men and women was keenly felt by some of the early believers. 'Abdu'l-Bahá was also very interested in the suffragette movement. Many of the suffragette leaders went to His talks and had audiences with Him. The ones we know about include Charlotte Despard (1844–1939), one of the founders of the Woman's Freedom League; Emmeline Pankhurst (1858–1928), foremost suffragette leader who founded and led the Women's Social and Political Union (WSPU); Emmeline Pethick-Lawrence, one of the leaders of the WSPU and Annie Besant (1847–1933), president of the Theosophist Society. 'Abdu'l-Bahá also spoke at suffragette meetings in London, always stressing peaceful, non-violent methods of seeking women's rights. It is likely that Elizabeth Herrick introduced Marion Jack to Annie Besant during one of the many meetings that were held in London.

Marion Jack was a witness – and not always a passive

witness – to many of the demonstrations. Among her papers is this short, undated essay of how she remembered the suffragette movement.

A Few Suffrage Experiences in London

While a student of painting in Paris I met the Bahai group and became interested in that wonderful Movement, so, when I went to London, I was introduced to the friends there, one of whom, Miss Elizabeth Herrick, author of *Unity Triumphant*, let me a studio in Kensington. She was also a milliner for the country people in England, who liked their hats to be of good material, but not too smart.

One of Miss Herrick's greatest interests, for she had the good of humanity at heart, was to attend Mrs Pankhurst's lectures. I, too, became interested, by the help of an American man who told me I should not miss hearing this fine speaker. She certainly was convincing, and so I joined a group, but not a militant one, because Abdul Baha taught that woman would take her place through efficiency & when she showed her worth. Also, his idea was that evolution is preferable to revolution.

Soon after this, things began to stir among the militants and although I was not quite in accord with their tactics, I admired their courage and pluck, and had no wish to criticize them, at all events, to the sterner sex. One day while walking in Bond Street, London's smartest shopping street, we noticed a very disturbed atmosphere. Many of the exclusive shop owners were at their doors, talking excitedly with the passing pedestrians. As this was an almost unknown occurrence, my friend and I stopped also to see what was going on. We were told that some of the naughty suffragettes had broken some valuable shop windows. It seems they had selected the ones of those who were not kind to their assistants, or who had worked against the Movement. Soon we saw policemen coming hastily down the street to the police station, scurrying along these unfortunate & naughty young ladies, who went at that time submissively. None showed the white feather, all were quite courageous. Had I been alone I might have doffed my hat to them, but my very conventional friend would have been outraged! This was the beginning of the militant tactics. Soon this form of expression became quite common, and in consequence the police became more & more vigilant. At first a very short prison sentence was given. This increased later. As the thirst for smashing windows increased, so did the sale of hammers, the implements for this form of warfare. In those days when ladies wore muffs they were easily concealed. I believe this accounts for the decline of popularity of this item of ladies wear.

At the lectures, graphic accounts of the exploits were given, and the susceptible became imbued with the desire to shine courageously too. No one was luke warm any longer. Some of the maidens began to despise their married friends who would not act contrary to their lords and masters and who were apt in turn to criticize instead of championing their more daring sisters. As a Bahai I could not take part in militant tactics, but I could not criticize those who felt it their duty to do as they were doing, and I certainly admired their pluck. Abdul Baha has said: 'as the faithful, fearless and undaunted arise with absolute detachment to exalt the Word of God, and, with eyes averted from the things of this world, engage in service for the Lord's sake, and by His power, thereby will they cause the Word of Truth to triumph.' He too was for suffrage, and when in London, met with many of the heads of the Movement and spoke on their platform. Among other things he said that 'Humanity is like a bird with two wings, the one is male and the other is female. Unless both wings are strong and impelled by some common force, the bird cannot fly heavenwards.' According to the spirit of this age, women must advance and fulfil this mission, in all departments of life becoming equal to men. They must be on the same level with men and enjoy equal rights.[125] In fact one of the first suffragettes we know of arose in Persia after the appearance of the Bab. Her name was Kurat ul Aine or Tihereh[126] – a beautiful young woman and a poetess. She was persecuted and put to death, but she did her work for women nobly & well, and will never be forgotten for her extraordinary courage. Abdul Baha also says that girls are to receive as good an education as boys, and that their education is even more important, for as mothers they will be the first teachers of the next generation. Dr Esslemont[127] says that children are like green and tender branches, if the early training is right they grow straight, if it is wrong they grow crooked; and to the end of their lives they are affected by the training of their earliest years. So you see the Bahai teachings are certainly for the advancement of woman, & that she should take her place in the world. Of course I did what little I could to help along the good working such as speaking privately to those I met, & pointing out to women the unjust laws which were made by men for men. One of which was that a mother was no part owner in her own child. I took part in selling suffrage papers in the streets, and was vastly amused at the different attitudes meted out to me. Some asked me if I were 'not ashamed to be doing such work'. . . This amused me tremendously. Once in a while I received a word of commendation, but more often people passed by with disdain.

Before the militant outbreaks the biggest woman's parade on record took place in London,[128] where 50,000 women marched from the Thames Embankment near Charing Cross to Albert Hall, a matter of over two hours, because of the disturbance of traffic. Crowds, crowds of people lined the streets, and great cheering took place.

As we stopped for the carriages to go by, we had ample opportunity to speak with the crowds, and invite them to join us. A few were saucy, but most seemed kindly disposed and willing to listen. Miss Herrick was in great feather. She had prevailed on two men friends to carry her banner which bore the word 'Individuality'. When we reached the Albert Hall the meeting was well under way. Mrs Pankhurst & Mrs Besant were the most striking speakers, and the voice of the latter rang out loud and clear in that enormous gathering. This truly was a triumphant march & a great meeting.

Meetings continued in all parts of London, but Mrs Pankhurst seemed most to inspire Miss Herrick. She would come home in great excitement and I soon saw that she meant to take steps. One evening she said as she closed her Bonnet Shop, 'Tonight I am going to break a window.' I did my best to dissuade her, but she was by this time convinced that it was a moral obligation that she should take part, in spite of the fact that, as I pointed out, her business might suffer. She said that she would choose a small window in a back street post office, so the sentence would not be more than three days. So, off she went, with chosen friends. Next thing I knew, about ten o'clock, she was busily packing her suitcase to return early in the morning to the Old Bailey from whence she was allowed out on bail for the night.

Her friend, the Hon Mr Forbes and I went up to the Police Court to see what would be done with her. We were surprised at the Magistrate, who was enjoying his own witticisms at the expense of his victims. I complained about this to a distinguished gentleman standing near. He said, 'I too am disgusted at this levity in the Courts.' I suggested that he should do something about it. He said, 'Well you see that is not possible as I too am an official.'

To our dismay instead of getting three days' sentence, poor Miss Herrick received six weeks. Always plucky, she received this untroubled, asking demurely if she might have back her hammer as it was a family heirloom. This request was ignored. Then we went around to the prison yard, to see our little friend packed into a Black Maria, the ugliest & most forbidding of vehicles. I made many attempts to see her in Holloway Jail. This meant hours of waiting about the courtyard & waiting rooms were always packed. Many notable people were there to see relatives & friends – clergy from the fashionable Kensington Churches – W. W. Jacobs[129] the story writer to see his wife, Miss Haigh, sister of the great general, to see her sister, and many others one could mention. One of the most forbidding women I have ever seen was one of the wardens. I had heard of people having faces like a meat axe, and hers was truly of this description; but not all wardresses were so hard. Some were really sympathetic. Poor Miss Herrick tried to prevail on them to give her fruit, since she was a vegetarian, this request was taken to the doctor, who said that only in hospital wards was this permitted, & that if Miss Herrick wanted to go to the hospital she could have it. She refused, but later was forced to go there because of her insistence for fruit. She would not go willingly & thought she would raise her voice in demonstration, so they carried her screaming to hospital, where she continued to disturb the peace. A friendly inmate came & whispered advice to her, telling her that she might be put in a worse place, if she did not keep quiet. So Miss Herrick got a touch of hospital life. This did not interest her, so she soon returned to the more sporty part of the prison, where the victims were learning a play written for them by a Miss Smythe, an American also a prisoner.

Having no theatrical costumes they tore up & re-arranged their extra garments and when all was in readiness they proceeded to act this in the yard, in the recreation hour. Lloyd George, one of the heroes, was supposed to be shovelling coal to stoke the fires of hell, accompanied by Asquith.[130] The play did not get very far, for the prison chaplain was too shocked to allow it to proceed. Many other little incidents transpired in prison to pass the monotony of the six weeks. Among other things was the forbidding of the trespassers to take part in holy communion. A petition was at once sent to the Archbishop of Canterbury, demanding that they should be permitted this opportunity. The answer came back that all those who had acted as they had done for the sake of their fellow beings and not for selfish motives were to be given communion. On the next Sunday not a place was vacant in the chapel, and every Episcopalian in prison received communion.

When the six weeks were up Mrs Douglas Hamilton sent her beautiful motor, and the Hon Mr Forbes and I drove in it to bring home our heroine. She came gaily out of the prison waving a little Suffrage flag. Mr Forbes placed her in the seat of honour & we drove off while Miss Herrick sang a little Suffrage song & waved her flag. She told us that she had the first real holiday since she was thirteen years of age & that if one wanted a real rest one should go to prison.

To go back a bit. When we left the Old Bailey, I returned at once to break the news of the lengthy sentence to the apprentice in the Bonnet Shop. She nearly wilted, for she was but a young girl. I did my best to buoy her up, telling her that this was her opportunity & that as she knew all about everything she must assume full responsibility, but that I would stand back of her. I even tried to manufacture a few hats, one of which Miss Herrick wore herself later & made an attempt to trim the shop. We did not long have to worry on that score, as the kindly Mrs Douglas Hamilton sent to Paris, and had five crates of Parisian millinery presented to the shop. There all the friends came along to open the boxes, and several of us decked ourselves out in our purchases. One dear dame, a clergyman's widow whose usual garb was a shabby cloak & bonnet, joined in this dress parade. She donned a blue tricorn which was adorned with a soft red feather edging. Seeing the transformation in her appearance she eagerly asked, 'Could I wear this?' It was really becoming, but when I looked at the rest of the costume, I was forced to remind her that she might have to purchase a complete new wardrobe to go with it. As the dear soul was one of those whose lives were dedicated to good works, she decided to turn her back on these new temptations of the world and relinquish that new beautiful Parisian head gear.

Never was the Bonnet Shop more gay, for in those days the fair sex wore feathers, flowers & ribbons galore. The country customers, not being told where the head of the establishment was living, were quite perplexed at her lengthy absence. They little guessed in which castle the poor prisoner was languishing.

Whether all this suffering helped the Cause or not, one cannot tell. It certainly aroused the people, many to intense opposition, so much so that the various non-militant societies decided to prove to them that there were innumerable numbers of women who believed in peaceful methods. We then proceeded to march again, and this time huge processions came from the four quarters of London into Hyde Park. Another friend and I walked in the one from Charing Cross, but we were not in such favour as on the former occasion, as the populace was not sure that we were really harmless & rather mistrusted us. Then came the war, and the enduring efforts of women was such as to win the male hearts, until they could no longer resist the urgent appeal, and Votes for Women became a matter of real importance and the fair sex went back to its normal occupations. They had won the day by real worth, and had truly become the strong second wing of the bird of which Abdul Baha had told them – and, from so doing, they came into their own, fairly and nobly. Not forgetting, we hope, the strenuous efforts and sufferings of their indefatigable and courageous sisters, whose initiative in starting the ball rolling, and whose splendid unselfishment & hard work, was surely the beginning of this great ending. This recognition of women as man's equal. And, now that they have won out as such, may they never be content to sit back with their well won laurels – but push forward to help man to win an equally important thing, the peace of the world, without which neither progress nor happiness can ever be realized on this earth.[131]

In a contemporary reference work Marion Jack was described as a sympathizer of the suffragette movement and a member of the 'Women's International of England'.[132]

It is not known how many other Bahá'ís participated in the campaign for 'Votes for Women', however we do know that some were quite active. Mary Esther Blomfield,[133] daughter of Lady Blomfield, made a demonstration before King George V and Queen Mary on 4 June 1914, shouting out, 'For God's sake, stop forcible feeding.'[134] She and her sister, Rose Ellinor Cecilia Blomfield, were quickly bustled out. It was reported that Lady Blomfield apologized for her daughter's behaviour and immediately left for Switzerland.[135]

It was only in 1928 that women received full voting rights in the United Kingdom.

The Traveller
1912–1931

The North American years (1912–1930) were for Marion Jack years of almost constant travel – or so it would seem from the chronological record, for she stayed no more than a year or two at any one place. The information is scant but we know of her epic travels in Alaska, her first journey in the Maritime provinces, her stays in Vancouver, Green Acre and many other places. There is also a record of at least one dash across the Atlantic to Italy. It has not been possible to weave a continuous picture of her life during these years with only broken threads before us but through the loom of time a pattern does emerge.

1912: South Carolina, Chicago

Even though Marion Jack lived in England from 1910 to 1914, her ties with Canada were never completely severed. There is reason to believe that she visited Canada and the United States several times during this period. In 1912 a short biography of her appeared in a Canadian biographical dictionary called *The Canadian Men and Women of the Time*, edited by Henry James Morgan. Her brother, David Russell Jack, probably submitted the article. The article states that

Marion, 'owing to ill-health, forgoes the studio and paints in the open air'. The article must have been written many years earlier, for it refers to '4 decorative panels of landscape, recently contributed to the "Nationale", attracted much attention, being noticed in the *Strand* and other publications; resides in Paris'.[136]

There are only two recorded sightings of Marion in America in 1912. From correspondence from the Bulgarian period, it seems that in 1912 she was in Sumter, South Carolina, visiting Carl Witherspoon and Josephine 'Josie' Pinson, early American Bahá'ís. Also in 1912:

> Marion was living in the city [Chicago] and held general education classes for children in that deprived area. Leroy [Ioas] felt proud to be a small part of it.[137]

This was the year that 'Abdu'l-Bahá made His historic trip to North America. He arrived in New York City on 11 April and departed on 5 December. Did Marion Jack accompany Him, as her friend Louisa Mathew did? Did she meet Him or go to any of His talks? Was she at the ground-breaking ceremony for the House of Worship in Wilmette? It is hard to believe that Marion Jack would not have met the Master at some stage of His travels, yet these two sightings of her in North America are the only ones that have so far come to light.

1913: Saint John

In this year Marion had two of her English landscapes selected by jury for the Thirtieth Spring Exhibition of the Art Association of Montreal. Through the titles of her paintings we can gain an insight into the areas of England which touched her most: Rye, the Suffolk coastal villages, Bedfordshire and the small village of Benfleet, Essex, at the mouth of the Thames. Her address at this time was given as '162 Union Street, St John, N.B.' indicating either that she paid a short visit to Canada in 1912/1913 or that she was assisted by one of her many friends in Montreal. If the latter, then the friend was probably either Mary B. Pomeroy or William Sutherland Maxwell, both local Bahá'ís. Maxwell, an architect, also took part in the exhibition and, along with his brother Edward, was represented by two architectural designs: 'Design for Executive Building, Winnipeg' and the 'C.P.R. Hotel, Calgary'.

1914: Saint John, Montreal, Green Acre, Toronto

Shortly after arriving in Canada in the spring of 1914, Marion Jack participated in the Art Association of Montreal's Thirty-first Annual Spring Exhibition which was held 27 March to 18 April. Eight paintings, including six scenes from England and one from New Brunswick in oils and watercolour, were selected by the jury. There was also a portrait of 'Abdu'l-Bahá in pastel, which was probably one of the earliest publicly displayed painted portraits of 'Abdu'l-Bahá. Also participating in this exhibition was Mary B. Pomeroy, at whose home in Montreal Marion stayed for a while the following year. The titles of Mary Pomeroy's three watercolours were: *Morning Hour in the Forest, Dancing Sunshine in the Pine Trees* and *The Lecture Pine, Green Acre*. These titles reflect the influence the Bahá'í summer school at Green Acre had on this artist, as it would in the future on many more.

The Montreal showing was one of the two most prestigious annual art exhibitions in Canada. The other exhibition was the Royal Canadian Academy of Arts Exhibition in Toronto. Of the artists who participated in the 1913 and 1914 Montreal exhibitions, 41 were deemed important enough by J. Russell Harper to be listed in the biographical section of his *Painting in Canada. A History.*[138] It should be noted that of these 41 artists, only three were women and only three had even a tenuous connection with the Atlantic provinces, John Hammond being the only one who actually lived and worked there as an artist. Therefore Marion Jack was a minority among minorities.

Later that spring Marion attended the sixth Annual Convention of the Bahai Temple Unity,[139] which was held at the Great Northern Hotel in Chicago from 25 to 28 April. Marion Jack was designated as the delegate from London, England. An account of the convention reports that 'Far away London sent its greetings in the much enjoyed presence of Miss Jack.' The same account records that Marion Jack was present along with many other delegates at a celebration of the fiftieth anniversary of the Feast of Riḍván hosted by the Chicago Assembly on the evening of Saturday, 25 April at the Noontide Club in Chicago. The meeting was chaired by Albert R. Windust, one of the editors of the *Star of the West* magazine. On Sunday morning the delegates and other Bahá'ís gathered at the site of the future Mashriqu'l-Adhkár[140] where prayers and Tablets from the Bahá'í sacred writings were read. Later in the afternoon began the first of three sessions in the Masonic temple. During the convention Marion 'gave a progressive account of the work in London and England'.[141] Among the delegates were several whom she had previously met, including Louis G. Gregory of Washington DC, Kate C. Ives[142] of Salem, Massachusetts, and Elsie Pomeroy of Montreal.

Later that summer Marion Jack was at Green Acre, where on 21 August she presented an informal conference. Also at Green Acre that summer were her friends Stanwood Cobb[143] and Kate Ives.[144]

An unprecedented artistic event occurred in New Brunswick on 5 September with the opening of the art exhibit at the Provincial Exhibition. The art exhibition was sponsored by the Saint John Art Club and must have been especially welcomed by the artists of New Brunswick and the general population of Saint John, since there were no large galleries in the city. The National Gallery in Ottawa, the Toronto Art Association and the Art Association of Montreal loaned a large number of paintings for this exhibition, as did several individuals. Marion Jack loaned 15 of her paintings, including works in oil, pastels and watercolours. Among them were landscapes from Ireland, New Brunswick, England and the Holy Land. Two paintings in particular were singled out in a newspaper article as noteworthy:

> Miss Jack's collection, in which Saint John takes especial pride, is not large, but includes some very lovely pictures. Church Interior (124) is an excellent example of the quality of Miss Jack's work along certain lines, while Beeches and Maples at Rothesay Park (125) shows another phase of her art.[145]

Whenever Marion was in Saint John she invariably took part in the activities of the Art Club. For example, at the annual meeting held on 22 October she was thanked for supplying plaster casts for the exhibition and for supplying art magazines.[146]

In November one of Marion's paintings from Green Acre was selected for display at the Thirty-sixth Annual Exhibition of the Royal Canadian Academy of Arts in Toronto.

1915: Montreal, Green Acre, Boston

Landscapes from Maine and New Brunswick were Marion's contribution to the Thirty-second Spring Exhibition of the Art Association of Montreal, held 26 March to 17 April 1915, which contained three of her paintings.

Marion Jack spent the summer of 1915 at Green Acre. The published programmes from Green Acre state that on 4 August, during the Green Acre Conference, Marion Jack, then living in Montreal, gave a piano recital at a concert.

In September, during the Green Acre Festival, Marion was chairman of the Sports and Games Committee. She also provided the piano accompaniment, along with Miss Alice Toby, for the 'Folk Dances on the Lawn'. The programme also names her as one of the dancers. Another dancer listed is Miss Ghodsea Ashraf, a Bahá'í and the first Persian woman to travel to the United States.[147] A photograph dated 1915 might be of this performance and lists the dancers as Elizabeth Barker, Marian [sic] Jack, Julia Hadaway and Ruth Spinney.[148]

Bahiyyih Ford provided one of the very few pen sketches we have of Marion from this period:

I knew Marion Jack in Green Acre when I was a little girl, about the years 1915, 1916, along in there. She had a summer cottage. She used to teach painting and I took some lessons. I was hopeless, had no talent at all. She would let me struggle and then would come with a brush and in a few strokes would make my picture right. She said I always picked such hard things to paint like flower arrangements. But her kindness in fixing my terrible efforts, and then telling me to take it home as if it was all my own! She was stout, had the casual approach to dress and to life. She used to buy a large piece of material, cut a hole in it for her head, slip it on and then tie a sash around her waist. Somehow she always looked colorful and sweet! She was a happy person, loved to laugh. As a child I loved being with her for all these reasons, but most of all because of the tenderness and kindness she never failed to give. I can see her now walking down the road at Green Acre, ready to be jolly. I can imagine Jackie, as she was called, putting up with great hardship, as she must have in the last years of her life, and yet having a ready smile.[149]

In December, while living in Montreal, Marion wrote a letter to Helen Goodall concerning a painting of hers that was sold for $250. She wished to donate the entire amount to the Temple Fund, minus five per cent to buy Bahá'í literature. This was apparently one of several paintings she did especially for the Temple Fund. Marion described her scheme for a travelling exhibition for the purpose of selling paintings for the Temple Fund and remarked that she had returned from the Boston area, where she had been for quite a long time for eye treatment. While in Boston she came to know the metaphysicist W. W. Harmon and highly praised him and his book *Divine Illumination*.[150] Of her activities in Montreal, Marion wrote:

> The Montreal Assembly is not large but it is full of spiritual love and unity. It is a joy to be back in its midst again. And dear May Maxwell is always so lovely & so loving I am indeed grateful to the Heavenly Beloved for allowing me to be a worker in this Assembly in which she is the teacher. I have what May calls the social instinct and can gather the people together for her to talk to and teach so we do beautifully. You see I do not care whether I am second or fifty-second fiddle so long as I have the joy of playing in God's orchestra at all. There is use for each one of us – and particularly if we keep in tune – and there lies the difficulty in some assemblies. Thank God all is harmonious here.[151]

In an addendum written two days later Marion states that, in consultation with May Maxwell, it was decided that perhaps it would be better to send the money to 'Abdu'l-Bahá for the relief of the destitute in Palestine. It is not known whether this was carried out. Perhaps the letter from 'Abdu'l-Bahá sent in 1919[152] is a response to this query.

Marion Jack always felt close to May Maxwell and when in Bulgaria wrote to Anne Lynch:

> I have often wondered why Mrs Maxwell was so loveable. I see now it was because she was so loving herself. Her love was so great that it prevented her from seeing faults in others. It was that blessed eye of hers. True she was generous and kind, but so were others, and others had lovely qualities, but still she stood out in my mind far dearer than them all.[153]

1916: Montreal, Lake Chautauqua, Saint John, Fredericton

In May 1916 Marion Jack was still living and painting in Montreal. In her letters she gave her address as 32 Lincoln Avenue. Three of her paintings were selected for the Thirty-third Spring Exhibition of the Art Association of Montreal. Two were landscapes from Palestine and one from Maine. Little else is known of her activities other than from the following recollection of Elizabeth Hackley of Urbana, Illinois.

In 1916 when Miss Hackley was a college student, her friend Cora Gray[154] was asked to be in charge of the dining room at Green Acre. Elizabeth went to wait on tables. The girls went by way of Montreal, hoping to meet at the home of the Maxwells, but they found that the Maxwells were out of town. They were told that there would be a meeting in the apartment of Marion Jack.

They met in the large 30' x 30' room in one corner of which was a sink, stove and table behind a screen, another corner a cot and dresser, and a third corner for easel and canvases. There were folding chairs in the center of the room with quite a few people. Miss Jack spoke. She was very warm and friendly, quite heavy with a dear round face, a lovely smile. She was easy-going and took things in her stride. She gave us a benediction when we left.

The girls had to take an early street car ride to get to the train for a 6:30 a.m. departure for Maine. There on the platform was Marion Jack. She had prepared a large lunch for them and taken a trip of at least half an hour to get there. They appreciated her thoughtfulness even more later when they discovered that there was no diner on the train and that they would have had no food until evening without her box of sandwiches and fruit.[155]

Marion Jack did not go to Green Acre that year. She states in one letter:

May[156] may have told you that she wants me to go to Chataqua[157] this year for the purpose of helping to start a Bahai opening in that place. I suppose I should not realize my own inadequacy for such a part, but I do, at the same time I am profiting by a lesson I learned from my painting Professor which was 'Don't be afraid to dare', and am pushing forward, hoping that other more capable Bahais may come to my rescue. The plan is to have a cottage there which will be a Bahai centre for meetings.[158]

December 1916 found Marion in Saint John from where she made at least one trip to Fredericton, New Brunswick, with Grace Ober. In a letter written to her hostess in Fredericton, a Mrs Gregory, Marion corrects several misconceptions concerning the Faith that were then circulating. Among these were that Bahá'ís did not believe in the divinity of Christ, that Bahá'ís were Muslims and that Bahá'ís believed in 'free-love'.[159] This last would, a few years later, throw a shadow over the teaching work in the Alaskan southeast.

Marion Jack visited Fredericton quite often. Another person in Fredericton who knew her was Mary Montgomery Campbell, the mother of Hand of the Cause John A. Robarts.[160]

1917: New Brunswick, Nova Scotia, Prince Edward Island, Newfoundland

At a regular meeting of the Saint John Art Club on Thursday, 17 February 1917 at the Studio on Peel Street, Marion Jack and Edna McKinney[161] gave a talk on 'Green Acre, Eliot, Maine: Its Beauty and Ideals'. A newspaper account of the meeting stated that:

> The principal feature of the evening was the addresses by Miss Marion Jack and Miss Edna McKinney of Boston. The subject was Green Acre, Eliot, Maine; Its Beauty and Ideals. Miss Jack told of the great natural beauty of the surroundings of the well known community settlement there. The balopticon[162] views added interest to the bright comments. Miss Edna McKinney of Boston also gave a pleasant address. She narrated the formation of the settlement by Miss Sarah G. Farmer formerly of Newport, R. I. The place has since become a gathering place for the great minds of the country, she said, and the names of several prominent persons who were visitors were mentioned. Mr W. Frank Hatheway, in moving the vote of thanks, which was seconded by Mr Geo. A. Henderson, spoke appreciatively of the work done at Green Acre, having spent some days there some years ago . . .

The display of about 50 oil paintings by Miss Jack gave added pleasure to the meeting and her work was very favourably commented by many of the members.[163]

The same newspaper account mentions some of the regular business of the club, including the acceptance of new members. One such new member recommended for admission was a Mrs Henry S. Culver. This was most likely Mary Diana Culver, wife of the US Consul Henry S. Culver. Both of them were Bahá'ís.[164]

During World War I Marion Jack toured the Maritime provinces of New Brunswick, Nova Scotia and Prince Edward Island. With Kate Ives she visited Saint John's, Newfoundland, in 1917.[165] It is likely that she visited her cousins, the children of her Aunt Elizabeth Neville, née Jack, and her husband John Thomas Neville. Later in Moncton, New Brunswick, Kate Ives spoke at several public meetings. At one of these Marion had an exhibition of paintings to benefit the war workers.[166]

Thank God however the little town of Moncton has been less prejudiced, and maybe from there several seeds may spring up. I had the bounty of accompanying a beloved sister who was a fine speaker to that spot during the first terrible war – and though we found folks a wee bit responsive there was then no great result. I have always felt that the outer ear has to get accustomed to the (then) strange though glorious sound of the word 'Bahá'í' – and maybe our wee pioneering trip, and Kate Ives' forceful presentation of the blessed teachings helped prepare the soil for the more successful later efforts.[167]

This same year with Rhoda Nichols of Upper Troy, New York, Marion visited Prince Edward Island and Nova Scotia, holding meetings in different villages, again with no visible results.[168]

The 1917–1918 *Programme* of the Saint John Art Club contains the following entry for Tuesday, 13 November 1917:

> 'Starving Syrians', an Entertainment by Miss Marion Jack showing her Oil Paintings in the Lantern.[169] Admission 25 cents – Members 15 cents.

No further information is available. Presumably these are paintings Marion sketched while in Acre in 1908.

1918: Boston, Saint John, Chicago, New York, Winnipeg

Marion again spent the winter in Boston and was a witness to a crisis in the Bahá'í community concerning the metaphysical teachings of W. W. Harmon.[170]

The Tenth Annual Convention of the Bahai Temple Unity was held in Chicago at the Auditorium Hotel from 27 through 30 April 1918. Marion Jack was the delegate from Saint John, New Brunswick; the alternative delegate was Grace Ober.[171] A letter addressed to 'Abdu'l-Bahá from New York City and dated 2 May indicates that Marion must have left Chicago immediately the Convention ended. Her movements in the United States after that date have not yet been established.

Later that year Marion began to work in the United States as a portrait artist. It is reported that during 1918 she had a solo exhibition in a large department store in Chicago, where she was living that December.

Marion Jack was among the earliest to respond to 'Abdu'l-Bahá's Tablets of the Divine Plan, the first five of which were received in North America shortly before the First World War broke out and which were published in *Star of the West* in September 1916. In the December 1918 issue of *Star of the West* we read that 'Marion Jack is soon to leave Chicago for Winnipeg'.[172] There is, however, no further information about this Winnipeg trip.

1919: Chicago, New York

During her stay in Chicago, Marion Jack participated in art classes, though whether as a student or as a teacher is not clear.[173] She had an exhibition at the YWCA in Evanston, Illinois, on 27 January 1919.[174] It was at these art classes that she met Wanda Wyatt of Prince Edward Island, her sister Dorothy and her mother and that a warm bond of friendship developed. They would spend time shopping, sewing or tinting photographs together. Wanda recorded in her diary:

> Sunday, April 20, 1919
> Easter Sunday & it was a gorgeous day, altho as usual windy. We did not go to church. Miss Jack had to leave early so that meant dinner between 12 & 12.30. Miss Jack is such a dear. She gave Mother an awfully cunning incense burner & D & me each a darling vanity bag for Easter presents. I gave her a brown embroidered collar that looks well on a brown tunic she is making & we put a little spool & needle case in her shoe. She had to leave right after dinner – we had lovely new beets & cauliflower.[175]

At the Eleventh Annual National Convention of the Bahai Temple Unity held in New York City at the McAlpin Hotel in April 1919, Marion Jack served as a member of the National Reception Committee.[176] Among the other members of the Committee were two of her past and future travelling partners, Kate Ives and H. Emogene Hoagg. It was during this Convention that the series of letters, or Tablets, from 'Abdu'l-Bahá addressed to the Bahá'ís of the United States and Canada directing them to spread the Bahá'í teachings across North America and around the world were publicly unveiled, though some had been previously published in *Star of the West*. These were later published as *Tablets of the Divine Plan*.[177]

1919–20: Alaska and Yukon

In one of the Tablets of the Divine Plan dated 8 April 1916, 'Abdu'l-Bahá points out the importance of propagating the Faith in Alaska and teaching the local people:

> Hence the mercy of God must encompass all humanity. Therefore do ye not think it permissible to leave that region [Alaska] deprived of the breezes of the Morn of Guidance. Consequently, strive as far as ye are able to send to those parts fluent speakers, who are detached from aught else save God, attracted with the fragrances of God, and sanctified and purified from all desires and temptations. Their sustenance and food must consist of the teachings of God. First they must themselves live in accordance with those principles, then guide the people. Perchance, God willing, the lights of the Most Great Guidance will illuminate that country and the breezes of the rose garden of the love of God will perfume the nostrils of the inhabitants of Alaska.[178]

In response to this Tablet, Marion Jack and Emogene Hoagg sailed from San Francisco in July 1919 aboard the Alaska steamship *Victoria* for Nome, Alaska, where they arrived on 15 July. On the way, they apparently stopped in Seattle:

> In Seattle I spoke to some people, but put them in touch with the Assembly there.[179]

Marion and Emogene chose Alaska because it was referred to so powerfully in the Tablets of the Divine Plan. They were not, however, the first Bahá'ís to go there: Mariam Haney in her article on 'Travelling and Teaching in Alaska' published in 1924[180] records the names of earlier adventurers.[181]

Emogene and Marion got off at Akutan, a whaling station on one of the Aleutian Islands 'to give them a pamphlet . . .'[182]

> Our first stop was at the Whaling Station in the Aleutian Islands called Akutan. There we met the doctor to whom Imogene [sic] gave literature and three men on the wharf, to whom we mentioned the Message. The one most receptive and possible hopeful was Mr Cundy, Acutan, Aleution Islands, Alaska. He and the group of men working at the Station are so destitute of any means of getting reading matter that what they have is read and re-read, so as he told me what we gave him would not only have the same treatment but be passed on to other Whalers. So I gave him Mr Veil's book, Wisdom Talks, Jean Masson's paper on the Mashrak-el-Askar[183], Martha Root's article on What the Bahai Movement means to the Colored People. So if literature could be sent to the Station I think it would be appreciated.
>
> Mr Cundy said that Mr Malone the bookkeeper was a deep student, but we did not see him. So please have things sent to Mr Cundy or Whalers at Acutan. The bulk of the men remain only six months, but there was a group

of eleven there last winter building a big wharf. This is a very important Whaling Station, more so than those of Newfoundland. Letters would be much appreciated.

Our journey on the 'Senator' ended at Nome, and there we met the Sathers. Mr and Mrs Peter Sather [or Sater], Nome, Alaska is the address. Both were most receptive and will gladly welcome anything further on the Revelation.

Mrs Campbell, c. of Mr Davis, Nome, Alaska is also a receptive soul. Her brother Mr Davis also evinced interest. Mrs Campbell's inclinations seem to be towards Astrology and probably toward the Occult as well, but she appeared to accept the idea of the coming of the Great One and the fact that this was the dawn of a New Day. We left her Unity thru Love, some small literature and 'Ten Days in the Light of Acca'.[184]

Mrs Throline Ingwaldson, Box 63, Nome, Alaska, wife of the judge of the Probate Court I found receptive altho Emogene did not feel quite as warmly towards her as I did. I left the 'Compilations on War and Peace'[185] with her for Mrs Sather and Mrs Campbell as well and have written asking if they could have it put in the A.B. (Alaskan Brotherhood) Library.[186] She also has 'Wisdom Talks', Mr Veil's Book, Big Ben,[187] etc.[188]

After staying in Nome for a few days Marion and Emogene sailed for Saint Michael near the mouth of the Yukon River, and the beginning of a 4,000–kilometre river adventure lasting four months. They travelled from Saint Michael to Tanana on the riverboat *Julia B.*, stopping at many settlements on the way. From Tanana they went to Fairbanks and from Fairbanks again by riverboat to the Yukon Territory, Canada. Emogene Hoagg kept a detailed diary of her trip. In it she described the countryside, the people, the weather, the movement of the various riverboats and the injustices suffered by the native peoples. In this 45–page diary, as in published accounts, there are only a few entries referring to Marion Jack but these, along with a few others, paint a fair picture of this adventure.

Excerpts from the Diary Notes of Emogene Hoagg 1919–20, Alaska[189]

26 July left Saint Michael on board the *Julia B.*

30 July, Marshall

At Marshall a Mrs Jones (colored) got on with a first class ticket. When she came to be seated at the table the steward said there was no seat. She walked out of the room very much hurt.

Jackie and I informed the Steward and also the Purser that we would sit at the table with her. Miss McGown the blond who was on the *Victoria* objected to sitting with her at table. Quite a conversation took place at table in a pleasant way. At noon with a Mrs Young who got on here at Holy Cross, and with the 'sourdoughs' we commenced our meals at the 'second table'. Since then I have acted as though nothing had happened. This person is pleasant and interesting. She came into Alaska in 1898 going to Dawson when the rush was on there, walking from Bennett over the Pass, the first woman to do this. She has kept road-houses in various places and has evidently made money. Mr Mutchler who is going to Iditerard has left with a bunch of literature to distribute. Jackie did his portrait today.

1 August

Took on wood for five hours yesterday, so did not today.

Jackie did the portrait of the first Officer, Neil Carroll, who is the joke of the ship. We call him Snorobus because he snores and sleeps next to us. Later she painted the Steward, Mr Crocker. After them she did two of the natives, one is an Eskimo named Pete, who is the best packer in the country.

3 August, Lauden

Peter Frummer is a young man of twenty-nine on board. He goes to Nenana. Yesterday he gave me a small pair of moccasins and Jackie a wallet made of moose hide.

4 August, Ruby

This eve we discovered an organ in the barge in front and had a little concert. Jackie paints and talks to all. The mail launch caught us last night and has gone on with the mail.

7 August, Tanana

Mr Donnell gave his boat to Jackie to go out to the Mission and paint an old Indian woman.

8 August, Tanana

Rainy this morning but it cleared up and was cold later. Jackie and I took a walk and called in at a little drug store to find Mrs Davis the owner, who is interested in Christian Science, willing to listen to the Teachings. The *Yukon* arrived about ten o'clock.

14 August, Fairbanks

Up at eleven and out to the Model Cafe for breakfast. Found a lot of letters at the Post and the Postman said that he knew we were 'Mrs Hoagg and Miss Jack'. He did not say how he knew. I wonder if we had a pious look.

15 August

Went shopping this morning for Jackie, found a dressmaker.

16 August, Fairbanks

A Base Ball game today with the Nenana team and this eve a dance. Jackie has offered to paint the 'Most beautiful woman and the most popular man'. Had to get a winter hat for mine was rakish. Went to the dance with Mrs McKinnon and a friend. A Miss Creamer won the picture and Mr Pinsky. Scotty and Peter came from Nenana.

The style of the evening was the 'shirt-waist' men. Mr Pinsky won the picture. Now Jackie is wondering how she will get his nose on the canvas. Miss Creamer was voted the most beautiful.

20 August, Fairbanks

This eve Jackie created quite a sensation by painting the Indian Chief in the Lobby. People passing would come in to look at her. We were there until half past eleven.

..ugust, Fairbanks

Jackie is painting Mr Wilson's portrait. The *Alaska* came in last evening and leaves today.

24 August, Nenana

Jackie went out for to conquer and found Mr Steven at a store, I am to go and talk to him . . . At Mr Stevens' shop he invited us to see his wife and there we found Mrs Guys. She is much interested in the Teachings and so is Mrs Stevens and her sister-in-law who lives here. In the store we found Mr W__ of Fairbanks and while he is an agnostic we had an interesting talk about the Teachings; so we felt our trip was not altogether useless.

26 August, Fairbanks

Last eve Jackie met a Mr Gleeson, Terence, who became quite interested in the Cause. With Mr Pinsky we walked out by the Farm and then had ice cream, meeting also Mr and Mrs Roth. Today Mrs Whitney and Mrs McGown called and we went to see the Masonic Hall, where I might give a talk. It rained hard. When I returned we talked to Mr Gleeson until after two a.m.

28 August, Fairbanks

Jackie's telegram with money arrived today. I had my suitcase fixed and talked some with the man Mr S__.

3 September, Nenana

At supper time Jackie got hold of some of our doughs that knew Mr Hunter and Scotty and led them to me to talk to. We had a good talk and they were delighted. Mr Heins said that they had concluded they believed what we said.

8 September, Circle

Arrived at Circle about eight in the morning. Dr Parker got off here to investigate some cosa for tuberculosis. A Mrs Bayliss got some literature. Then Jackie painted Mrs Kuhn's house and I talked to a Mr R__ to whom we will send some literature.

13 September, Dawson City, Yukon Territory

We have not decided whether we shall stay on or go in a day or two. Jackie is wanting to go to Canada to teach and may leave me. I feel the necessity of staying in Alaska until more of the places have heard the Teachings.

14 September, Dawson

Jackie went to Science Church[190] this morning and to Presbyterian tonight.

17 September, Dawson

Judge John Black called to see Jackie. He comes from New Brunswick and knows her people. We are to go to a Concert with him Friday at the Presbyterian Church.

21 September, Dawson

A bleak day, rainy and cool. Jackie painted and I wrote.

25 September, Dawson

A beautiful clear day. Jackie and I walked to the top of the first slope and had a fine view of Dawson.

Gave a talk in Lowe's Hall which was attended by about fifty. A good crowd the people said. The Presbyterian minister, Mr McGuggin, asked a number of questions. He asked what was the theology of these Teachings, and the philosophy; also if we did not believe in Nirvana. And to explain the number nine and the square of 19. Mr Black came home with us and we went to the restaurant for supper.

The *Dawson* left at midnight. The *Yukon* is waiting for the *Casca* and freight. Letters came from Mason[191], Lech, Poldo, Rosenberg.[192]

30 September, Dawson

Jackie is to give an exhibit of her sketches at the Soldier's Club in the afternoon for the children and in the eve for the grown ups. I am to talk to them both afternoon and eve. Lovely clear day, ice on the streets.

2 October, Dawson

At Dawson . . . two public talks were given. One was in the Lowe Hall and the other at the Soldier's Club House under the Auspices of the Ladies' Auxiliary of the G.W.V.A.[193] –

whatever that is. At the Club Miss Jack gave an exhibit of her paintings for the benefit of the Soldiers and the talk was given in the eve. In the afternoon the children came and Miss Jack gave rapid colored drawings and talked about Abdul Baha to them.[194]

The Northern Lights were wonderful tonight. At times great broad streaks would stretch across the sky, sometimes three or four, then this would change and commence to wave in colors, again it would spread like a filmy pointed edged curtain waving in streaks up and down, then a great wave would spread over the sky, and then it would change continually, sometimes circling, and sometimes in lines. At times from the horizon the light would seem like a torch.

4 October set sail for Whitehorse.

7 October above Selkirk on the Yukon River

To see the Five Finger Rapids Jackie and I went up to the pilot house. We did not reach there till 2 a.m. It was certainly worth the staying up. These rocks, five fingers, extend across the river and leave a narrow passage way for the boat. It seemed as we approached that there was not room to pass, as the boat had to turn after entering the narrow way. It was snowing and that made the scene more weird. The Pilot, Mr Burruss, threw the search light on the sides, so as to guide the boat, and it seemed that there was not more than a few feet between the rocks and the boat on each side. The current is swift at this point.

8 October, arrived at Whitehorse

Temperature −2°F.

13 October, Whitehorse

Clear, somewhat warmer. Called to see Mrs Wilson with Jackie. Mrs Gordon was there and asked Mrs Wilson to call with us some eve. Reception to the returned soldiers, two, and a dance after. Mrs Wilson came and took us. We met the principal of the school, Mr Galpin, and he asked us to call at the school.

17 October, Whitehorse

Gave the Talk in the Moose Hall which was donated by the Order.[195] About thirty present. Talked of Oneness of Manifestations. Not nervous as before. Jackie said it was the best I have done. The article in the paper was just as I had written.[196]

21 October, Whitehorse

Went to the school where Jackie is painting the Mr Galpin portrait for the children.

25 October arrived at Skagway, Alaska by train on the White Pass line.

30 October, Skagway

Awoke this morning to find seven inches of snow on the ground and still snowing. It stopped about noon. Jackie and I went to see about a Hall, but did not see the parties. The Elks[197] Hall is too large.

7 November arrived by boat at Juneau.

8 November, Juneau

Wondering about the south-western coast, if I will have to go alone. I feel that I must if Jackie will not go.

9 November

Jackie said that she is not going to Anchorage, so I will go alone.

11 November

Jackie would wait for me here. Too expensive for her to come just for that trip.

[Apparently Marion Jack's money ran out. She stayed in Juneau and earned money painting portraits, including one of Mrs Herbert Faulkner.[198] Marion charged $50 to $250 for a portrait. She apparently painted quite a number while in Alaska but the Bahá'ís there have been unable to locate any of them.[199]]

12 November

[Emogene Hoagg left for Anchorage and made stops at Cordova and Seward and on the return journey at Seward, Valdez and Cordova.]

21 December, Juneau

Arrived at ten this morning. Jackie at wharf to meet me.

31 December

There has not been anything of particular interest in these past days. I have met Mrs Faulkner whom Jackie is painting . . .

1 January 1920, Juneau

A very quiet day, rainy. Georgia Ralston[200] came on the *Watson*, arrived at 11:30 last night. She had a good trip. Jackie and I were at Mrs Garnero's talking, I was and she was painting Roma when we heard the whistle of the boat. In the eve went to the reception given by the Gov. and Mrs Riggs.[201]

9 January, Juneau

[Emogene Hoagg and Georgia Ralston left for Sitka, Petersburg and Wrangell.[202]]

17 January arrived in Wrangell.

Sent cable to Jackie saying we were sidetracked.

25 January arrived back in Juneau.

2 February left Juneau on the *Watson* for Ketchikan.

Saw Jackie away on the boat for Vancouver.

15 February arrived in Vancouver via Seattle.

No way to find Jackie. Hope to see her at the *Princess Mary* when she gets in from Alaska. Left a note at P.O. Nothing to do but watch the natives.

16 February, Vancouver

Jackie materialized about noon. She came from Seattle on *Seattle*, so no work has been done. Seems loss of time. Jackie has found that there is a Bahai near here. She called on her today But J__ was out.

***

On 21 February Emogene Hoagg left Vancouver for Seattle and then travelled onwards to San Francisco where she arrived 27 February. Marion Jack remained in Vancouver.

Over 20 years later Emogene Hoagg wrote a letter summarizing her experiences which sheds more light both on this historic trip and on the people involved:

> My dear: To my tardy reply to your request for items of Alaska trip, please diagnose as mental, physical and moral decrepitude – each one the result of the other. This acknowledgement would indicate the disease and signify that although the 'patient' is not patient it certainly requires patience from others.
>
> Memory is one of my weakest qualities. However, I shall try to think back. We must remember that in 'those days' before radio and air services female visitors to Alaska in the town were looked over critically to be sure they were not 'sporty'. Recognized as the 'proper sort', the elite of the town received them gladly. So it was with us. At Fairbanks, our first stop-over on the trip, the

Judge and his family, the 'society' of the town, entertained us, and after three weeks' visit when leaving we
gave a tea and there were, as I remember, about 25 or
30 ladies present.

Our trip up the Yukon on a freight boat, no other being
available, brought us in direct contact with the 'sourdoughs' and we found them willing listeners to what we
had to tell them, so much so that one or two always
introduced us to their friends as 'ladies having something
interesting to tell them'.

When we got out at the villages and towns en route
many heard of the Faith and received the pamphlets. On
this trip I gave my first 'soap-box' oration just outside a
little store where one of those friends had asked questions,
and as I answered people gathered until there were 20 or
30 surrounding us.

One remembers the mosquitoes of Alaska – poetry has
been written of them. We wore mosquito netting over our
broad brimmed hats and newspaper under our stockings,
gloves on our hands. It took us 3 weeks to reach Tanana,
travelling one mile an hour at times where the river was
shallow, and less when we bogged at times, and it takes
hours to back, forward and sideways out.

Our second stop was at Dawson, Canada. There the
Governor's wife[203] took us for a four-in-hand drive into
the country. Jackie, being Canadian, no doubt had its
influence. She had, too, a distant relative, or some friend
of a relative there, so we were well received and had
numberless opportunities to speak of the Faith besides the
public talks given. We were always invited to teas, concerts,
dances, while there. I forgot to say that the sourdoughs
(prospectors) corresponded with us, at least three, for some
years. My going to Europe rather cut me off, as I might
have contacted some of them when they 'came out' to make
a visit.

At all the places I mentioned in my last we had similar

experiences. Had the sled ride, too, when the first snow fell, while we were at the last Yukon stop after Dawson – Whitehorse, I think.

We reached Nome the first of August and the sun set about 11:00 p.m. Cold weather we did not experience until we reached Dawson really; and while at Fairbanks 60 below is not unusual, in the summer it gets very warm with 19 or 20 hours of sunshine.

We were at Juneau in December and along the southern coast were the lowest I remember was 30 degrees below, so I bought a long fur coat for $150. Imagine it now!

. . . Must confess that for real interest the sourdoughs expressed the greatest. Juneau had many opportunities and many, of all classes there, heard about the Faith, but no deep interest was shown. We had meetings weekly for a group on Sunday in a barber shop, and these were of the 'déclassée' – some of them . . .

Going from Nome to Fort Gibbon, as the boat was for freight, we stopped at every small village, and we always got off, visited the little store, and left literature. Often the town would have a store, a church, and only a few houses. Stops were from an hour to two or three, according to freight to be delivered. Most of the small places were called 'settlements' – not large enough even to be called villages. White people were always to be found there, stores kept by white men, probably educated but who had not 'made good' (financially) so had remained lost, many of them, to their families.

One of the features of our visit always remains with me. Hotels provided only rooms. Our meals were taken out, and that meant sitting on a high stool at a long counter or bar, feet dangling or resting on the rounds of the stool. One chose his meat – $1 or more – and vegetables canned, and usually blueberry pie was the dessert. In larger places this was not necessary. It was a new experience and rather colorful – the surroundings – only

men and sometimes most interesting specimens of sour-
dough . . .

In towns where we stopped the newspapers would take
anything we would write. Newspaper offices were usually
our first contact, and they were always ready to give advice
as to people to see and places for talks . . .

Whenever travelling on the *Yukon* or *Tanana* our
sleeping hours were shortened by talking to groups
gathered to hear about the Faith. Jackie was the 'scout' and
never ceased to attract listeners. If not one way, then she
would paint them on canvas, and while posing she had a
listener.[204]

Another description of this trip is provided by a newspaper
report of a lecture given in 1923 by Marion Jack in Saint
John, New Brunswick:

It was the privilege and great pleasure of the members of
the Art Club to attend the illustrated address given last
night by Miss Marion E. Jack in the Natural History Society
rooms when she spoke of 'Alaska the Wonderland', told
of its varied population, its marvellous scenery and its
strange customs. Miss Jack had visited Alaska in the
company of Mrs Hoagg, who was carrying a message of
Universal Brotherhood and so left the beaten track and
sought to reach as many of the large centres as possible.
Miss Jack had sketching as her chief aim in making the
trip and the splendid water colours and oil paintings which
she showed to illustrate her address were a delight and
a sufficient proof that she had made good use of her trip.

She related how she had met Archdeacon Hudson
Stuck,[205] who had devoted so many years to missionary
services in the Yukon, and in the course of her address she
quoted from the Archdeacon's book, *Voyages in the Yukon
and its Tributaries*.

On her journey Miss Jack had first touched at a whaling

station where a cargo of harpoons was unloaded. The harpoons were fitted with bombs. Nome, the former gold rush colony, was another early point of call and there the unstable houses made a vivid impression. At St Michael's, the Yukon port, the boneyard of abandoned steamboats proved a fascinating field for exploration, and when the trip was to be continued up the river, the weather was so stormy that a five day delay was necessary.

The trip up the river Miss Jack described as being made first through flat, stale and uninteresting scenery and then reaching a feast of the beautiful. She painted a glowing word picture of the scenery which her paintings so well reproduced.

In her address she spoke of the people she had met, told of the characteristics of the Eskimos and the Indians and described the peculiarities of the ever present dog.[206]

In 1951, more than 30 years after the journey, Marion Jack herself summarized her experiences:

It was in 1919 or 1920 dear Emogene Hoagg asked me to go with her to Alaska. So we set sail for Nome I think early in July from Seattle. We were 9 days en route. Dear Emo got off at the Aleutian Islands to give them a pamphlet – maybe more. At Nome we encountered some Spiritualists, but decided to remain a short time as we wanted to catch the Yukon river boat at St Michael's. In the latter port we spent but a few days, and then en route up that long long river. It gave one a chance to boost up our Emo and introduce folks travelling with us, as I felt I knew too little about the Cause in those days, so I was happy to have such a fine speaker to refer them to. At Tanana we changed steamers for Fairbanks (after 17 days on the Yukon), which was quite a thirsty town and dear Emo gave a public talk which was well received. It seems that another dame had tried to do the same thing before, but had not succeeded in explaining the Message, so they were glad to hear Emogene's lucid discourse. Folks were most hospitable and we received several private invitations. After several days we embarked for Dawson City which also treated us kindly then on to Whitehorse and finally, for me, Juneau. Emo wanted me to go along the South Coast with her but my money gave out and I decided to await her return in the meantime earning a little money by painting a few portraits – one of Mrs Faulkner, a charming woman. She was recently in Washington with her husband. We then went to Vancouver where we parted, but in the meantime Emo had done good work along the South Coast as she had done all over, but these non-stop pioneering trips are not really satisfactory . . . Although Emogene spoke splendidly I don't know whether any Bahá'ís resulted from all her efforts. The seed was undoubtedly excellently sown. But I was a very minor part in it all, a mere accompanist. It is true I did much in presenting people to her as the exponent of the Teachings but alas I fear she left no traces of the result of her efforts – Who knows?[207]

In these various reports and letters there are many references to the fact that the women gave out literature on the Faith to anyone who was interested. In only one letter do we have any idea of what type of literature was used or what titles the women felt it appropriate to distribute.

During this trip Marion and Emogene were able to meet people from all strata of society, from all professions, and they did not keep aloof from the Native Americans, the Chinese or the African-Americans.

Theirs was a marathon trip covering over 6,000 miles and taking eight months, in conditions not exactly ideal, undertaken by two women in their fifties, for their love of humankind.

1920–1: Vancouver

After Emogene Hoagg left, Marion Jack settled in Vancouver, where she continued with her painting.

On 18 September the British Columbia Society of Fine Arts opened its Annual Exhibition in Vancouver and on display were three paintings by Marion Jack. One of them was a portrait of Miss J. Fripp[208] and the other two landscapes. One of the landscapes is of Savary Island[209] and the other is mysteriously titled 'Old Favorites'. Among the other artists who participated in this showing were Thomas William Fripp (1864–1931) and Charles Hepburn Scott (1886–1964), Vice-President of the Society and Director of the Vancouver School of Decorative and Applied Art. He is known for the illustrations he provided to the journal *School Days*. Another illustrator to *School Days* who was represented at this exhibition was Spencer Percival Judge (1874–1956), a British-born teacher.

Simultaneous with this exhibition was the Art Section at the Vancouver Exhibition. A weekly newspaper reported:

> The Vancouver Sketch Club was well represented in the Art Section of the Vancouver Exhibition this week. In the amateur list, Mr S. G. Abbott won third prize for portrait in oils. Miss Jack got second prize for landscape in oils, and Miss Maud Sherman carried off first prize for landscape in water colors.[210]

Unfortunately there is no further information on this award-winning painting. At the next monthly meeting in October it was reported that:

> Miss Marion E. Jack showed two portrait studies, done at the club's evening life class, and also landscapes in oil and water color, two of them being sketches in Palestine.[211]

It can be assumed that Marion Jack's participation in the activities of the Vancouver Sketch Club was not limited to the above events. It was probably through her art circles that she met the reporter Mrs J. L. Dunn, who was a member of the B.C. Art League Publicity Committee. Dunn later wrote several very good articles about the Faith in various magazines and newspapers in Vancouver.

We know of Marion Jack's Bahá'í activities in British Columbia through several articles in the *Bulletin* of the National Teaching Committee, then called the Teaching Committee of Nineteen. The first is from July 1920. Here is Marion Jack's own account, interspersed with the editor's comments:

Miss Marion Jack has written a most interesting letter about the work in Western Canada. We quote excerpts as follows:

'The soil is extremely fertile, and the Great Gardener is surely busy in this field, otherwise the souls who are receptive would not be found so frequently, for it is very wonderful how a stranger who does not consider herself either a teacher or a speaker, could meet and give the Message to well over a hundred. The Pres't of the Women's Canadian Club has, at the instigation of a former President I met, invited a Bahai speaker to occupy their platform when one comes this way. Then a Mrs Dunn, a brilliant woman in the world of letters, has given us a good write-up in "Fair Play", a weekly publication that is widely read, and the Editor has, through this article, become interested.'

In addition to this, we gather from Miss Jack's letter that she had twice been able to display her pictures of Acca at Art Exhibitions, and through this many, many people have learned of the Cause. The great interest manifested everywhere, at every meeting, public and private, and through all personal interviews, shows that the district in

94

Canada where Miss Jack is working – Vancouver and its environs – is very promising indeed, and as Miss Jack writes: 'Proofs are in evidence all the time of the truth of the statement of the Heavenly Beloved One that everywhere people now have capacity. Never since it has been my joy to serve have I seen so many thinking and unbiased souls as in the West, – and all I ask is that if possible for any Bahai friends who are seeking for a new field of labor to come as far west as British Columbia, that they come and live in Vancouver. When a Bahai home is opened up here, meetings can begin.'

It is Miss Jack's hope and desire to open a studio in Vancouver, and there have the Bahai meetings, but it has not been possible thus far.

This is but the Springtime in British Columbia, but the crop which is beginning to sprout is in a very healthy condition so a big wonderful harvest may be expected.

From here, as elsewhere, come letters full of joy over the prospects for the future, and Miss Jack adds: 'It is with joy that I read of the probability of a visit from our dear Persian brother, Mirza Fazel.[212] It is a great thing to have something like this to direct the new friends' attention to.'[213]

The next issue of the *Bulletin* contained the following excerpts from Marion Jack's letter to the secretary of the Committee, Mariam Haney:

I cannot tell you what it means to be in this far off place to be able to know what some of the field workers are accomplishing . . .

As for my service: As soon as some dear souls are interested, I cannot wait until I share the good news with some of the friends. The Beloved is indeed good to me: two women who seemed to have turned against the Cause because they could not bear to think Jesus Christ as having the One Holy Spirit that has come through all the other Mediators, speak to me now as if they were again interested; they are reading the books, and want to accompany me to Green Acre should I be able to go next year. My 'fifty or sixty' visits to them have not been in vain: not that I have done anything, only I had begun to feel I might have spent the time differently.

Dear Brother Roy [Wilhelm] was with us for a visit during the last of July. He gave one very delightful talk to a small company of people in the hotel parlors. There was a great feeling of sincerity in the meeting, and he said he much preferred to speak to just such a little group rather that to a vast audience. Those who came were immensely pleased, and I have not heard a critical word from any of them.

Some one told me I was most fortunate in getting the people to read the Revealed Word. (Indeed there is a great confirmation in this).

One lady holds on to the portrait of the Beloved and is going to copy it. She feels she will thereby absorb the spirit, so I am only too anxious to have her begin.

You dear people in the U.S. may think me very slow to wait five months for the first meeting, but if my methods are like the old tortoise, God grant that the results will be the same. When I read of the thrilling rapidity and brilliant results of the more expert and talented workers, I feel absolutely dazzled by their success. But we cannot all work alike – nor have we all ten talents – so I just pray that in time I may acquire greater speed, and more than that, – that I may become detached and selfless like some of those same blessed brothers and sisters. Their heavenly example speaks volumes. Truly an ounce of living the life is worth a pound of mere talk.

One thing this separation from the friends has done for me, and doubtless for all the others: it makes one lean more on the Beloved Friend. One may not be able to talk

things over with the Bahai friends, but one can tell
everything to Him. And I feel I can never tell Him often
enough how grateful I am for permitting one so incapable
to become His instrument. Some day you will see the
miracle He is performing in making use of the apparently
useless.

My immediate prospects appear to be very good, as I
am to meet new and interesting people in three different
directions. I pray they may not only be interesting, but
interested. And if it be His Will, I hope to have good news
for you in time. So far the surface only is being scratched.
But if the dear Persian brothers come, there will be real
news, – a real digging to the depths. In the meantime pray
for us. It is the prayers and the work from the Heavenly
Concourse which is going to do nine-tenths of what will
be done.[214]

Laura Luther of Washington state joined Marion Jack early
in January 1921 to help prepare for the forthcoming visit
by Jináb-i Fáḍil-i Mázandarání.[215]

On 30 January 1921 the *Vancouver Sun* announced that
Jináb-i Fáḍil-i Mázandarání,[216] a Persian philosopher,
would be in Vancouver to give a week-long series of
lectures[217] at the Hotel Vancouver and was accompanied
by Ahmad Sohrab. The newspaper carried a sketch of 'Dr
Jenabe Fazel Mazandarani' by Marion Jack and four of her
line drawings from the Holy Land which she sketched in
1908. This is the only time that Marion Jack's sketches were
published. Along with these sketches the newspaper
published photographs of 'Abdu'l-Bahá and Laura Luther
of Seattle, who, it stated, was an expounder of the 'Bahai
Movement' and was a guest of Marion Jack's at the Gros-
venor Hotel. Under the illustrations appeared another
article with the strange title 'Occultism to Hold Sway for
Devotees of Bahai', written by Mrs J. L. Dunn. This article

contained many peculiar bits of news about the Bahá'í Faith, such as the idea to build a Canadian temple for a sum of $200,000 along the lines of the one in Chicago; and 'in the year 1912 more than 23,000,000 adherents had accepted the cause . . . of almost every nation and two-thirds of Persia'. The article mentions the various societies and organizations where talks would be held, including the Theosophists, New Thought Centre, the Psychical Research Society, the Gyro Club and the Get-Acquainted Club. In describing the teachings the article is surprisingly accurate and sympathetic.[218]

Among the contemporary descriptions of the visit by Jináb-i Fáḍil-i Mázandarání to British Columbia and Marion Jack's involvement is this almost prophetic laudatory statement about Marion.

'Praise be to GOD the field of the Cause is vast and limitless.' A continuation of the sweet story of the proclamation of the Message of Glad-Tidings by Jenabe Fazel, brings us to Western Canada. Miss Marion Jack is the pioneer in this corner of the Vineyard. We will see how through Divine Confirmations she has taken some virgin soil and brought it under cultivation. We will see also how radiantly she responded to the Call. Abdul Baha has instructed us in detail about the work in Canada and the need for teachers, and in three or four of the Tablets he has told us that 'the future of the Dominion of Canada is very great'. 'Her future is most brilliant.' Miss Jack has demonstrated that she has wonderful pioneer qualities, and that she is a loyal, magnanimous and devoted teacher. From all reports we believe she has tried 'to achieve some new service every day' and has 'removed every obstruction from the path of the promulgation of the Word of GOD'. The long weeks and months that she stood with firm feet serving alone in that City called for intense sincerity of purpose, miraculous efforts and extraordinary exertions. The Knowledge of GOD was her guide and the Creator of the Covenant her Protector.[219]

Jináb-i Fáḍil-i Mázandaráni's visit lasted from 31 January to 6 February, and the Teaching Committee dedicated practically an entire issue of its *Bulletin* to a detailed description of the events. This was based mainly on Mirza Ahmad Sohrab's 'Diary Card' reports. Little is mentioned of Marion Jack in these reports, other than her joy at the success of the visit, but there is reference to the work she and Laura Luther put into organizing many of the meetings. On 4 February they accompanied Jináb-i Fáḍil-i Mázandaráni to Victoria, on Vancouver Island, where a successful meeting was conducted which attracted extensive press coverage. In Vancouver the Faith was presented to a Chinese audience, apparently a group that Marion Jack had very much wanted to reach.

Also in the *Bulletin* we have Marion's own report of the events of this historic week:

This campaign – shall I call it? – of the beloved brothers in Canada has so far exceeded anything I could possibly have imagined or pictured to myself, that I am absolutely spellbound at the wonder of it all . . . But we have not done this; the Hosts of the Supreme Concourse have been at work . . . When you think that we are both strangers in the place, with absolutely no backing and very little money, you can see that it is indeed God's work . . . It was heavenly to witness the arising of the various people who came to our assistance to promote the Cause. For instance, the Unity New Thought friends hired a big hall, and as they are not by any means a rich body, this was a beautiful expression of their great faith in the All-Power and Bounty of GOD. The good Theosophist friends banded together

99

and gave their biggest hall. Both of these meetings were packed. Mr Durnin, Unitarian Minister, hired an expensive theatre both morning and evening, and paid for it from his own pocket, and he, too, is far from well-to-do. The Psychic Research Society took the big hall in the biggest hotel here, and the money in payment for it was subscribed by four of its hard working members. This meeting was also packed, and the Society and its President were delighted. One man who had promised the most, almost danced with joy outside the door as we were leaving, so happy was he at the response. The Get-Acquainted Club, under the Unitarian group here, were very happy over the visit of Dr Jenabe Fazel, and they, too, had a big gathering. But the one who assisted us most, perhaps, was the brother of Miss Goodstone of Montreal, a brilliant young lawyer here, who, although not a Bahai as yet, braved everything (in the way of eccentric behaviour meted out to us by our misunderstanding friends) and worked with astonishing zeal.

Through the efforts of our dear brother, George Latimer,[220] we had an opening at the Kiwanis Club[221] in another City in British Columbia, Westminster.

Then our kind friend, Mr Durnin, who never met any of us before, offered his services to go all the way to Victoria to see Dr Butler who is leading the Unity New Thought there, and he was so successful that Dr Jenabe Fazel was invited to speak to their group, – not in numbers like our huge Vancouver audiences – because of the shortness of time given for preparation, but it was a most appreciative audience. They eagerly asked questions, the atmosphere was simply charged with the intensity of their concentration . . . Again the kind Mr Goodstone served us most faithfully, although he might have subjected himself to the misunderstanding and ridicule of the 'smart set' in his own private hotel or apartment hotel, the home of many of the bridge–whist–dancing people of Vancouver.

Here he arranged a most successful meeting for Jenabe Fazel and insisted upon the subject of the Bahai Teachings. The large hall was full and many of the guests were invited to a supper by Mrs Mollison, the owner of the hotel, in her beautiful museum-parlors after the lecture and reception. From the way the guests stayed on and hung about, we could see that this group of people were as charmed as the other Vancouverites who had the treat of listening to our wonderful brother.

I could continue this little exposition for a much longer period . . . I only wanted to emphasize the point that it is not we who accomplish the work, neither are we the authors of results which come about. We are simply the obedient (or as near to obedient) servants as our state of development permits, who arise to put forth our best efforts; and to prove this I have gone into the details of what was done for us by all these dear friends who were not even friends of ours previous to this work. So if this is not encouraging to other followers of the Beloved who, like myself, are among the most inefficient of the undergardeners, I do not know what more is needed. As the dear, sweet-souled Jenabe Fazel said last night before he left, 'what we must do is work, work, work.' This is the greatest message I gained from him. Since dear Laura Luther came, we have indeed worked heart and soul, and gone forth when we were so sick we should have been in bed. I tell you this not to praise ourselves, for I, for one, deserve no praise, but just to encourage others who may feel themselves ill-prepared or inefficient. We do not have to rely upon ourselves; we have but to pray for guidance, and, above all, those prayers written for the whole western world at this moment, in the Divine Plan, and then just arise and 'get at it'. The rest is not in our hands. This visit here is the greatest evidence I have ever known and the most complete fulfilment of the promise of God's Assistance. So please tell the dear friends to 'take courage in both hands' and as our beloved brother tells us 'work, work and work'.

Another wonderful day has dawned for we are beginning to see the harvest already, and these signs are so heavenly that we are even more radiantly happy than we were this morning. I am not going to tell you all just now, but know this much, that there is forming one of the most angelic groups of Bahais in all America . . . People were all charmed with our dear brother Jenabe Fazel and who could help it! They also liked brother Ahmad tremendously; so many people complimented him on his fine diction and scholarly interpretation.

The visit to the Chinese Labor Ass'n, conducted by the fine Japanese, Mr Geo. Kaburagi, was the most thrilling of all the meetings to my mind, but Laura is going to report this and other meetings.

It is great that four different Cities in British Columbia were visited by this Flame of the Fire of the Love of GOD – Jenabe Fazel. Who could have expected such a victory!

Dear Roy Wilhelm has been one of the seed-sowers here. Also I must tell you how delighted we were to see George Latimer at the station with the friends. His cheerful smile attracted many people and they all want to see him again. Both he and Mrs Luther will I hope be the real sponsors of British Columbia since they have been here at the spiritual birth of this part of Canada and live near enough to come here often.[222]

During this short but intensive week hundreds heard of the Faith in and around Vancouver:

And the first five believers were confirmed. These were Mrs Rhoda Anne Harvey, Mrs Grace Ethel Joyce, Mrs Frances Elizabeth Collin and Austin F. L. Collin,[223] who were joined by Mrs Christine Monroe,[224] a Seattle Bahá'í who took up residence in Vancouver at that time.[225]

1921: Winnipeg, Chicago

After leaving Vancouver in the early spring Marion Jack went to Winnipeg, Manitoba. A letter in the United States National Bahá'í Archives concerning one of her sketches of 'Abdu'l-Bahá's garden in Acre bears the rather abstruse statement, 'presented by Miss Jack, apparently at Trinity Hall in Winnipeg, Canada, April 16, 1921'.[226] Mrs Nina B. Matthisen donated the watercolour to the Archives in 1964.

Between 23 and 27 April 1921 Marion attended the 'Bahai Congress and Thirteenth Annual Mashreq'ul-Azkar Convention', Chicago at the Auditorium Hotel during which it was reported that 'General Jack told of the work in Vancouver and Victoria, B.C.' She was appointed to the National Teaching Committee. Others representing Canada on this Committee included May Maxwell, Laura Luther and J. H. Hougen.[227]

Later in the summer of 1921 Marion Jack was living in the Chicago area with the family of Elfie Lundberg. While at the Lundbergs', with her paints and canvases scattered about, Marion Jack painted a portrait of Elfie's mother, Emma Lundberg.[228] Among the places she visited that year with the Lundbergs was Rockford, Illinois. Emma Lundberg also acted as Marion Jack's picture agent.

1922: Chicago, Winnipeg, Ontario, Prince Edward Island, New Brunswick

In March and April Marion was again in Winnipeg, teaching the Faith and staying in the Royal Alexandra. She was generally very discreet about her personal life but there is one letter which does hint of a romance:

103

I have come here to Winnipeg alone & struggle with the Message – but I hope when I return to have someone with me, as we know the Beloved wants us if possible to come in twos. I am not at all satisfied with myself. Oh to be one of those who are so shining that their very presence speaks.[229]

One wonders if this could be the same person Marion refers to in a letter from the Bulgarian period:

I also met a jolly witty man, but too late. Alas he was younger. However I have done pretty well alone for I had my paintings, and adopted humanity instead of a family, so all is well.[230]

In the spring of 1922 Marion Jack was an alternative delegate from Vancouver to the National Convention.[231] However, this does not mean she was living back in Vancouver, as strict residential requirements for delegates had not yet been introduced. From Chicago Marion apparently went to Ontario, where in May a very long interview with her was published in the *Hamilton Spectator*.[232] Excerpts from this article were later published in *Star of the West*.[233] There is no indication of why she was in Hamilton or whom she met there, although it was probably about this time that she visited Mrs Mary Wright in London, Ontario.

During the summer Marion went to Summerside, Prince Edward Island, to paint. This was at the invitation of Wanda Wyatt,[234] whom she had previously met at art classes in Chicago. There she stayed at the Wyatt residence at 85 Spring Street. During one of Marion's many visits Wanda and her sister, Dorothy, arranged an exhibition in Summerside of a hundred of Marion's paintings for the benefit of the IODE.[235] 'The exhibition was held in E. H.

Rayner's fur room in the McArthur Block.' The local paper, *Pioneer,* stated: 'Those depicting scenes in the vicinity of Summerside, at Stanley's Bridge, Clark's Mills, etc. are exceptionally interesting, as they so truly depict the scenes represented.'[236]

In the winter of 1922/1923 Marion Jack was living in Moncton, New Brunswick, where on 9 November she had a solo exhibition at the YWCA. There appeared a very favourable and long article in the local press describing her education, career and the fact that she had taught English in the home of 'Abdiel Baha, a noted Persian reformer of very refined and exalted sentiments'.[237] The exhibition showed landscapes from most of the countries and areas that Marion Jack had visited. There were scenes from Palestine, Italy, France, Ireland, Alaska, Yukon, British Columbia, Prince Edward Island, New Brunswick, Flanders, Maine and England. The reporter commented specifically on a few of her paintings, those depicting Irish peasants and landscapes, and makes this very interesting comment:

> In addition some very excellent portrait paintings were observed, one of which, a masterpiece, depicts an early settler of New Brunswick.

1923: New Brunswick, Green Acre

On 23 April 1923 Marion Jack travelled to Saint John where she gave a lecture called 'Alaska the Wonderland' and exhibited her paintings at the Saint John Art Club. Again this was well received by the press, which reported that her detailed lecture was accompanied by 'about 200 water color sketches [which] were shown by means of reflectoscope being thrown upon the screen. The oil paintings and large pictures were exhibited about the room.'[238]

'Miss Marion Jack was a recent visitor at the school [Saint John Art Club Art School] and she expressed herself as much pleased with the work of the pupils,' reported a newspaper on 6 June 1923.[239]

Marion spent a lot of time in Green Acre, where on 17 October she even bought a small cottage with an adjoining studio. The cottage consisted of one room on stilts reached by a suspended gangway. Her small two-storey studio was located behind the cottage. Nothing of these two buildings appears to remain today.[240]

There are many who remembered her at Green Acre during those summers. William Sutherland Maxwell wrote:

> My mind goes back to the Ivy Cottage in Greenacre. Guess it was there that I last saw you – all bedecked in a painter's smock & swinging a paint brush. This recalls my last visit to Bahji and the fact that I had a good look at your paintings. They form splendid treasured decorations – and are as fresh as on the day you completed them. Thank goodness you were there to do them.[241]

Another memory of Marion at Green Acre is found in this anonymous statement 'from one of her Green Acre friends':

> She was such a lovely person – so joyous and happy that one loved to be with her. Her shining eyes, red cheeks and beautiful smile, with dimples proved how much the Bahá'í Faith meant to her . . . We used to love to go to her studio and talk with her, and to see her paintings of the Holy Land and familiar Green Acre landscapes . . . She always entered into any plan with zest . . . If we could all radiate happiness as did Jackie, I am sure we would attract more people to the Faith.[242]

Marion was also active with the Christian community in Saint John, as this fragment of a report indicates:

> During the 1923–24 winter, a more opportune time arose when a new pastor of the Black church, Rev. Stewart,[243] 'a wide awake, radiant soul', had 'gladly consented' to Bahá'ís speaking to his congregation. Dr Edna McKinney of Philadelphia spoke five times and Miss Jack gave an exhibition of her paintings. This was the first church ever to open its doors to the Bahá'í Faith in the East Coast of Canada. There was even interest in starting a group 'among the colored children' in that church.[244]

One of the early believers in Saint John and a close acquaintance of Marion Jack was Mrs Dealy, who wrote to 'Abdu'l-Bahá when her two little boys died.[245]

1924: Prince Edward Island, Toronto

In 1924 Marion is listed as a Canadian member of the Children International Protective Council of Friends. Other Canadian members included Siegfried Schopflocher, Elizabeth Greenleaf and Elizabeth Cowles.[246] We know nothing of Marion Jack's activities with this society other than the fact that from time to time she sent contributions to it.

A photograph published in Kessler's *A Century on Spring Street*[247] shows Marion Jack in Prince Edward Island with Wanda Wyatt and her sister Cecilia, probably taken in the spring or summer of 1924. It seems that Marion often went to visit the Wyatts in the 1920s.

Sometime in 1924 Marion Jack, by special request, had a solo exhibition at the Women's Art Institute of Ontario in Toronto. Unfortunately we have no description of this exhibition or any of her work done in Toronto. One attraction that the city held for her was that in the 1920s Toronto was famous in the art world as the home of the Group of Seven. This was the name of a circle of painters who discovered a common bond in their love for Canada and their ability to express this through their paintings. They were especially attracted to the rugged northern landscapes of Ontario with its distinct light and the intense bright colours of autumn. The Group had a like vision about art in Canada. 'They [were] all imbued with the idea that an art must grow and flower in the land before the country [would] be a real home for its people.'[248] From the exhibitions in which both she and the Group participated, Marion Jack would have been familiar with the artists' work, especially that of A.Y. Jackson, who lived in Montreal. Jackson also studied in Paris and was there in 1907 at the same time as Marion. Did they meet then or later, in Montreal or Toronto? It is possible to speculate that they did. We do not know Marion's reaction to their work or how it influenced her. Another member of the group, Lawren S. Harris, is purported to have been a Bahá'í in the early 1940s.[249]

Marion lived in Toronto, where she held Bahá'í firesides, for about two years.[250] Thus she fulfilled a request that 'Abdu'l-Bahá made of her in 1914: that she teach the Faith in Toronto. Not much is known about this period of Marion's life. However, a letter written by Laura Rumney Davis[251] states that she lived at the corner of College and McCaul Streets – which would put her practically in the centre of the city – and that she associated with Laura Davis and 'Mother' Rumney. There is also a possibility that Marion visited Ottawa about this time.[252]

An anonymous believer tells us:

Marion's friends remember this jolly wholly dedicated soul – impressed by her gracious charm, her understanding, her twinkling sense of humour . . . everyone who recounts some association with her does so with a smile which seems to spring spontaneously from the mention of her name. 'Jackie' was ageless in her complete at-homeness with young and old alike, was beloved wherever she went, drawing all to her and to each other through the quality of her faith, love and devotion to the Cause of her beloved Guardian.[253]

It was in Toronto that Marion was struck by a bicycle and sustained a back injury which was to bother her for the rest of her life.

1925: Green Acre

When the Annual National Convention was held at Green Acre in 1925, Marion Jack was present. A photograph shows her with several of the friends in front of Fellowship House: Mariam Haney, May Maxwell, Ivy Edwards, Mrs Nayom Cobb, Stanwood Cobb, Ruth Randall (Brown), Bahiyyih Randall,[254] Louise Boyle,[255] Barbara Allting, Roshan Wilkinson,[256] Dr Yunis Khan,[257] Paul Haney, Elizabeth Greenleaf, Howard MacNutt, Louis Gregory, Louisa Gregory, Lorel Schopflocher, Doris Lohse, Dr Susan Moody and Mary Maxwell.[258] Of this group, which included three future Hands of the Cause of God, four were to die serving the Faith in foreign fields.

It was at Green Acre that George D. Miller was introduced to Marion Jack by Laura L. Drum[259] of Washington DC. George Miller later acquired several paintings by Marion Jack, including one of Laura Drum, and presented them to the United States National Bahá'í Archives.

In this year Marion Jack was elected to the first Spiritual Assembly of the Bahá'ís of Eliot, Maine.[260]

1926: Italy, Green Acre

In 1926 Marion returned to Europe for a few months:

> Miss Marion Jack sailed for Italy during January to serve with Mrs Imogene Hoagg in Florence.[261]

In the summer of 1926 she was back at Green Acre.

1927: Montreal

From 28 April to 1 May 1927 Marion Jack attended the Nineteenth Annual Convention of the Bahá'ís of the United States and Canada, held at the Windsor Hotel, Montreal.

1928

Marion Jack's whereabouts in 1928 are unknown.

1929

In 1929 Marion was photographed getting into an automobile with Cecilia Wyatt and a John Jack. This was probably taken in Prince Edward Island.[262]

1930: Green Acre, New Hampshire, Florida

In 1930 Marion Jack organized at Green Acre a Fine Arts and Crafts Club, which had an exhibition at the Rockingham Hotel in nearby Portsmouth, New Hampshire.

Information about Marion's activities and whereabouts from about 1924 to 1931 is scanty. It can be surmised that she travelled a great deal and it seems that her favourite regions were New Brunswick, Montreal, Green Acre and New England in general and the area around Chicago. But she did go further afield. There is a photograph dated 1930 which shows her and Ivy Edwards in front of 'The Gift Shop' in St Augustine, Florida.[263] During this period and until she left for the Holy Land, Marion lived with the family of Dr Walter B. and Frances M. Guy. She also had a winter studio in St Augustine, probably at the Guys'. Francis Guy relates that Marion planned to come back to Florida in the winter following her pilgrimage but she never returned. During the winter of 1942/1943 Francis Guy attempted to sell Marion Jack's paintings with the aim of sending the money to the National Bahá'í Fund. Two paintings were sold for a total of $25: a portrait of Lua Getsinger and a scene of the gardens at Bahjí.[264]

1931: Illinois, Green Acre

According to one of her letters, it seems that Marion was in Illinois in 1931 and that she again had trouble with her eyes. Many years later, when she was in Bulgaria and writing to friends, she would reminisce about Green Acre and her friends in America. Here is an excerpt of one such 'gossipy' letter:

> Thank you for forwarding my letters. Three this week from Green Acre Eliot are most welcome. Ivy Edwards is looking for a job & hopes to land one soon. Isabelle Rivers has just left for Washington where she will pause en route for St Augustine to join the Guys who are valiantly working for the Cause in spite of a several years' ostracism.

Do you remember that campaign in Boston in which dear old Fanny flourished her fists. She still keeps up that positive and forceful attitude, this time fortunately on the right side. She has become quite a noted speaker in a modest way and is President of the WCTU.[265] She has spoken well for the Cause at the big Colored School, which is well attended by whites on Sunday afternoon, who go there partly out of sympathy and largely to hear the students sing the Spirituals. Dr Guy has brought her forward quite a little. When he has been asked to speak he asks to have her take his place, as he does not like to push himself forward too much. What he has to say goes much deeper and really speaks to the heart, but his delivery is poor, whereas Fanny has real oratorical powers and speaks in a colorful way, as they would say in America.

As you may know Shoghi Effendi was most urgent that we should take a greater step in social intercourse with the colored friends, who he says are in no way different from ourselves. In fact he said we ought to intermarry more – and that, as there must be a beginning, it might as well be now, even if there are difficulties on that path.

A letter from Mrs McKinney speaks of Edna's husband's last wife and says she is interested in the Cause and helpful to Frank.

Kitty[266] has started by now for South Africa via Mexico. I don't know whether she is alone or has her Secretary (?) with her. She may drop in on you on the way back. It is extraordinary the capacity of a sort which she possesses. If the poor soul could only forget a few things that some flesh is heir to, she would be a real help to the Cause. – Maybe she is more of a help as it is than some of us realize.

Isabelle Rivers writes that Green Acre has had 'some lovely spiritual this summer but like most cases the best came at the last'. I think she refers to the Willard Hatch visit. She says 'of course there were difficulties – (I know them of yore). Klebsy[267] has given two concerts – one at

Bahá'ís of Bulgaria

Bahá'ís of Bulgaria, 1939

The funeral of George Benke

George Benke's grave

Marion at the Esslingen Summer Week, 1933

At the Esslingen Summer Week, 1933

Marion Jack in the kitchen

Esslingen Summer Week, 1934
Left to right, standing: *Eugen Schmidt, Frau Eugen Epple,*
Fred Kohler; seated: *Louisa Gregory, Marion Jack, Max Greeven,*
Amelia Collins

The swinger
Esslingen Summer Week, 1933

The train staion at Sofia, April 1933. Second from left,
possibly *Howard Carpenter,* next to him *Marzieh Carpenter
(Gail),* then *Marion Jack.*

Marion Jack, far right, *and Martha Root,* third from left,
in Adrianople

Marion Jack's grave, Sofia

Old Varna (circa 1930s)

Birches and Maples, Rothsay Park (1914)

the Grange Hall – the other at the Inn, of her pupils – Both successes – She had a beautiful meeting at her camp before returning South 'all spirituality and harmony' and in a letter from the South she says that 'her heart and soul were still singing and it made up for everything she had suffered all summer'. They think she is failing – the dear soul. She certainly strikes the high spots.

The Thompsons are in their winter quarters near Ivy, & it is a really cozy wee place – bless their dear hearts.[268]

In 1931 Marion Jack left North America on pilgrimage to the Holy Land. She was never to return.

8

The Pilgrim
1931

Marion Jack left the United States in January 1931 on board the 35,000–ton White Star liner SS *Homeric* on what would be her last transatlantic voyage. Sailing with her was Mrs Alice Doolittle, a Bahá'í from Cleveland, Ohio. The ship stopped at the Portuguese island of Madeira on 31 January. Marion visited the cathedral and the flower and fish markets in the town of Funchal. This was probably not the first – nor the last – time that pilgrims had stopped at this island but it would not be until 1953 that Bahá'ís would permanently reside there.

The next day Marion and Alice sailed for Morocco. They arrived at the port of Haifa on 17 February. Emogene Hoagg and Effie Baker were already in the town.

Marion Jack did not write any 'pilgrims' notes' as such but she did write about her pilgrimage in several letters to friends and relatives. It is through these letters and other contemporary accounts that we are able to follow her on her second visit to the Holy Land.

The pilgrims spent most of their time in Haifa at the Pilgrim House. Marion states that Effie Baker looked after the pilgrims:

She was looking after the [Western] Guest House and did everything to make things comfortable for us who were staying there.[269]

Marion provides a pen sketch of the Western Pilgrim House:

The Pilgrim House is a beautiful place for us all to be in. The six of us have our own bedrooms and there are two more for you girlies just opposite each other. There is the big hall in the middle. At either end there are smaller halls with a bedroom out of each. At the very end are sitting rooms with 2 bedrooms out of each. Then there is a library and a writing room all on this top floor. The front door is up here too, approached by marble steps (broad ones) from the street. Down stairs, on the ground floor, the entrance from the street is up a little stone passage. There is also a hall there in the middle – the dining room, and a little square sitting room to one end, and Fujita[270] and Effie[271] each have two rooms. The kitchen is not very big because not very much cooking is done in this house. The meals all come from Abdul Baha's house – except breakfast – which consists of eggs, toast, nice whole wheat bread, butter, tea and coffee. We have wonderful food I think, and I am always ready for it. Lunch at one and dinner at half past seven.[272]

From the Pilgrim House it was a short, steep walk to the Shrine of the Báb. The Shrine at that time was only a low, one-storey building, consisting of the six rooms built by the Master and an additional three rooms added by the Guardian. A vault under the centre room contained the sacred remains of the Báb.

The middle room of the three which have been constructed adjacent to the Shrines of the Bab and Abdu'l-Baha on Mt. Carmel have been so arranged by the Guardian as to contain some of the pictures and writings reminiscent of the early Baha'is both in the East and the West, and will by and by become a place that the friends will visit with great and increasing interest. The gardens around the Shrines are now in full bloom with the coming of spring and they form a heavenly surrounding for the last resting place of those much loved and much adored leaders of the Faith.[273]

It was much later that William Sutherland Maxwell, under the direction of Shoghi Effendi, designed the beautiful colonnaded structure around the Shrine crowned by an ornate drum and golden dome.

About a week after her arrival, on 23 February, Marion Jack accompanied Louise Wright and Alice Doolittle on a trip to Jerusalem 'by motor'. The party stayed two or three days in Jerusalem before returning to Haifa.[274]

The Mansion of Bahjí, the last home occupied by Bahá'u-'lláh, had fallen into the hands of the enemies of the Faith, who had occupied it from 1892 to 1929. In 1929 Shoghi Effendi was able to take possession of the Mansion. Such was the sorry state of neglect that the building had fallen into that it took over two years to complete the restoration. Shoghi Effendi ensured that the reconstruction was as faithful as possible to the original. Afterwards he adorned the Mansion with historical photographs, paintings, Chinese vases, Persian carpets and books in order to convey a sense of the unfoldment of the history of the Faith and to maintain an air of beauty and respect. He made it into a Bahá'í Holy Place in whose precincts is the Tomb of Bahá'u'lláh, the Most Holy Place of visitation, an object of pilgrimage for

Bahá'ís around the world.

The first group of pilgrims who had the privilege of staying overnight at the Mansion of Bahjí after Shoghi Effendi had completed renovating it included Louise Drake Wright; Marion Jack; Thilde Diestelhorst from Berlin, Germany; Alice Doolittle; Effie Baker; and Mary Olga Katherine Mills. They were accompanied by Munavvar Khánum,[275] Zahrá Shahíd,[276] Thurayyá Afnán,[277] Mihrangíz Khánum[278] and Ḍiyá'iyyih Khánum, Shoghi Effendi's mother.[279]

A contemporary account reports:

> The Pilgrims visiting are already appreciating the rare experience which is now available to all to spend the night in the Mansion of Baha'u'llah in Bahji. They find it still another opportunity to visualize the atmosphere in which Baha'u'llah spent His closing years and to drink deep from that ever-flowing fountain of inspiration.[280]

From the Mansion itself Marion wrote this account of her pilgrimage:

> At present I am residing in a beautiful palace which has just been renovated, and re-decorated in the old style in which the first owner was pleased to have it. I know you would like.
>
> The upper half is very lovely with arches & pillars – very big – 60 feet long & very wide. Eleven big rooms and two corridors empty out of, or into it. And the wide arched galley on the outside is all painted with quaint groups of figures, flowers, boats, etc. This runs around three sides of the building and is a beautiful place to sit for the view is superb all out over the valley of Achor and groves of olive trees and on the front a few hundred yards away an orange grove.

117

As you look past this delightful scene you see Acca all white or shrouded in mist & atmospheric effects at other times, and beyond is the bay of Acca & further on the slope of Mount Carmel with the port of Haifa nestling at its base. Then to the left are the hills of Galilee. Sometimes covered with a haze and again disclosing the various little hamlets and villages nestling in their midst as the mist lifts and the air becomes clearer. These mists are not of the Scottish order but just soft atmospheric veils.[281]

Here we have another pen sketch of Marion's pilgrimage, this time from Bahjí, in the form of a letter to Auntie Victoria Bedikian:

Dearest Auntie Victoria,

Yatola Sisami wants me to send you a line of loving greeting from the Behji. So I hasten to do his bidding – Zahara[282] and Esfendiar[283] are also anxious to be remembered to you – They are all standing around me in the new writing room of the Behji – Yatola wants me to tell you that Shogi Effendi is very very happy that the Behji is now restored to its former beauty – and that it is so wonderfully illuminated with electric lights – The two Thompsons[284] are here with me now and also send much love. The reason I am staying out here is to paint some pictures for Shogi Effendi. One which is about 12 feet long is the view of Acca & the Sacred Shrine – a panorama – the other is almost half as long and does not take in the Shrine.

Yatola wants me to thank you for the many letters you have sent to the Acca Assembly – He certainly has a grateful heart – and a very warm spot for his dear Auntie Victoria – He has mentioned you several times and the friends who were with you here. If he could I know he would write you himself.

He also wished me to say that several of the friends have

lately had the joy of staying in the Behji for a couple of nights. The first group included Miss Wright, Emogene Hoagg, Olga Mills from St Augustine and Germany (near Munich), Mrs Distlehorst of Berlin, Alice Dolittle of Cleveland, & yours truly – Shogi Effendi's Mother, Mrs Ahmad Yazdi (Monever Khanum), Saroya Afnan, Jahara Jalel & Muharanges Khanum were also of the party. Some slept down with Sahara where you often stayed and the rest of us upstairs in the Mansion which is the name Shogi Effendi has called the Palace. Some of the big rooms are fitted up as bed rooms and some have too [sic] beds in them. Several of the rooms are as yet unfurnished, but that will all come some day.

The second party included Mrs True, Mrs Harding[285] of Urbana, Miss Burton[286] of Evanston, Miss Dolittle, Olga Mills, Emma & Louise & myself and the beloved Monever Khanum & Marangies were with us. The Thompsons & Alice leave Wednesday for America – Olga & I sail on Wednesday week for Triest, and I shall join Mrs Gregory in Sofia where she is trying to spread the Cause. I hope Olga will come too for she is a fine linguist.

Shogi Effendi is so lovely to Emma Thompson and this evening just before leaving, at twilight he took us into the shrine for prayers – and after chanting himself took the three of us into the inmost Shrine and had Emma recite the Tablet of Ahmad. He said this is a great privilege, a very great privilege. Later on he told Emma that he enjoyed her prayer & that she recited with such fervor, sincerity & devotion, I think the third word was.

It is glorious to be in this Holy spot & to visit that holiest of all places on earth, the resting place of the remains of the Blessed One. How can we thank God enough for this visit.

We spent the Naurooz[287] with the Holy family[288] and all the women & children Bahais of Acca, Haifa, Rizwan[289] and so on.

There was a group of Persian pilgrims who spent one night at the Behji during my stay here – One would not sleep all night & began to chant about three oclock. It was lovely to hear his lovely prayer ascending in these early hours.

Dearest Auntie I am sorry indeed that I see so little of you, but I always think of you most lovingly – Again with special love from Zahara & all of us here, lovingly in His Name & Service. Jacky (General).[290]

The painting mentioned in this letter was hung by Shoghi Effendi in the main hall of the Mansion at Bahjí.

Louise Drake Wright was with Marion Jack as she painted. Here is her diary note from Thursday, 5 March 1931.

Miss Jack & I sat above the Shrines while she painted a landscape for Shoghi Effendi. Her picture is from the back of the Shrines on the . . . side. She gets half the Shrine, gardens, Haifa, sea, Acca, Mt. Hormon & hills. She is such a true dear! Noble! I hope that Shoghi Effendi will be pleased with what she is doing. He likes careful, detailed work & chose the view. She is going to Bahji to paint what Baha'u'llah saw from the balcony there . . .

Another diary note for the same day reads:

Sat up above Shrines with Miss Jack & read to her from 'The Ighan'.[291] She is making a large painting of the Shrines, sea, Acca & Haifa below. Lovely time.[292]

Marion Jack must have met the Guardian several times during this pilgrimage, however in her letters only one such meeting is described:

We have just had lunch with Shoghi Effendi and he stressed some points quite emphatically. The first was that in making friends with the Ahmad group[293] there should be no compromise for he said the Administration is as important as the spiritual – and we must be loyal to both, and he went on to point out that the Administration went further back even than Abdul Baha to Baha O'llah and the Aqdas.[294]

He spoke quite at length on the question of mixing with the Colored friends socially, and even of intermarrying with them. He feels that we in America are not without prejudice and that we have carried on that inclination from our early days. He says we are very little different in our attitude from the non-Bahais in our conduct towards that race. He says it is not enough to meet them formally, but we must go out of our way to have them in our homes. He said there was no difference whatever between the black & white race and we must realize that, but must if there is a choice give them the preference. He said that Green Acre was an excellent place to demonstrate this, that the Amity Conferences[295] were good, but they were a little formal, too . . . He spoke of the Gregorys' marriage[296] and said that Abdul Baha must have had great wisdom in joining these two, and that it would have been an excellent thing if more people would follow suit . . . He also spoke about the motion picture taken of Abdul Baha in the United States.[297]

The pilgrims spent a considerable amount of time with the members of 'Abdu'l-Bahá's family: His sister, the Greatest Holy Leaf; His widow, the Holy Mother; and his daughters.

A very special event during this pilgrimage was the celebration of the Bahá'í New Year, Naw-Rúz, on 21 March. The local newsletter provided a report:

On the 21 of March the Baha'is of Haifa celebrated the Nawruz at a meeting on Mt. Carmel which was attended by the Guardian. Among others were Jenab Motlak and Dr Hakim[298] from Persia, Mr Mushukati from Port-Said. We have also had with us a large group of American friends among them Miss Wright, Miss Doolittle, Mrs True, Mrs Harding, Mrs Burton,[299] Mrs Mills, the Misses Thompson, Miss Jack, Mrs Hoagg and others.[300]

Louise Wright and Marion Jack both mention another visitor at that time, a Mrs Halderman (or Aulderman) from northern Italy who was, according to Louise Wright, a pupil of the Theosophist Krishnamurti.

At the time of Marion Jack's pilgrimage, Shoghi Effendi was editing and translating Nabíl's chronicle of the early days of the Bábí revelation, *The Dawn-Breakers*.

Emogene Hoagg has been typing it in the mornings and Muhrangies his sister has been working with him in the afternoons . . . Effie Baker went to Persia on a very extensive tour and photographed many many places where these terrible events had transpired . . . She has only been back a couple of weeks and has been developing them herself ever since.[301]

In this same letter Marion Jack describes how the Guardian let the pilgrims assist him in choosing the photographs of the relics of the Báb which would be most appropriate for the book.

It was towards the end of Marion's pilgrimage that the Guardian suggested she should go to Bulgaria to help Louisa Gregory, who was pioneering there at the time, and that she should travel via Germany. Marion found out in Jerusalem that it would cost her $75 for the ticket.[302]

Marion Jack along with several other pilgrims left Haifa around the end of March. They stopped at Cyprus and visited some Crusader ruins and St Nicholas Cathedral. From Cyprus they sailed through the Greek islands and the Ionian Sea and then into the Adriatic to Brindisi, where Emogene Hoagg and Mihrangíz Rabbání disembarked. They then sailed to Trieste, where

Mrs Mills left me in the clutches of Cook's[303] man & after a night came on here [Sofia].[304]

Part Two

Veni, Vidi, Vici

9

The Bringers of Light
1926–1932

O ye close and dear friends of 'Abdu'l-Bahá!
In the Orient scatter perfumes,
And shed splendours on the West.
Carry light unto the Bulgar,
And the Slav with life invest.[305]

This verse was composed around 1893 by 'Abdu'l-Bahá. It is the introduction to a lengthy Tablet on teaching and seems very appropriate for the Balkans with its war-weary history.[306]

In *God Passes By* Shoghi Effendi alludes to the prophetic import of the poem in writing about the establishment of the Faith in the West:

A year after the ascension of Bahá'u'lláh, 'Abdu'l-Bahá had, in a verse which He had revealed, and which had evoked the derision of the Covenant-breakers, already foreshadowed an auspicious event which posterity would recognize as one of the greatest triumphs of His ministry, which in the end would confer an inestimable blessing upon the western world, and which erelong was to dispel the grief and the apprehensions that had surrounded the community of His fellow-exiles in 'Akká. The Great Republic of the

127

West, above all the other countries of the Occident, was singled out to be the first recipient of God's inestimable blessing, and to become the chief agent in its transmission to so many of her sister nations throughout the five continents of the earth.[307]

'Abdu'l-Bahá again referred to Bulgaria in a Tablet addressed to the Bahá'ís of the United States and Canada, dated 11 April 1916:

Therefore, O ye believers of God! Show ye an effort and after this war spread ye the synopsis of the divine teachings in the British Isles, France, Germany, Austria-Hungary,[308] Russia, Italy, Spain, Belgium, Switzerland, Norway, Sweden, Denmark, Holland, Portugal, Roumania, Serbia, Montenegro, Bulgaria, Greece, Andorra, Liechtenstein, Luxembourg, Monaco, San Marino, Balearic Isles, Corsica, Sardinia, Sicily, Crete, Malta, Iceland, Faroe Islands, Shetland Islands, Hebrides and Orkney Islands.

In all these countries, like unto the morning stars shine ye forth from the horizon of guidance. Thus far ye have been untiring in your labours. Let your exertions henceforth increase a thousandfold. Summon the people in these countries, capitals, islands, assemblies and churches to enter the Abhá Kingdom. The scope of your exertions must needs be extended. The wider its range, the more striking will be the evidence of Divine assistance.[309]

The recorded history of the Bahá'í Faith in Bulgaria before the monumental changes of the 1990s documents that there were four pioneers to the country – Louisa Gregory, Marion Jack, George Adam Benke and Lina Benke – and about a score of travel teachers. Before Marion Jack's arrival in 1931 Bulgaria had received only one pioneer – Louisa Gregory – and, despite its proximity to Adrianople,

Bahá'u'lláh's 'Land of Mystery', and its being on the land route for pilgrims between the Holy Land and Paris, only one travel teacher – Martha Root. That is, there are documented records of only one travel teacher, though there are fleeting whispers of others. One of these is related in a letter from Louisa Gregory to Marion Jack:

> He [Mr Stoyanov] was very pleased & said he remembers he heard of the teachings some 15 years ago at Samokov, had a pamphlet in English given him. He could not remember by whom but thought some English visitor. I think it must have been Mr Cobb[310] unless perhaps Lady Blomfield as I have an idea she came to Bulgaria. I had heard from her maybe at the time A.B.[311] went to Budapest or just after. Anyway he says he knows it was before the war so I do not think it was Martha. He says he remembers he was much impressed especially with 2 things, the abolition of war & the oneness of humanity . . .[312]

At this point it would perhaps be useful to have an overview of this pioneering field so close to the Holy Places in Turkey.

Bulgaria: Background Notes

Bulgaria lies in the Balkan Peninsula and is bordered by Romania to the north, the Black Sea to the east, Turkey on the southeast, Greece on the south and Macedonia and Serbia, both part of the former Yugoslavia, on the west. The 1934 census showed a population with the following composition:

Bulgaria – 1934 Population					
Ethnic groups			**Religions**		
Bulgars	5,274,854		Orthodox	5,128,890	
Turks	618,268		Muslim	821,279	
Gypsies	80,532		Jewish	48,398	
Jews	28,126		Roman Catholic	45,704	
Armenians	23,045		Armenian	23,476	
Romanians	16,405		Protestant	8,371	
Russians	11,928				

The main cities are the capital Sofia, Plovdiv, Veliko Turnovo, Pleven, Varna, Burgas, Stara Zagora and Ruse.

In the 1930s Bulgaria was mainly an agricultural country, with wine and tobacco as the main exports.

The worldwide depression of the 1930s hit Bulgaria hard. Strikes occurred up and down the country and continued off and on for the next five years, with various degrees of violence and clashes with the police. It seems that everyone went on strike at one time or another: in 1931 textile workers, tobacco workers, metal workers, rubber processing workers and glass blowers; in 1932 it was the unemployed and the Sofia tram drivers. Politically, Bulgaria was a monarchy, with Boris as the tsar. In 1930 he married Princess Giovanna of Saxony. General elections were held in June 1931, which the Popular Bloc won. Bulgaria was generally politically unstable and a continuous battle raged between nationalists, socialists and fascists. In 1932 the Bulgarian Communist Party won the Sofia municipal election. On 19 May 1934 there was a *coup d'état*. During the 1920s and 1930s in Bulgarian Macedonia there were many incidents of banditry carried out by Macedonian fascists.[313]

The Bringers of Light

Martha L. Root (1872–1939)[314]

Martha Root was an American journalist who accepted the Bahá'í Faith in 1908. She met 'Abdu'l-Bahá when He was in America in 1912. In 1915 she began her first round the world trip, teaching the Bahá'í Faith wherever possible. Three more such trips followed, despite pain and illness owing to a back injury and advancing cancer. Martha Root's audiences with Queen Marie of Romania, eight in all, resulted in the Queen embracing the Bahá'í Faith.

This oft-quoted statement by Shoghi Effendi appropriately sums up Martha's life and service to the Faith she so ardently adopted:

> . . . [Martha Root] not only through her preponderating share in initiating measures for the translation and dissemination of Bahá'í literature, but above all through her prodigious and indeed unique exertions in the international teaching field, has covered herself with a glory that has not only eclipsed the achievements of the teachers of the Faith among her contemporaries the globe around, but has outshone the feats accomplished by any of its propagators in the course of an entire century. To Martha Root, that archetype of Bahá'í itinerant teachers and the foremost Hand raised by Bahá'u'lláh since 'Abdu'l-Bahá's passing, must be awarded, if her manifold services and the supreme act of her life are to be correctly appraised, the title of Leading Ambassadress of His Faith and Pride of Bahá'í teachers, whether men or women, in both the East and the West . . .
>
> [She] transmitted the message of the New Day to kings, queens, princes and princesses, presidents of republics, ministers and statesmen, publicists, professors, clergymen

131

and poets, as well as a vast number of people in various walks of life, and contacted, both officially and informally, religious congresses, peace societies, Esperanto associations, socialist congresses, Theosophical societies, women's clubs and other kindred organizations . . .[315]

Martha Root first came to Bulgaria at the beginning of February 1926. She stayed for twelve days giving lectures and meeting with university students. She also sent a book and a letter on the Bahá'í Faith to the king, Boris III, and his sister Princess Eudoxie.

On 17 October 1927 Martha Root returned, staying until about 24 November. She was able to give lectures in various cities and towns throughout Bulgaria. She first visited Ruse on the Danube River, where the local Esperantists had organized a lecture in a theatre and five hundred came to hear her speak. Two days later, on 11 October, she arrived in Sofia. Here she addressed the National Convention of Women's Clubs in Esperanto. Her talk was entitled 'Woman and Peace'. This is how the chronicle of the development of Esperanto in Bulgaria recounts this historic visit:

> En la komenco de novembro 1927 oni arangis verdan semajnon. En la publika kunveno parolis la usona esperantistino f-ino _Marta Rut_ (Root), ku vizitis la kongreson de la Bulgara Virina Asocio kaj referis je temo: '_La virino kaj la paco_'. [At the start of November 1927 a green week was arranged. The American Esperantist Miss Martha Root, who was visiting the Bulgarian Women's Association spoke in the public meeting and dealt with the subject 'Women and Peace'.][316]

After this meeting Martha received many invitations to speak. In Sofia she managed through the good offices of a local paper and with the assistance of Slav Dilkmov to get the first pamphlet published in Bulgarian, *What is the Bahai Movement?* Martha reported:

> One paper is using as supplement 'What Is the Bahai Movement?'[317] in Bulgarian language[.] I got out 10,000 for $20. (couldn't afford the booklet so just put it all on one page[.)] They did the printing & sent out 3500 for me gratis, and next week they will at their own expense get out a *Bahai Number*.[318]

As usual Martha Root visited several newspaper offices and had articles published in the local press. She also spoke at the two universities in Sofia, at the Tourist Club and at the Red Cross Training School for Nurses, having been invited there by the assistant director, Miss K. Pachedjieva. Martha also spoke to a group of youth at the home of Professor Dymitry Katzarov, a Tolstoian, whom she had previously met in Switzerland. She made several trips out of Sofia, visiting Samokov, a small town to the south of Sofia, and Vratsa [or Vraca] to the north of the capital. In Samokov she gave a lecture to four hundred at the American School, through the assistance of Mrs Black, the wife of the president of the school, who was away in America at the time. The Esperantists in Vratsa organized a meeting that was attended by over five hundred people in a heavy rainstorm. On 19 November she arrived in Plovdiv where the Esperantists and the Arts and Press Club jointly sponsored a meeting. Again the Esperantists sponsored a meeting with Martha Root in Stanimaka (now called Asenovgrad), 15 kilometres southeast of Plovdiv. Martha Root left Bulgaria around 23 or 24 November for Constantinople.

From 14 to 18 July 1933 Martha attended the National Esperanto Congress in Ruse. Later in October she left Sofia with Marion Jack for Edirne (formerly Adrianople) in

Turkey. They returned in November to Sofia, where Martha spent a month assisting Marion. And in December 1933 she went with Marion Jack to Plovdiv. Marion wrote of Martha:

> Martha Root is without exception a princess of the royal blood as a teacher & worker. She has the greatest of all gifts, the loving heart which draws with a mighty force people of all ranks.[319]

In June 1934 Martha visited Bahá'ís in Dragoman, a small town near the Serbian border, apparently on her way from Belgrade to Athens.

Martha's next to last visit to Bulgaria was in 1936 when she stayed for several weeks, arriving 17 January in Sofia and departing 31 January.[320] There were informal meetings almost every night. A formal meeting was held on Sunday 26 January and over 50 attended. On Wednesday 29 January there was a meeting at the Esperanto Club, with Petar Yordanov chairing, which about 50 people attended.

Again in February 1936 in Sofia *en route* to Belgrade, Martha Root spoke at one large meeting which Marion Jack organized and again over 50 people attended. She also attended two afternoon teas, one a meeting at Mr Nikov's and one with the Esperantists. This was her last visit to Bulgaria.

Louisa Mathew Gregory (1866–1956)

Marion Jack described the first pioneer to Bulgaria:

> Louise, a noble pioneer of great devotion, is a quiet little mouse, but perhaps the few she teaches may be so strong & spiritual that they may move mountains.[321]

Louisa Mathew, born in England, a social worker by education, was pursuing musical studies when she first encountered the Faith in Paris and met Marion Jack. This would have been around 1903. Louisa later travelled to Egypt to meet 'Abdu'l-Bahá and in about 1912 moved to the United States. In contemporary Bahá'í history she is known for the fact that she was the wife of Louis Gregory, an outstanding American Black Bahá'í, posthumously raised to the rank of Hand of the Cause of God by Shoghi Effendi. Their marriage was performed by 'Abdu'l-Bahá Himself, the first interracial marriage among the Bahá'ís of America. Her 'highly meritorious' pioneer services have been somewhat overshadowed by those of her husband. Because of the cruel, inhospitable and bigoted social conditions in America and parts of Europe, the couple were often apart. Louis Gregory spent much time teaching the Faith in the southern states of the United States and Louisa travelled in Europe.

As with so many events in Bahá'í history, the beginnings of Louisa's connection with Bulgaria are lost. Why she went to Bulgaria, and why Varna, a resort on the Black Sea, is unknown. It is known that she arrived in Varna in November 1928, thus becoming the first pioneer to Bulgaria. However, it is possible that she was in Bulgaria even earlier. We know that she was a frequent visitor to Europe in the early 1920s. For example, she was in Manchester, England, in July 1924[322] and in 1926 she was again reported to be in England *en route* to Vienna and Budapest.[323] In 1928, with Martha Root, she attended the Esperanto Congress in Prague.

Louisa Gregory stayed in Varna from 1928 to 1931. It is likely that she travelled in Europe during that time and even visited America. In January 1930 it is recorded that she was in Sofia. In December 1930 she visited Romania and arrived back in Sofia on 7 January 1931. Wherever she was she taught the Faith. Literature in Bulgarian was non-existent so she used whatever she could. She had Lubin Dobrovsky translate into Bulgarian the paper *The Baha'i Religion* by Ruhi Afnan sometime before 1931. He also translated part of a pamphlet by Horace Holley (1931).

In January 1931 Louisa wrote to Marion Jack and asked her to come to Bulgaria to help her teach the Faith using her 'chalk talks'. Apparently she and Marion had taught the Faith together in America in the 1920s using this method.

In January 1931 Louisa Gregory wrote about an article that appeared in one of the Sofia daily papers in the form of a letter from Ankara, Turkey. The article mentioned that there were 2,000,000 Bahá'ís, that the Temple was built and that it cost $2,000,000 and said something about a home for orphans. The article was used by Louisa Gregory to interest other people in the Faith. A bank teller brought it to her attention.

Louisa's activities as a Bahá'í did not go unnoticed by the government:

On April 1 [1931] I was sent for by the American Legation & informed that the police said through my work on behalf of a religious movement they considered non-Christian they object to it & this came through the Foreign Affairs who asked them to let me know that if I asked for an extension of my 3 months' permit to stay which expires April 7, it would not be granted.[324]

On 8 April 1931 Louisa left Sofia by train, passing Marion Jack going the other way about 2:30 p.m. From Sofia it is likely that Louisa went to Belgrade. She had already planned to leave Sofia in mid-May at the latest so that she could be with Louis, as she considered his needs important when he returned home from his long travel teaching trip across the southern states. However, she also wanted to be in Bulgaria when Marion Jack arrived.

Louisa returned to Bulgaria in October 1931 and went to Varna to meet Marion Jack. She has left this fragmentary report of her activities:

> At Varna where I went in the late autumn of 1931 to meet Miss Jack I was able to teach two students whom the first believer, a poor Armenian youth taught by Miss Jack through her smiles & Bahai literature in Bulgarian, sent to me after Miss Jack left Varna. Later an elderly Armenian who translated some of the teachings into Armenian became a believer, unfortunately he died later . . .
>
> These youths became believers but – being obliged to leave to go to teach the Cause at Belgrade often am [beyond call] & when the students were too busy to come to me . . . their home is Burgess[325] . . . one of these youths [is] Nicola Vassileff . . .[326]

In 1932 Louisa was back in America for a short period, returning to Bulgaria in October via Hamburg, Leipzig, Vienna, Salzburg and Budapest. From various records it is known that she was also in Varna from 27 February to 9 April 1933. On 15 April she arrived in Sofia. It is not known how far afield she travelled in Bulgaria, except for the fact that she did visit Samokov at least once. Before returning to the United States for good she travelled widely in Europe, especially in the Balkans and Germany, and she often visited Belgrade for several months at a time, the last occasion probably being in 1935.

Details of Louisa's teaching activities are scarce. However, when she left Bulgaria there was a small group of Bahá'ís in Varna and the ones she had interested in the Faith in Sofia later became the nucleus of the community Marion Jack developed, which in 1934 elected the first spiritual assembly in the Balkans. Among these were Professor Katsarov and Lubin Dobrovsky, both of whom wrote and translated pamphlets; Mrs Belopeteva, who became a very close friend of Marion Jack; and Leon Minassian, who later worked on some Armenian translations of Bahá'í literature; and many more.

On her way back to the United States Louisa spent a few weeks in England visiting her relatives and an early Bahá'í, Mrs Kinnethy in York, who was introduced to the Faith by Louisa and Ethel Rosenberg.

Many years later Marion Jack wrote this appreciation of Louisa Gregory:

> How many people get & even accept the Message, but they need the inspiration of seeing other folks carrying on, and denying themselves as she [Draga Ilich] has seen you and Martha, before the aspiration for service take a deep hold on them (not always of course – but very very often). See how you inspired me! If you had not come to Europe, maybe I never should either. I read with awe of Martha's achievements in meeting this & that great one, & in doing all sorts of stunts. I used to wish I had her capacity of journalism & so on, but it was <u>your firm determination to stick to your work in a modest way</u> which carried the day with me, so I thank God for my dear Louise.[327]

In 1949 Marion Jack wrote:

> It was through her [Louisa Gregory] that I came here and she is the Mother of Bulgaria. She and sweet Martha – twin mothers – a new species.[328]

Perhaps one day a full-length biography of Louisa Mathew Gregory will appear that will bring to light her extraordinary pioneering services in southeast Europe.

George Adam Benke and Lina Benke[329]

Lina and George Adam Benke accepted the Bahá'í teachings in 1920 as a result of a meeting held in Leipzig. A biographical article about Hand of the Cause of God Hermann Grossmann describes that spiritually charged meeting:

> Hermann's earnest search for meaning and purpose eventually led him to the Teachings of Bahá'u'lláh; he met Harlan and Grace Ober in Leipzig, Germany in the summer of 1920. This well-known American Bahá'í couple were returning to the United States after being on pilgrimage in the Holy Land where they had visited 'Abdu'l-Bahá. It was at the behest of 'Abdu'l-Bahá that Mr and Mrs Ober were in Leipzig where they accepted an invitation from the Theosophical Society to speak about the Bahá'í Faith. Here it was that Hermann first encountered the Bahá'í Teachings which were to have such an important bearing on his future life. In later years he would frequently recount the circumstances of that fateful encounter.
>
> Arriving late at the gathering, Hermann entered the softly lighted room and saw a woman of radiant countenance standing at the speaker's table. Mrs Ober at that moment was voicing the Utterance of Bahá'u'lláh that all men are the leaves of one tree and the flowers of one garden. The truth of these words struck a responsive chord in the young man. Later, Mrs Ober approached Hermann and said, 'I think I was speaking your thought.' 'Yes, indeed,' he replied, 'but tell me what it is.' His recognition of the truth of the Message was instantaneous; his acceptance, wholehearted.

The same night Mrs Lina Benke also spontaneously embraced the Cause. Shortly afterwards her husband, George Adam Benke, also accepted . . .

Soon the three – Hermann and the Benkes – were eagerly visiting each day with Miss Alma Knobloch who was residing in Leipzig at that time. Miss Knobloch had accepted the Cause in 1903 and at the request of 'Abdu'l-Bahá had settled in Germany in 1907 to assist in the firm establishment of the Faith in that country.[330]

Marion Jack recorded the following notes about Adam Benke:

> Frail health. Went by train to Esperanto Congress at Stara Zagora and on the train he met the President of the Congress, who was so much taken with his spirit that he invited him to be vice-president of the Congress.[331] When the Congress met in Sofia the following year the same honor was conferred upon him . . . He visited Varna and gave two talks in Russian there, and on his return journey he called at Stara Zagora to contact friends of the previous year, and then went to Plovdiv where Mr Tchervenkoff had suffered for the Faith. Adam Benke's greatest desire was to have the Faith registered in Bulgaria. However, the time was not right for it as there was an insufficient number of deepened believers in Sofia. There was also the potential opposition from the Church.[332]

Little has been published about George Adam Benke. He was born in Russia and went to live in Leipzig, Germany. There he learned Esperanto and became very fluent in it. In 1931 he travelled from Leipzig to Sofia and was elected vice-chairman of the Bulgarian Esperanto Conference. In May 1932 the Benkes moved from Germany to Sofia.

At last the dear Benkes have come and I feel all is well. Although Mr Benke was exhausted after forty-eight hours ride on hard seats in the third class carriage, he courageously faced the meeting the day of his arrival, and everyone listened breathlessly, while he spoke fervently, & reverently, first in German, which was translated in Bulgarian by Olga Srebova, then by the request of a new enquirer in Russian . . . I was thankful that our meeting was well attended the night the Benkes came, we were sixteen.[333]

After a short illness and some strenuous travels George Benke passed away on 19 November 1932 in Sofia. Marion Jack was in Varna and received the telegram very late. She rushed to Sofia from Varna but was too late for the funeral. Louisa Gregory was also in Varna and owing to an inflamed throat could not travel to Sofia for the funeral. George Benke was buried in the German sector of the Sofia cemetery. Marion called his passing a calamity, adding:

How thankful we are to feel so secure of his welfare and happiness. We know for a surety that he has 'entered into the joy of his Lord.[334]

Such were George Benke's services to the Faith in Bulgaria that he was raised to a high station by Shoghi Effendi:

They must never forget that one of the first 'pioneers', before the days when that term was even in use, was dear Mr Benke, who sacrificed his life in the service of the Faith with such an exemplary spirit of devotion that the Guardian felt impelled to call him the first European martyr for the Faith.[335]

A year before his passing Adam and Lina Benke received

this message from Shoghi Effendi.

> Shoghi Effendi wishes me to acknowledge the receipt of your letter dated September 11th, 1931. He was overjoyed to hear of the work done in Bulgaria. Its fruits have already begun to show, for some of those souls that were interested have written to Shoghi Effendi and expressed their desire to be considered humble servants of the Cause. They are in turn bringing in other interested persons and we hope before long they will succeed in forming a properly constituted Assembly. All this work is undoubtedly due to you as well as a few others who were ready to venture into the wild, and open up new countries to the armies of God.
>
> The Balkans, Shoghi Effendi believes, are a very fertile field, their people very ready. They have so long and severely suffered from wars, and their aftermath, that they undoubtedly long to enjoy a reign of permanent peace. But the work is nevertheless not so very easy, and not free from its own stumbling blocks. There is undoubtedly much prejudice to overcome, and much religious antagonism to be faced. But these are the thorns that any new field will have. We should not mind them. We should concentrate upon the promise given by Bahá'u'lláh that the hosts of the Kingdom are ever ready to pour down and assist anyone who would rise with determined mind and a free heart.[336]

After Adam's death Lina Benke stayed in Bulgaria for another few months and taught the Faith in Varna, Sofia and Plovdiv, before moving back to Leipzig.[337]

10

The Pioneer in Bulgaria
1931–1940

1931: Marion Jack's Arrival in Bulgaria

The Cook's man did his job and Marion Jack arrived in Sofia, the capital of Bulgaria, on 9 April 1931. Unknown to her, at about 2:30 in the morning her train passed Louisa Gregory, who was in a train leaving Sofia.

Here are fragments of Marion Jack's thoughts on first coming to Bulgaria:

> It was to aid Louise in her difficult task, that the Beloved Guardian afforded me the bounty of joining her in the spring of 1931. I regret to say that I was rather averse to such a move, at the time. The wonderful & awful language of Bulgaria seemed an insurmountable obstacle. The Guardian however, would not take <u>no</u> for an answer. He assured me of the receptive nature of the Bulgarian people, and said many kind things about that nation. Seeing that I looked doubtful, he said two or three times 'Just try it and see.' You may imagine my positive dismay, when I reached Sofia, a few weeks later, to find that Louise had been forced to leave and I seemed to be a lost Robinson Crusoe without his man Friday on a desert island. I really had serious thoughts about taking a ticket back, some-where. Strange to say the fanatic landlady, who had been the cause of, we believe, Louise's departure, & who met

143

me at the platform gave me the same advice as the beloved Shoghi Effendi; for she said, 'Just wait a few days & see how things go.' She came the next day at Louise's request, and took me to a noted Vegetarian Restaurant, where I met a charming German lady & her son. They have been my best friends from that day to this and both of them are now on our Spiritual Assembly.[338]

Marion thought that she was going to Bulgaria for a short spell and she never seriously thought that she would stay long, as this fragment from a letter written to Shoghi Effendi testifies:

Beloved Shoghi Effendi.

Forgive my troubling you with a letter, but I should like to know if there is anywhere in a warm climate I could go to do my infinitesimal bit of service if I stay over for next winter (warm because of throat & bronchial trouble). Has the Cause been promulgated in Algiers or Tangiers? or would you prefer to have me go with Mrs Mills[339] to work among the colored folk.[340]

From Miss Edith Douglas[341], an American missionary in Bulgaria, Marion received this advice:

If you want to be happy here you have to like them no matter what, by heck.[342]

Marion arrived in the capital just before Easter and on Good Friday she decided to attend one of the Eastern Orthodox churches, of which she left an account:

This is Good Friday, services everywhere this evening. I went first to the Cathedral,[343] an elegant building with lovely wall paintings of the life of Christ. Most people were standing – no chairs except near the walls – I found one just watch me. Nearly everyone had a taper, to put in taper holder & light crossing himself or herself while doing so. I refrained just out of obstinacy. The priests were togged up regardless – no way to behave on Good Friday (theirs not ours). There was lovely singing up in the organ loft & chanting or intoning – Then they put out most of the lights – later they switched them on again – Richly robed priests came all thru the Cathedral with fumigators called incense burners – Then all lighted other tapers & held them in their hands & stood at attention. I could not see any crisis so left soon after . . . We have all these stunts in the high Church Anglican – probably the same in Portsmouth except the tapers and the lovely voices. Then I tried a smaller church where sole decoration was standing figures – probably of saints – The priest's voice was ordinary so I got out. Next I tried a Russian Church but it was so full I only got to the top step & then left for the Vegetarian Restaurant to regale myself & refresh the inner man.[344]

In July Marion Jack received a letter from Shoghi Effendi acknowledging her letter of 17 June. He stated that he was pleased with the teaching work which had resulted in several declarations and he encouraged her to travel to Germany and then to Geneva for the winter. He said that Germany was in need of travelling teachers.[345]

That summer Marion spent a week in the small mountain resort town of Borovets (formerly Chan Korea), about 70 kilometres south of Sofia.

In October she began to take French lessons at the Alliance Française. She also showed an interest in Esperanto. In November she wrote to Julia Culver at the Bahá'í Bureau in Geneva,[346] stating that 'I have joined an

Esperanto class, hoping to contact some new people thereby.'[347] Later she wrote, 'I also started to learn Esperanto and had a diploma . . .'[348]

In December one of the local believers, a Mr Krestanov, was able to get two articles about the Faith published in the press.[349]

Marion, following in the footsteps of Louisa Gregory, organized meetings and in a letter to Shoghi Effendi she described one of them:

> Mary Mitov read her translation from Beloved Abdul Baha's Talk on Women in the Scriptures, and Constantine Dinkoff read what he had translated from the chapter – What is a Bahai by Dr Esslemont.[350] Then we had in Bulgarian the quotation from His Holiness Baha'u'llah & Beloved Abdul Baha translated by Mr Krestanov . . . The rest of the meeting was in French with a little English, two prayers and the Shepherd Prayer from the Bible.[351]

In October 1931 Louisa Gregory returned to Bulgaria. She and Marion Jack would meet with interested people in hotel lounges, where over cups of Turkish coffee they would have quiet conversations about the Faith. Later Marion transferred her base of operations to restaurants, especially vegetarian restaurants, where she would initially receive enquirers or find new ones. It was probably there that she first met with the Tolstoians and the Esperantists. She found that both groups were friendly but not, apparently, inclined to go much further.[352] The Tolstoians were people who tried to follow the moral and religious teachings of Leo Tolstoy; they were also vegetarians.

In a letter to Julia Culver in 1931 Marion explained that the Bahá'í group decided to purchase a typewriter with the funds which they had received from Shoghi Effendi to assist with the publishing of literature. Marion Jack also used some of the money to settle the Benkes and the rest was used to publish *Bahá'u'lláh and the New Era* in Bulgarian.

Marion reported that over the Christmas season the Faith was introduced in five new towns. Aleksandar Lepchev went to two villages in the north in the Danube valley and was very successful; over a hundred people attended one of the meetings. Krestanov went to Pirdop, a small town 75 kilometres due east of Sofia, and spoke to many people. Mary Mitova spoke to a group of women in Nova Zagora, a town in the centre of the country, east of Stara Zagora. Marion Jack and Aleksandar Lepchev spent some time around 6 December in Veliko Turnovo, in the centre of Bulgaria.

In December Marion received a letter from Effie Baker, writing on the Guardian's instruction, with a photograph of the interior of the Mansion of Bahjí, showing Marion's landscape of Bahjí in place.[353] We can imagine what joy this must have brought her.

1932: Sofia, Ruse, Varna

The year seemed to start auspiciously when Marion Jack heard that visitors would be coming in February. Max Greeven and his wife Inez Marshall Cook Greeven planned to stop in Sofia for a few days to give a number of talks. On the night scheduled for the first talk, over 40 people turned up at the hotel in cold, snowy weather to hear them. However, influenza prevented the Greevens leaving Vienna. On 26 February they passed through Sofia and Marion and seven Bahá'ís met them briefly at the station.

Though Marion knew French, Esperanto and some German, not knowing Bulgarian was a constant source of complaint:

147

... Another difficulty is that many new ones speak neither English or French so you can see I can't help them much. Many are brought by friends and I can just welcome them & feed them & grin at them & try to arrange the program for them and let it go at that. We have only a few chapters (nearly 9) of Esslemont & a few other translations so far, so there is nothing further for them to study.[354]

In March Marion wrote to Shoghi Effendi, mentioning a number of people who were interested in the Faith. These included Mrs Griesshaber, née Fabre of Constantinople, formerly of the German colony at Haifa and the daughter of the director of the German bank. She had met 'Abdu'l-Bahá and had been given a ring and beads by Him. Both she and her husband were interested in the Faith. She had a room next to Marion's in the same hotel and often came to meetings. She interested a Russian-German lady, a Mrs Maidler, in the Faith. At this time three Armenians became interested in the teachings. One, Professor Martharin, had heard of the Faith at Roberts College in Turkey from Stanwood Cobb.[355]

One of the most significant events of the year was the publishing of *Bahá'u'lláh and the New Era* in Bulgarian.[356] Translated by Konstantin Dinkov and published by the International Bahá'í Bureau in Geneva, it was the first major publication on the Bahá'í Faith in Bulgarian. This achievement was highly valued by Shoghi Effendi, who immediately asked for a number of copies to be sent to him. He then placed them on display in the Mansion of Bahjí. News of the publication spread quickly and Marion even received a request from Emogene Hoagg at the Geneva Bureau to send a copy to an enquirer in Turkey.

Since Bulgaria was more or less under a totalitarian regime closely allied to the established church, which in this case was the Eastern Orthodox Church, it was accepted that the direct teaching of a new religion would draw a strong response. Apparently this was the source of intense differences of opinion on how to teach the Cause between Marion Jack and Aleksandar Lepchev. Marion took a firm stand on her idea that caution and restraint were necessary while Lepchev had that unbridled enthusiasm of youth. He even wrote to the Guardian complaining about Marion and how he saw her desire to rule. The Guardian urged harmony, consultation and forgiveness. It is characteristic of the Guardian that he was able to sense the disposition of a person, for even though Marion did not write to him of this situation, he responded through his secretary:

> Shoghi Effendi is sure therefore that Miss Jack has no desire to rule. It is against her spirit. If she by chance asserts her idea, it is because she consciously believes that it is best for the Cause: for she has no other motive but to serve & no other hope but to carry the message of Bahá'u-'lláh to as many Bulgarian houses as she can.[357]

Between 7 and 15 May Marion Jack was in Ruse, a city on the Danube, at the invitation of Miss Martinova, described as a 'near-Bahá'í'. Three talks were arranged through the English-Speaking League and many interested people attended, including three Bahá'ís. One meeting, attended by 12 people, was held in the gardens of the Casino, where the talks were given between outbursts of jazz from the band. The chairman of the League, Mrs Rodoikova, translated for Marion Jack.

Back in Sofia Marion continued her activities:

> I am trying to fall in line with any social activities suggested to me, as one never knows what the outcome may be, or

149

who one may meet. Tonight Mrs Belopetva, an Armenian lady, is holding a little musical evening which she asked me to get up. So we are a nice little group. Miss Douglas from the American School here will bring a group, Olga Radmova is bringing a young Bulgarian doctor, Alexander Leipcheff is bringing one of the stars of the Academy of Music and I am bringing Heinrich Shrebowa . . .

I have tried meeting at the Opera where I can get a seat for thirty-five cents, and less, but don't think I chose my seat successfully. It requires infinite patience for one can go again and again to a place before contacting anyone – then all of a sudden along comes the right person. Of course if it were not for the opposition of the authorities I should give out much more literature. I often feel that I may be passing over many right people – but I am not ready to leave yet, and so do not want to risk anything . . . It is not wise to attempt any meetings here so that is why I am obliged to work in this quiet unobtrusive way.

After all Shoghi Effendi seemed to think that people needed much preparation and to read the Revealed Word first before being brought to meetings.

One youth who I sometimes meet at the Restaurant is trying to practise his English on me, so I loaned him a no. 9.[358] *He wants to keep it . . .*[359]

Out of her love for Shoghi Effendi, Marion Jack penned many letters, describing in detail all the pertinent happenings. However, she did not send all of them:[360]

Beloved Guardian and Protector. There is always so much to tell you, that when a letter is finished the next incident transpires before it goes to post, so I write again, & history repeats itself. If I sent all the letters I write, you would be deluged, so I post most of them in my near-desk.[361]

At the end of August Marion Jack arrived in the Black Sea coastal city of Varna and stayed there until January 1933:

> . . . but at the very end of August I came back to Varna hoping I could do some work here. Now I find it so promising that I do not want to leave until I see it a little further ahead. Also, I am expecting Mrs Gregory to join me in a short time. Then if we can start a study class, we may make real headway here. I am not needed in Sofia for Mr & Mrs Benke are quite qualified to work there without me and I feel that I am really getting ahead here and meeting new people almost all the time, who either receive a little literature or hear about the Cause. You know what pioneer work is, and that is what I am at with all my heart and soul, just as you and dear Martha were at in Prague.[362]

Tragedy struck the Bulgarian Bahá'í community when, after a short illness, George Benke passed away on 19 November 1932 in Sofia. Marion Jack, who was in Varna, hastened to Sofia but was too late for the funeral while Louisa Gregory, who was also in Varna, was too ill to travel.

Shortly after the funeral Marion received what turned out to be a prophetic mimeographed circular letter from Victoria Bedikian:

> I 'met' our Jackie in Alaska, and I 'met' her again in Bulgaria. A great distance rolls between these two spots of Jackie's endeavours, and the fruits thereof are now known to all, and throughout the ages her name will be praised in the Light of Bahá'u'lláh's Kingdom! Blessed are you who assist her, confirmed are the hearts that listen to the music of her teachings! She is a disciple of Bahá'u'lláh, she is a steadfast and loveable heroine of His Throne! Gather Ye around her closely, and catch the words of the

151

Lord of Hosts from her lips! O, may the study of His Word in Sofia ignite that town and bring it into the Mercy of His Guidance, and may Ye each become a firmly planted tree in the Paradise of the Abhá BEAUTY![363]

1933: Sofia

It is not known when Marion Jack left Varna for Sofia but there is a record of her going to Ruse in January 1933 with Lena Benke.

Back in Sofia, Marion Jack again started meetings at her hotel. However, there were hindrances, some from very unexpected sources:

> ... it seems that some of the husbands of women who want to come will not permit them to attend because the meetings are in a hotel. Quaint! And this is one of the most respectable hotels here, no funny business is allowed. It is probably more respectable than the 'Brunswick'.[364]

As has been previously stated, establishing a concise and clear chronological order of events in the life of Marion Jack and her nearest friends is very difficult. It is known that Louisa Gregory was in Varna for the period between February and April 1933. Early in March Marzieh Carpenter (Gail) and her husband Howard were in Sofia for three weeks. During her stay in Sofia Marzieh spoke about 35 times. She and her husband left for Thessaloniki, Greece, by car on 31 March. In March Mrs Thilde Diestelhorst of Berlin came to Sofia and several meetings were held. Marion Jack first met Mrs Diestelhorst during her 1931 pilgrimage to the Holy Land. That same month Marion moved into the Union Palace Hotel in Sofia.

The meetings continued to be just as full and more so than before, and many new ones were brought to us. Mrs Quimjean brought a nice man, and he came and brought two young ladies and a young gentleman. The next day one of the young ladies brought a friend and her teacher who was here from Lovich . . .[365]

In April Marion Jack received a long letter from Emogene Hoagg, who was then in Geneva. The letter throws light on many past and future events:

Dearest Jacko,

Your diary-letter was most gratefully and joyfully received and read with great interest. I don't mind it coming that way except it is 'a long time between drinks'.

By the way, you probably know by this time all about Mrs Gregory, her being better and deep in the throes of converting her young students. I do not know whether she intends to go to Dr Goering or not this month. I gave her all necessary directions, also the place where I hung up and how she can manage her affairs there. I think you are right about Mr G. It has long been my opinion that these 'travelling teachers' should do less travelling and more earning, that their remaining in a place and earning their living is at first sight a great advertisement for the Cause. The old 'helped-over-the-hills' teachers need to do a little pushing of their own apple cart now and the time is ripe for that effort as the whole world is struggling in the throes of tight finance. Of course, Mr G. will come out all right as he has the right spirit. But I cannot imagine a strolling teacher getting around in an automobile when people have to walk or ride in streetcars to help give them the money!

Glad to hear that we have an Armenian copy of Esslemont.[366] Never mind Mrs G.'s lack of consultation with you about the book; that is the difficulty with these

153

'one-rail' people: they do not know how to go in double harness very well.

Forgot to say in the beginning that the books you asked for were sent today. Mrs Lynch who takes care of that part of the work usually, is on a little vacation, so the prices I am not positive of. The Iqan I know is $2.50. I think you have an account so that it can be arranged as soon as she comes back tomorrow.

I hope you have lost none of your letters. I gave your address to a Java man as your old address, but as he goes to Haifa first I shall probably hear and be able to correct it.

Mrs Sherman has not yet connected herself up with the Bureau in Geneva. When was she supposed to arrive?

Am so sorry that the Carpenters did not come our way. Everybody leaves us out in the cold. Dear me! we are sitting on an icicle meditating and trying to warm it. But it does not even melt here. We need some warm stuff like you, or some mixer for bringing together the different elements that might make a good bonfire. My bones are badly put together these days and with the routine of the Bureau about all my strength oozes out so that any outside work at the present time is almost impossible. I make a sudden dash occasionally then have to haul in my ropes and wait until the mercury rises in the boiler so as to permit me to spill over again. Trust your newly interested people will pan out.

How on earth did Marzieh ever hitch up to such a flaming companion! Perhaps she is wise, in these days when moral attitudes have changed and enthusiastic spirits boil over with the instantaneous fervour capturing the hearts of those already bound: perhaps she felt it was safest to have a well-made not over-entrancing companion.

You spoke of French prayer books. There is no such thing. Evidently the French Bahá'ís have not needed to pray in French. However, Margaret Lynch is going to make for you a collection of French prayers taken from the Esslemont book, and some others that I have, and will send you two or three copies so that you can have them in your meetings and give them away if you want to.[367]

Details of the Armenian translation of the Esslemont book are provided in this letter from Marion Jack to Shoghi Effendi:

After much prayer and deliberation we finally put the Armenian translation into the hands of the Kavifian family who with their secretary are starting upon the work. Mr Minissian is a capable man we hear, and Mr Gron Kavifian & his sister will assist. They have the Bulgarian, the Turkish, French & English New Eras. Until now they have all been up to their eyes in work, fortunately the slack-time is now upon them, so they hope to put everything through inside two months. The publication will be cheaper in Sofia. Here (Varna) they ask 40,000 levas for 3,000 copies. In Sofia 8,000 for 1,500, a great difference. However, we are concentrating on the translation. Mrs Gregory will see the friends from time to time to watch the progress.[368]

1933: Hungary, Germany, Turkey

Shoghi Effendi encouraged Marion Jack to travel in Europe during the summers. In May she went to Budapest and spent a month there with Martha Root. In Budapest she met Renée Szanto-Felbermann, who has recorded her impressions of both Martha Root and Marion Jack.

Martha Root stayed at the Pension Grimm, where she lived in a tiny room, probably the smallest and cheapest she could get. She hardly spent anything on herself. When I first went to see her, she told me that she was expecting the visit of a friend of hers she very much wanted me to

155

meet. Her name was Marion Jack, and Miss Root called her affectionately 'Jackie'.

Miss Jack, a Canadian, was now living in Sofia, Bulgaria, where she was teaching the Bahá'í Faith. She had become a believer in Bahá'u'lláh while studying painting in Paris during the early days of the Faith in the Western World. I met her several times. She was a very cheerful person with a commanding stature. During her visit to Budapest she gave a talk at the Feminist Association and spoke of her stay in the Holy Land, where, in 1908, she had lived some time in the household of 'Abdu'l-Bahá, teaching His grandchildren English. She gave a touching picture of 'Abdu'l-Bahá's goodness and charity. He used to call her 'General Jack'.[369]

In a letter written almost 20 years later, Marion Jack states that it was Martha Root who encouraged her to give that talk. In another letter she records an unusual experience:

> We found a sweet-soul in Budapest. Mr Polgar who had a similar experience. He learned that Mr August Forel[370] was a Bahai and went to the Library to find out about it. They sent to Germany for information & got him a small pamphlet. Then he wrote for other literature and became a radiant Bahai. We were the first Bahais he had seen.[371]

In another letter Marion Jack continues the story of Mr Polgar:

> He has been a Baha'i for three years and this is his first meeting with believers. How happy he was . . . The meeting was both glad and sad, for Mr Polgar is a sick man. Being a Jew he longs to carry the Message to his race, so he hopes to have strength long enough to write a pamphlet calling his people to the Revelation which he feels is their salvation . . .

Marion then goes on to describe some of the activities of Martha Root:

> Martha Root spoke many times in Budapest. She was always a shining light . . . She spoke before an audience of 600 people at the University. Her loving heart drew to her and to the Cause some quite eminent people.[372]

A major reason for Marion to go to Germany was her health. In June she was diagnosed by a physician as having angina pectoris, a heart ailment.[373] It is known that Marion went to Stuttgart, Germany, after leaving Hungary. There on 4 June she met Elsie Lea of England. Later in the summer she attended the second Bahá'í Summer Week in Esslingen, near Stuttgart. The lecturers were Dr Adelbert Mühlschlegel, Dr Eugen Schmidt and Dr Hermann Grossmann. Among those present were Helen Bishop, Charles Bishop, Louisa Gregory, Inez Greeven, Alice Schwarz-Solivio, Franz Pöllinger and Amelia Collins. In August she reported to Shoghi Effendi that she had gone with Annemarie Schweizer and Lina Benke to Heilbronn, north of Stuttgart, for several meetings. There they met Rizwaneah <u>Kh</u>ánum.

In the autumn, accompanying Martha Root, Marion Jack went to Adrianople. The two arrived by train on 17 October. The purpose of their trip was, in the words of Martha Root,

> . . . to look for 'traces of the Traceless Friend'. Their quest was 'to seek, to find and not fail' to portray Adrianople to the Bahá'í world . . . Miss Jack through her brush and the writer through her pen.[374]

In her life of Martha Root, M. R. Garis states that Marion Jack also took photographs of the sites at Adrianople, as well as sketching them.[375]

157

Adrianople, presently called Edirne, is of great importance in Bahá'í history for it was here, on the continent of Europe, that Bahá'u'lláh lived in exile from 1863 to 1868. It was from Adrianople that He began to write a series of letters addressed to the ruling monarchs of the world. One of the tasks which Martha Root and Marion Jack undertook was to locate the houses and other buildings associated with Bahá'u'lláh's stay and to photograph and paint them. Martha later published several articles detailing the trip and describing all the sites, then in ruins, illustrating the articles with numerous photographs. The two women were well received by the authorities, including the governor, the mayor and the prefect of police. They also found eyewitnesses who remembered in detail Bahá'u'lláh's stay in Adrianople. The activities of Marion Jack particularly aroused the interest of the local inhabitants:

> People were intensely interested in the paintings of Miss Jack; each time she went out to sketch they gathered about her, and I know the artist was pleased when the Turkish women would give her shoulder a loving little pat and exclaim: 'Áferin! Áferin!' (Bravo! Bravo!) Children flocked about her to see the pictures grow, and in the eyes of many men and women and youth was the question: 'Why are these sites so dear to you.'[376]

Marion Jack was also fascinated by the Mosque of Selim III, built in the 1500s and considered the masterpiece of the great Turkish architect Koca Sinan. Martha Root states:

> This mosque is so beautiful that my artist friend Miss Jack and I go to see it every day; she likes to have a view from different points, so she gets out of the carriage to see it from the river or halts the carriage, to catch new views from

the hillside. One reason she came to Adrianople was to paint this mosque.[377]

While Martha and Marion were in Adrianople a not uncommon incident occurred. It is interesting to see how the two women used it to strike a blow against prejudice:

> Miss Jack, one of the first days, when out sketching in the garden lost her English money. The man who discovered it knew from his mother whose money it must be for it was just where the painter had been making her sketches; he brought it immediately to the hotel. She said to me that night: 'I am glad I lost the money for it is an admirable example of the honesty of the Turk who has not always been fairly spoken of in some parts of the world.'[378]

The delicate nature of the women's task in Adrianople is made clear in Marion Jack's report to the Guardian about the trip, which was published as an addendum to Martha Root's report:

> She [Martha Root] kept on looking and asking and repeating the names of the places to anyone and everyone, so that finally we had many people looking and searching for us. Also she proceeded with excellent tact, at first particularly, until we were sure of the ground and that none was likely to make trouble and prevent the search. This caution until the latter part of our stay gave people time to become friendly, and to realize that our only purpose in coming was to find out about these buildings.
>
> Incidentally a good deal of propaganda was accomplished. And many were delighted and honored to be given little pictures of the Beloved 'Abdul-Bahá. People, some of whom had not heard of the Movement before our visit, will now be ready to know more when the time comes.[379]

A few years later Marion Jack penned this short statement about the visit:

> It was a grief to us to find that the buildings which had been occupied by Bahá'u'lláh had been destroyed during the war,[380] but dear Martha found the ruins & we got photographs & sketches of them.[381]

Marion went on to say that she and Martha had found two old men who had carried milk to the Holy Household and that they had testified to the majesty and grandeur of Bahá'u'lláh.

On 6 November Marion Jack and Martha Root left Adrianople for Sofia. From Sofia, on 19 December, Marion wrote to Charles Mason Remey:

> Dear brother in El Abha: –
> Greetings from Sofia! Have your ears burned these past weeks – if not they ought to have done so – Martha, the dear, and I have so often spoken of you, and wished that you could come over to help us in Europe – Now we are told that the Beloved Guardian calls the Bahais in America to concentrate on Europe, so we put our heads together, and I told Martha I would write & tell you how much we need, not only your concentration but your presence – She is sure you might do great things, not only here but in Adrianople – And right here & now I want to engage you first for Sofia – Later you can go elsewhere, but do give us a few weeks & then a few days in Plovdiv – a week at least in Varna and a few days in Lernova[382] (the quaintest & most lovely old town here) and a few days in Rousse[383] on the Danube – In fact you might float down the Danube from Budapest, or better still from Vienna – if you do not get here until May – Or, if you come via Haifa, you could reach us via Constantinople with ease – There is a train direct –

Our precious Martha has left us, and it seems so flat without her – We had friends all the time – and very sweet meetings always – She has the most tender heart in the Western world I believe – There are many adorable Bahais in the U.S.A., but Martha's tentacles are the most insidious of all I believe – Of course you will want to look in on our beloved Emogene, but save that until later S V P.

How you would adore the Mosque of Salim in Adrianople if you have not seen it – it is a dream I think –

We were asked to give our impression of it – It made me grin & purr – If I lived to be one thousand in America or Canada no [one] would care what I thought about Architecture there or anything else – It is worth coming to Turkey to be discovered – provided the discovery is satisfactory – We have not heard yet whether or no, as our friend Director of Mosques, went off to Constantinople to enjoy Kemil Pasha's[384] fete.

In Esslingen the words Mason Remey are 'sweeter than the honey & the huckleberry bee' like those of Jenne Johnson – All I had to do there was to say Mason Remey and everyone fell for me – I could not make myself understood as a rule, but those pass words did the deed – The little card enclosed should have reached you long since, but when Martha is around what else can be attended to but her wonderful & strenuous program? Anyone who has worked with her can testify of this – I simply let go all else & fell into line for her time was precious & as she was working for us here it was the least we could do as you will agree –

Bulgaria is a great place & the courage & initiative of the people only fifty odd years free will interest you – Never have I seen such a thirst for knowledge – If they are allowed a little more freedom they will soon step in line with the rest of the world – I like them fine, as they say in Scotland –

Eh Bien chere frere its up to you –

Lots of love to you and every one of the lovely Bahais
in Washington and everywhere you go S V P
In His Name & Service
Yours always devotedly
Jacky (Marion Jack)[385]

Before Martha Root left Bulgaria in December she and
Marion made a trip to Bulgaria's second largest city,
Plovdiv. Plovdiv lies in the mountains 150 kilometres to
the east of Sofia. It is famous for its unusual folk architecture, churches and mosques.

1934: Sofia

Marion Jack was in Sofia for the first half of 1934. Here she
helped the community to hold meetings. Sofia was visited
by several Bahá'ís that year, including 'Abdu'l-Ḥusayn Khán
Na'ímí,[386] who came in April. Forty-two people attended
the meeting on very short notice – altogether, 80 had been
invited. Marion reports that he arrived from Stuttgart after
two or three sleepless nights on hard boards in the third-
class seats. 'His gift to us was the most refreshing &
nourishing spiritual food.' Through inspiration derived
from the talk, Mrs Lesseva embraced the Faith and, after
a short stay in Sofia, left for her home town of Stara Zagora,
determined to spread the Bahá'í teachings.[387]

In June Helen and Charles Bishop were in Sofia for two
days. Marion Jack reported 'splendid meetings'.

One of the hall porters [at the Union Palace Hotel] has
been very good in bringing in many people. The director
& owner of the dining room told me that there 'was
something delicious about the Cause', and that it was the
greatest religion of all. Many say the same thing – but it

162

is always such music to listen to and one can never hear it too often.[388]

However, guiding and working with a diverse community was not an easy task. Marion wrote of some of the challenges posed by the Bahá'ís:

Four people gone to live elsewhere. One has turned communist, one has a very unfortunate sickness, one a sad weakness, one turned away because of a hopeless love affair, one is travelling in other countries & so on.[389]

Our smallest meetings number twenty-five and the largest nearly forty, if not quite. All however has not been *coleur du rose* in our corner for we have lost many members who have gone to live elsewhere either in Bulgaria or in other countries, coupled with this we have many who have previously been submerged in spiritism, reincarnation, vegetarianism, Dunovism, orthodoxism, Tolstoism and the like. Then we have a very few other ailments, and worst of all we are divorced of proper Bulgarian literature with which to educate the many who do not know French, German or English.[390]

. . . some of the finest near Baha'is are Theosophists with a few things to lay aside, some are followers of another man-made doctrine, others still cling to the superstitions of Mother Institution called Church. Some think meat eating a crime – among them Tolstoians . . .[391]

Louisa Gregory commented on the problems that Marion faced from the varied members of the Bahá'í community, with all their idiosyncrasies:

Dearest Jacky! I am so sorry for you, you poor dear! But I am not surprised you get anything with all you have gone through with your Bahá'í family! I am sure you have as much trouble as any mother with her brood! And what a mixture you have of good, bad & indifferent, yet all attracted by your dear mother heart that gathers all in & tries to make them good by love & kindness! If I had had charge of them I doubt if there would be one alive to tell the tale this time had they given me all the trouble they have given you![392]

A more optimistic report was given in a newsletter published by the International Bahá'í Bureau in Geneva:

From Sofia Miss Jack reports 'large and interested audiences. Friends bring other friends, so without any publicity, numbers to a remarkable extent. From twenty-five to forty are always present.' An interesting feature is the number who make the translations which furnish the material for the meetings. Mr Henrich Srebow has read his translations of Dr Grossmann's book before the Theosophical Society. Mr Schervenkof travelled to Plovdiv and addressed an audience of sixty.

Early in April Helen Bishop gave three initial lectures on the Administrative Order. Since then Mr Dinkof and Mr Strumsky, who is secretary at the American Consulate, have been translating selected texts from Bahá'í Administration to elucidate the subject. Then Mr Naimi[393] of Tihran arrived and confirmed several, and thus enabled Miss Jack to complete the instruction for the election of a Spiritual Assembly.[394]

It is a little difficult of course to steer this boat as I have to do it blindly – but as we receive constant assurance of the prayers of the Beloved Guardian, we know that we are simply holding the tiller, even when we may think we are doing much more. We pass many crags & find ourselves tossed hither & yore by the waves, but we know He is with us & that these are but little incidents in our journey . . .[395]

It was not only the believers that Marion Jack had to contend with:

> A policeman came on Friday to see if we were meeting & will come on Wednesday no doubt as he learned that Wed. was our night.[396]

> We have a list of 160 people to invite when visiting Bahais come, and for the past three years & more we have done as we were directed & held no public meetings & published no articles. So the dear friends have arisen to take hold of the work with heart and soul in a most inspiring manner.[397]

Sometime during the first half of the year an unfortunate incident took place involving the Bahá'ís in Plovdiv:

> I have news from Plovdif from Mr Lucca Kostadinof that through false information by people who accused the dear friends of conspiracy several of them were arrested and put in prison. Fortunately Mr Tchervenkof was in Plovdiv, and he is a reserve officer, with a special badge, so the next morning he had them released. Mrs Kostadinof, a dear Baha'i and a very fine character, was ill in bed, in a very weak condition. The shock of this arrest was so great that the dear soul sank and on December 30th passed away.[398]

It seems that the grandfather of Georgi Chervenkov (George Tchervenkof), a merchant, had met 'Abdu'l-Bahá in Adrianople and had spoken of Him as a saintly man.

The only trips outside of Sofia that Marion Jack is known

to have taken in June and July are those to the mineral baths at Bankya, near Sofia. In August she left Bulgaria for Germany, where she stayed for about eight months to help deepen the believers and for her health.

In August Marion was in Stuttgart and later in Belgrade. In Belgrade she visited the Bahá'í Serbian poet and translator Draga Ilich and Professor Bogdan Popovich. In September she attended the third Bahá'í Summer Week. The lecturers were Dr Hermann Grossmann, Dr Adelbert Mühlschlegel, Dr Eugen Schmidt and Emil Jorn. Marion was not left out – she presented a 'Report of Bulgarian Progress'.[399]

Shoghi Effendi considered the German summer school to be very important and wrote this description of it to the British Bahá'ís:

> Many Bahá'í travellers in Europe, mostly American, have had this summer the opportunity of attending meetings and classes of the friends in Esslingen. Mr and Mrs Greeven, Mrs Collins, Mr and Mrs Bishop representing the Bahá'í Bureau at Geneva. Bahá'ís from Austria and Persia attended. Miss Jack and Mrs Gregory came specially from the Balkans, and gave detailed reports on the conditions of the Cause in the Balkans.[400]

During the summer Marion Jack wrote to Charles Mason Remey:

> Dear Mason:
> I was so disappointed when you wrote that you could not come to Europe, but now Anna Koslin[401] tells me with joy in her heart that they hope and expect you in October or November. That is fine! I am delighted and so are the Esslingians and so will Miss Horne be and of course our

166

beloved Emogene. But, don't wait too long dear Mason, Emo is very thin and very frail, we were quite shocked to see how poorly she was. This is quite between ourselves but the Beloved Guardian told Helen Bishop that Emmy would not be long with her in the Bureau and told her to be good to her. I could weep over the poor darling. She is full of pep and ginger – just as spicy as ever and it is lovely to see her again.

Dear Mason I beg of you do go to Sofia this time. It may be a little out of the way, but you will do a world of good there. I may not get there myself because I have been told to try my hand elsewhere, but you will not be sorry if you go for we have now formed our Assembly, and have 24 believers. If the friends have not been able to start meetings on a good scale just take the big corner room in the Union Palace Hotel and get the friends to invite everybody. The hall man or his wife will get you some chairs. You can give him a shilling or two and tell him you are my friend. He listens in at the door himself very often and so do others in the house. If you could stay three days you could have a meeting each day. That would be great. You might have forty or fifty people. Also you might speak before the Theosophists and the Esperantists if you like. The latter body is luke warm towards us except their Bulgarian President who is a believer and one of the Assembly.[402] The Theosophist leader is now a believer and just missed being on the Assembly by one vote. Both these men are dears. Think this well over dear Mason. This new little group needs you, and you can help them so much. It gives me a thrill to think that you might go to them. After all they are your Spiritual Grandchildren Mason. If I had not met you at that reception just before you left Paris there might not have been this lovely group in Sofia.

We have other friends in Bulgaria. If you had time you might look them up some of them, but this may be too much to ask. If you are going to Haifa do go one way overland. Sofia is on the direct route to or from Constantinople. The people there too surely need you – and you can stop off in Adrianople and meet the Governor, the Mayor and others to whom beloved Martha spoke, and see that exquisite and delicious Mosque where the Blessed beauty worshipped and talk to Miss Fikret, the young secretary of the Governor, and to the proprietor of the hotel, Mme Marie and her daughter. This would be even more important possibly than travelling around Bulgaria. There is another little Mosque where Baha'u'llah used to worship out a bit on the outskirts where there are some lovely tiles brought from Persia which people come from Germany to see.

Then you can stop off in Salzburg at the Hotel Elizabeth and meet Fraulein Furth,[403] and in Belgrade meet Mme Draga Ilich and others whom Louise and Martha have interested in Budapest to meet several dear believers and in Vienna to see beloved Franz Poelinger, that dear angel. Paris seems hopeless. There is but one French believer, Mme Hess[404] – maybe one or two others – the rest are Persian and Edith Laura and Mme Scott[405] and the Kennedys. Germany is alive of course and is to come into its own one of these days. The other newer fields need you more. I do hope I shall see you myself dear brother. My heart is bothering me so God knows how long I shall hang on, but believe me I want to just so long as I can be of use to beloved Shoghi Effendi.

If you can get to these places I feel that great good will come of it, as it has from visits of the Bishops, Martha and others. And especially of dear Mr Naimi of the British Consulate of Teheran – a lovely soul. He just gave us eight hours but they were hours worth recording. He and the Bishops both had the big corner room in the Union Palace. I had the room next. The first is 46 – mine was – 48 on the fourth floor. The hotel people are lovely to us. Either Mr Barnard or Mr Assam the director or the proprietor will give you permission. I always add fifty cents to my bill for the staff. Money is scarce and a little goes a long way in Sofia.

Later

I saw Dr Goehring yesterday. He says our dear Emogene is very frail indeed, and she absolutely must not return to the Geneva Bureau. This he is emphatic about. He says he is afraid if he puts her up too much, she will be wanting to get back to work there again. So dear Mason do come over and use your influence. If you come maybe she would go back with you. Dr Goehring says she ought to go back there. It is too hard for her over here. She is very thin and worn. It is so sad to see our dearest Emogene looking like this. She is still full of jokes and fun, thank God. It is refreshing to see her believe me. Margaret Lenz[406] came with her but goes to Hamburg for a few days. I knew you would want the truth about dear Emogene. So come soon dear Mason. She needs you and we all would love to see you. I don't know where I am going to be but Dr Goehring wants me to stay with Emogene and not leave her alone. Que faire?

Miss Horne and I are the best of friends and especially since we know that we have the same spiritual Daddy. She seems to think it no wonder that we are so chummy. She is kind and so is Frau Schwartz,[407] but it is the Esslingen group I feel more at home with. They radiate so much affection.

Lovingly in His Name and Service with the love of everybody,
Yours, Jacky

[PS] Love from Miss Horne to all Alla'o'Abha. Best love from Emogene, Margaret Lenz, Louise Gregory and myself – All here at once – Devotedly in the Service, Jacky.[408]

The concerns that Marion Jack had for the health of Emogene Hoagg were reciprocated. In a letter to Mason Remey, Emogene wrote:

> And what do you think: Jackie is here! She came for the summer school and is staying on as she needs rest and treatment. Her heart is very bad. Of course, she is too fat and she eats a terrible lot of starches and sugars; but it's useless to try and persuade her that she must change her diet. It is nice to have her here and have our old confabs.[409]

Marion stayed the winter in Germany and spent Christmas in Stuttgart with Edith Horne and Emogene Hoagg.

1935: Leipzig

In February 1935, at the request of Shoghi Effendi, Marion went to Leipzig to help Lina Benke deepen the community there. On 18 March she was in Salzburg visiting Steffie Fürth. From Salzburg Marion went to Belgrade, arriving there 21 March. In Belgrade she met Louisa Gregory, who was living there for a short period and who had four or five students from Russia. On 2 April Marion arrived back in Sofia after an absence of over eight months.

On 6 May Lorol Schopflocher paid Marion the first of several visits to Bulgaria. She stayed until 9 May.

> Mrs Schopflocher is with us for a few days and gave an excellent and very strong talk last evening. I agree with her that the time has come when we must speak forcefully, and no longer cater to this & that whim of the populace. As we are not registered here, because of the narrow ideas of the Orthodox authorities, we can have no public talks or publicity.[410]

Mrs Schopflocher was followed by Jeanne Bolles,[411] who arrived on 3 June with her mother. They stayed until 15 June. Sometime later Marion wrote about these meetings and other activities to a friend in Paris:

> When Mrs. Schopflocher was here we had about fifty at the three general meetings. My room is far from adequate for these big groups, but if it needs to be, no doubt Bahá'u-'lláh will find us other ways & means. We did hire a hall, but the friends did not care for it, they like the atmosphere and the cordial greeting I like to extend when they come to me. Formality does not appeal, that is evident from the lack of success of the two winters in the hall . . .
>
> We elected our Assembly a few days ago, and I hope this year it may have more initiative than last. Our lack of funds of course is a great hardship, but the greatest mission is of course to spread the teachings, and as we are rarely without two, three or more new people, some two or three hundred must have heard of it from this humble hotel room – and we have given away several hundred Esslemonts also in the Provinces, so in spite of not being registered, we are doing fairly well in obeying instructions from Haifa.[412]

Life for Marion continued as normal, that is, meetings and more meetings. She also made visits to the mineral baths at Bankya. Although Marion was not on the local assembly of Sofia for most of the years she lived in Bulgaria, she continued to guide and consult the local assembly. In one letter she called herself 'a consulting engineer'.

From the sporadic entries in Marion's diary we learn that she had the opportunity to meet some very interesting people:

Aug. 15. Martha's dear young Roumanian friend, Mr Napatgana phoned & called at 4 & brought 1 R. book by Esslemont[413] & small literature translated by Princess Helene[414] and corrected by him.

Aug. 17. Mrs Belopitof called me up & I went to meet Mr Luther Lee from Peking, China & gave him Roy Wilhelm's address & book of principles. Asked Roy to introduce him to Saffy Kenny.[415]

It was probably about this time that the Bahá'ís of Sofia formed a musical choir. The first hymn translated into Bulgarian was the very popular American hymn 'Benediction' by Louise R. Waite.

1936

Marion Jack's diary for 1936 begins with this entry for Friday, 3 January:

Mrs Kasandjeva called at 11. Took me for a drive. Miss Roseva came for lessons at 12:45. Meeting – Mrs Srebrow, Mrs Gemera (?), Mrs Kowatchev, Miss Dontcheva, Mr Jordanof, Mr & Mrs Rouslctief (?), Miss Bagadunva (?), Mrs Molhoff & . . . Mr Jordanof spoke on the principles. Mrs Belopitova, Mrs Shrebova came & later Micky. The latter returned with Mrs Kinitsheva for a visit.[416]

Meetings, meetings, meetings – it seems that Marion Jack's life revolved around meetings. The following table of meetings attended by Marion in the first three months of 1936 is constructed from her diary entries:

THE PIONEER IN BULGARIA 1931–1940

Month	Day	Attendance	Notes
January	3	13	
	7	14	
	10	10	
	14	21	
	17	14	
	19	25	
	21	35	
	24	25	Martha Root
	26	50	Martha Root
	29	50	Martha Root
	31	14	
February	4	21	
	7	13	Meeting at 11, Clementina
	7	most	19 Day Feast at Hotel
	11	21	
	14	12	
	18	32	
	19	3	
	21	16	
	25	19	
	26	5	
	28	15	
March	3	27	
	8	35	
	10	50	Dr & Mrs Mühlschlegel
	11	27	
	13	16	
	17	29	
	20	19	
	21	45	

During this three-month period Marion attended 30 meetings, at which there was an average attendance of 22.8 people. It is not clear how long this hectic schedule was maintained but it seems that it was for several years, at least during the winter months. And this despite intermittent police supervision.

In April Leon Minassian, the Armenian translator in Varna associated with Louisa Gregory, passed away. In May regular study classes began and the first meeting was attended by Mrs Belopeteva, Mrs Sconsun, Miss Polt, Petar Yordanov and Mr and Mrs Henri Srebrov.

From 3 June to 7 June Lorol Schopflocher was back in Sofia with Jeanne Ruhanguiz Bolles and Jeanne Bolles. They stayed until 15 June.

On 7 June Marion Jack made another trip to the mineral baths at Bankya and recorded in her diary:

> Went to Bankia at 2 and coming back met the omnibus director & spoke of the Cause – said I would take him a book. Had supper at Elite. Mr Marinof sat with me on the sidewalk. At the meeting Mr Srebrow read a Tablet of 'Abdu'l-Baha. Then gave a speech & said he now had permission to go to Persia & bade us farewell. We felt very sad to think of losing him. Seventeen came, Mrs Sreb. & Olga & Miss Coralova, Mrs Dantcheva & friend, a girl advocate, Mrs Grossef, Mrs Poll & the boy who came to see Martha & a pretty girl who sat near Miss Ivanof, Helenke, Mr Jordanof & small man with a beard who used to come with 2 friends. Met Mr Strumsky.[417]

From 10 to 12 July Marion went to the Bohnivsyhov Monastery with Mrs Kinticheva. On the Saturday they were invited to a baptism feast at which Marion Jack refused the wine.

Meetings were usually held on Tuesdays from 6:00 to 8:00, then Marion Jack would serve tea, sandwiches and biscuits. Later there was an Esperanto class. Another local believer opened her home for the Nineteen Day Feast and Mrs Belopeteva opened her home for choir practice.

It is possible that Marion was in Ruse on 19 June, while on 24 July she was again in Varna. From 1 to 8 August she was in Borovets (then called Chan Korea).

The next eight months Marion spent travelling in Europe: Austria, Switzerland, Germany and Serbia. On 17 August she left Sofia for Salzburg where she arrived 15 August. The next day she left for Stuttgart. From 13 to 15 October Marion Jack was in Geneva where she met Anne Lynch, with whom a long-lasting friendship developed. Anne was the permanent secretary of the Bahá'í International Bureau in Geneva. Marion wrote to Anne:

Now Honeybells don't go worrying yourself about being a 'weak washed-out rag of a personality'. You are one of God's chosen helpers in this glorious service of the cause. You have worked nobly and bravely in the teeth of all kinds of difficulty to keep the Bureau running when during the war all the 200 h.p.s where snugly enjoying life in the U.S.A. You were holding the fort in spite of ill health and struggle to support life and family – dragging along to work & back home to the Bureau to do the work there and keep up with the News Letters & personnel letters to keep the rest of us going . . . So brace up little Anna darling. You are a brave courageous soul and the beloved of Haifa must know it . . . Whenever you want to belittle your dear self, remember that God called you, and if He wanted you He knew just <u>how</u> you were capable and <u>what</u> you <u>could do</u> to help along in His Great Cause.[418]

A major publishing event in this year was the appearance of an article on the Faith in a Bulgarian encyclopedia.[419]

1937

By 15 December 1936 Marion was back in Stuttgart. Here she stayed until 26 February 1937, when she left for Belgrade. She stayed in the Yugoslav capital until the beginning of March, arriving in Sofia on 6 March.

In Belgrade she again met Draga Ilich:

> I was charmed with dear Draga Ilich's efforts. She sat bravely in her wheeled chair smiling and directing things, and such nice people came to the various little meetings . . . There were only four or five believers.[420]

Political tensions in Europe grew and the Bahá'ís were not immune to the effects of the growing tempest. In 1937 the National Spiritual Assembly of the Bahá'ís of Germany was dissolved by government decree and all its activities forbidden. There was no Baha'i summer school this year as the Nazis had closed the Esslingen school.

There is a strong likelihood that Marion Jack was only a short time in Sofia before she started to travel again. On 13 March she was back in Belgrade and on 29 May she was in Geneva. The summer of 1937 she spent in Bulgaria, mostly in Sofia.

Marion's travels in Europe at this time gave her a clear understanding of the political situation. In a letter to a friend she wrote:

> . . . Yes, it will be if they can shake a loose leg and get away from that old blood hound [Hitler] who is sapping the forces of his country just as other wild beasts are sapping all initiatives and progressive inspiration from Italy, Russia and elsewhere.[421]

Ruins of the House of Riḍá Big, Adrianople (1933)

Adrianople. Ruins outside the city (1933)

*Sarah Farmer (*circa *1920s)*

*Street scene, Bulgaria (*circa *1930s)*

'Abdu'l-Bahá

'Abdu'l-Bahá

Shrine of the Báb, Haifa (March 1931)

Prison and Citadel of Acre (circa 1908)

Door and stairway, House of 'Abdu'lláh Pá<u>sh</u>á, Acre (1908)

Town scene

Adrianople (1933)

Ruins of House of Izzat Áqá, Adrianople (1933)

Adrianople (1933)

Bahjí (1931)

Marion would sometimes get very frustrated at the inability of the members of the local spiritual assembly to grasp the rudiments of Bahá'í administration. Her frustration is illustrated by a passage from a letter written to Emogene Hoagg:

> I am up against the elements that the dictators are planting elsewhere, lack of initiative. Gee its fierce. Little children in America could give these folks cards & spades on 'Procedure'. They are like Esquimeaux before some invention which is beyond their wildest expectation. If I took each by the hand and said now you do this or you stand there maybe they might see a glimpse of light.[422]

Unable to get meeting rooms in a new hotel, Marion Jack wondered if it was because of the 'unrepentant Magdalene, or the poorest Jewish family, or the poorer Russian one who frequent the meetings'.[423] However, not all was gloom:

> We have three young girls 13, 14 & 15 that love to read, so I try & let them so they may feel they are helping & taking a part.[424]

Over Christmas, 25–6 December, Emeric Sala was in Sofia where he took two meetings. At one, over 50 people attended, some standing out in the hall:

> Everyone was most pleased with dear Mr Sala, he gave a remarkably fine talk on Justice which I hope he will some day write up . . . the talk was forceful and big & fine . . . It was quite satisfactory that we had over fifty in this busy season with very few invitations . . . It was a real treat to have a visit from such an earnest & enthusiastic believer.[425]

During the year troubles with the authorities continued:

It was such a come down to have to look after a handful after the over-crowded meetings of two years ago, when we had from 35 to 50 people. At first I decided to hold Bible Classes & study the prophecies. How I worked at that! After two or three months I heard that we were teaching a 'perverted Christianity' so I gave up that tack & went back to the same methods as before, only making a greater effort to have enough translated so we need not have to have talks which the police forbade.[426]

Nationalism was very strong in Bulgaria, not only as a political theory but as government policy. A fragment of another letter by Marion shows the difficulties the Bahá'ís had and hints of a bleaker future.

Thank you so much for the Esperanto pamphlet. We have that translated into Bulgarian, but because of the name, we hesitate to publish it, as we have had a little sort of warning lately. Victor says we omit not speaking against Nationalism. It seems he translated one of Stanwood's chapters in which that matter was brought up. The Chief of Police told him they did not want to make a move or harm me, but if the clergy demanded it, they must obey. He said he would again send a plain clothes man. So I am cautious.[427]

Despite these restrictions, the Bulgarian translation of *The Hidden Words of Bahá'u'lláh* was published in Sofia.[428]

In December Marion wrote again of the problems with the local Bahá'ís but this time also had some good news:

. . . some of the least desirable have been weeded out. I have ceased to be a fighter. I believe in leaving it in prayer of course in higher hands. You would be amused at those who have been removed . . . At one time there were those who were inclined to be snarly dogs, one left for America, one for the Provinces. There was a spiritualist . . . who believed that God was directing him to lead the Cause through Spiritism. He got huffed over nothing and withdrew. Another was an unrepentant Magdalene. She has gone to Paris. Another a good looking rather charming kleptomaniac, he has gone for two years to do military service . . .[429]

1938

In 1938 the situation in Europe grew darker. During that year all Bahá'í activities in Austria were forbidden.

In Bulgaria, on 12 February, Marion reported that the group in Plovdiv – about 20 in all – had recently been arrested and imprisoned for conspiracy. They were freed the next day by an influential friend from Sofia who was there.[430]

Opposition from the Orthodox Church continued, as Marion related:

> Things have been all topsy turvy here for months. No big meetings since March. Only the friends – but we kept up & still keep all feasts. The Holy Synod is against us. We are against them in consequence. If we were a more robust group with the blood of the martyrs in our veins OK but we are only kids and not a sign of a drop of that holy article, s'elp the Bab.[431]

But the meetings continued, even though the conditions were not ideal:

> During the hot days we are hiring the Theosophical Hall, where we can meet in comfort . . . And I am having a holiday from the regular baking of the meetings in this

179

room, which at times is only possible with both doors open, and some elderly people cannot stand that . . .[432]

On 18 and 19 June Aḥmad Samímí was in Sofia.

1939

Marion Jack's decision not to complain about her adopted homeland was upheld through many crises. However, it broke down when it came to bedbugs.

> Alas yes flat bugs are bed bugs. Bulgaria is overrun with them. They are the bain [sic] of one's existence. They get in the books & everywhere. I bought some stuff, creosote & so on, but I doubt if it did much good. They have now bought some English Flytox. What they have here does nothing whatever. The old chairs & sofa & beds are alive & of course the walls. There is no paper on these walls, but they get in the cracks & everywhere. The worst of it is that some have come out at the Wednesday afternoon meetings where we have a nice class of women. Neither Mrs Belopitof, nor Mrs Srebow & Olga will sit in the stuffed chairs. I must because of my back. It is much worse in the summer.[433]

Marion Jack sent a report to the Guardian that the local spiritual assembly had been elected two months late in July owing to the illness of Petar Yordanov. Shoghi Effendi agreed with this decision. Marion was elected chairman for the first time; Petar Yordanov vice-chairman, or vice-president as she reported; Olga Srebova treasurer; and Ernestine Süssmann secretary. The other members of the assembly were Mrs Kinticheva, Nineva Rozeva, Miss Daneva, Mrs Deykova and Mrs Nussen.

Apparently the state of Marion's health deteriorated during the year, for she wrote:

> I would like to visit provincial towns, but for one thing I can't get away; and for another my old back keeps me from venturing away from an old easy chair, so I must just stick to Sofia & trust to the Supreme Concourse to pass on the Glad Tidings.[434]

Writing to a close friend, Marion Jack made this comment on teaching the Faith:

> It is so dangerous to pull up young slips to see the condition of their roots that I hesitate to enquire as to their progress.[435]

> In fact I have found America & Canada even more difficult sledding than Bulgaria, except for the sword that hangs over our heads & keeps the fine brainy & interesting men away from our meetings, and makes one hesitate to invite new folks in case they may be a menace to the continuation of the meetings. This uncertainty has gone on for more than a year now so we ought to be getting used to it – What?[436]

However, the hanging sword did not stop Marion Jack:

> One of my fondest hopes in the work has been to see a lovely group of young law students join up with our Youth Group. Tonight they came, eight of them, all seemingly serious minded young men.[437]

Marion also used the indirect method of teaching the Faith:

> Mrs Verbenova, the president of the Woman's International [Club] gave a fine speech – mainly culled from

181

Baha'i World & other Baha'i teachings – on interdependence at the close of our Club for the holidays. It seems too bad that she could not come out frankly & declare the source, but as some members are a little anti-Bahai, they need this indirect education first – and they seemed to drink it in & enjoy it, whereas if I read the paper there might have been opposition. So much for 'drops of water, little grains of sand'.[438]

On 1 September 1939 Germany invaded Poland and started a conflagration that swept across Europe and engulfed the world.

He [Shoghi Effendi] first advised Canada, but I suggested Geneva thinking I had found a man who could replace me . . . Shoghi Effendi wired 'approve Switzerland', but . . . I was now disillusioned with those who should have replaced me, so a few days ago he advised remain Sofia. There is one fine man who could do much better than I, but there is a law forbidding any government official to take part in anything other than the Orthodox Church religion, so this gentleman cannot be either president or anything else, though he has the courage to attend. And the young have no place, in one way, there is no one in a position to hold the fort. And so there goes, Mary Anne still at the old post.[439]

1940

On 19 and 20 April 'Inátu'lláh Suhráb (Colonel Sohrab) visited the Bahá'ís in Sofia. He was one of the last travel teachers to come to Sofia before its doors were closed.

Marion Jack continued to have trouble with the police. She wrote in her diary that on 23 April she went with some of the friends to Kenatova (near Sofia) to sketch and that 'policemen took sketches from me'. It is not known what

Marion was sketching and there is no further information about this incident.

The local assembly was elected by postal ballot because the Bahá'ís could not meet. The ballots had to be counted somewhere other than Marion Jack's room.

In May the hotel management prevented people coming to see Marion Jack for some time. This could have been at the instigation of the authorities. At this time Marion Jack had a large number of students coming to her flat.

On 15 July Marion moved to the Imperial Hotel. In October and November she visited the mineral baths at Bankya.

Her last outside visitor was Gustave Lowe, who visited her in October 1940. He has left this report:

I met Miss Jack in June, 1938, in Sofia. I had left Austria when Hitler took over and found a temporary position in Sofia, waiting for my visa to the United States. I noticed her in the restaurant where I took my luncheon and she impressed me immediately with her friendly smile that she had for everybody. One day when her regular waiter who spoke English had his day off, the hostess asked me to serve as interpreter and from that day on, I shared the luncheon table with her regularly. It did not take long before she invited me to join a small group of her friends with whom she had discussions in her hotel room, and that was how I met the Faith.

Her room was a museum, full of her pictures, books and papers all over. We sat wherever there was some place – on 'the' chair, the bed on the floor, and she always had some refreshments for her guests. The discussions of the Faith were handicapped by the complicated language question. Marion had nothing in the Bulgarian language, few people understood English, and her favoured book 'Abdu'l-Baha's *Paris Talks*, had to be translated by one person from French into German or English and by somebody else into Bulgarian. It was fun, but how much of the original spirit remained was questionable.

Marion had to be very careful in the choice of her guests. Bulgaria had one official State religion, the Greek Orthodox Church, and only a few other religions were permitted, like Catholic, Jewish, Lutheran, Baptist, Seventh-Day Adventists and Islam. Every Faith that was not permitted was forbidden and meetings like ours were illegal. State employees had to sign loyalty oaths stating their adherence to the legal Faith and we had one girl who worked for the government.

When World War II broke out, she had to discontinue her meetings. Sofia became the centre of European spy systems. Neither she nor I (a German citizen of secondary quality) could dare be seen together. I kept contact with her indirectly through 'neutral' Bulgarian citizens. She was in financial difficulties because her funds did not get to her. But her spirit was unbroken.

In October, 1940, when I finally got my visa for the United States, I dared to call upon her on the phone and even to see her. She had moved to a cheaper hotel. Her room was probably too small for two people and we met in the hotel lobby. I told her of my plan to go to the United States by the complicated way, crossing the Black Sea to Odessa, through Russia on the Trans-Siberian Railroad and crossing the Pacific from Japan to the United States. I invited her to come along and promised that I would take care of her. But she declined. She told me that the Guardian had permitted her to go to Switzerland rather than to wait for the German invasion in Bulgaria that was expected daily. She considered it her duty to stay in Sofia and would neither seek security in Switzerland nor in her native Canada, nor the United States.

We exchanged letters until Bulgaria became part of the Iron Curtain and she indicated that it was too dangerous to receive my letters and to write to me.[440]

Marion Jack never gave up trying new ways to meet people. Some time during the year she was elected president of the English section of the local Woman's International Club. The first subject she introduced was an article by Emeric Sala entitled 'Thirty Years After'. She reported that all enjoyed it and looked forward to more.

She also mentioned that she had to get her identity card renewed every three months; she apparently did this without difficulty, despite all the business with the police.

Marion might have had problems but boredom certainly was not one of them, as this typical entry from her diary illustrates:

> Took Mrs Beltcheva to dine at Imperial & for café glace & cakes at Savoya. Mrs Gonlebrova came at 4 for messages about the vote tomorrow at the Veg. Res. At 5 we went to the W.I. club, Miss Douglas talked, at 7 we went to the E.S.L. I took supper at the Veg. Res. – No friends.

Without a doubt the vegetarian restaurant remained Marion's favourite haunt, as can be seen by this statement:

> Est-ce que je vous ai parlé de Mr. David Madjar dont Mme Kintisheva et moi ont parlé a l'autre Restaurant Vegetarien.
>
> Je crois que le Restaurant 6ème Septembre doit être célèbre un de ces jours.Surtout à cause des réunions de notre chère frère Saint [sic?] Mr. Adam Benke et la chère famille Srebrowa que j'y ai trouvé n'est-ce-pas?[441]

1941

In July Marion Jack moved from her sixth floor flat at the Imperial Hotel to a fourth floor flat at the Station Hotel.[442]

There is no information available for the years 1942 and 1943.

The Letters of Shoghi Effendi

Between 1931 and 1940, Shoghi Effendi wrote a number of letters to Marion Jack and to the Bahá'ís in Bulgaria. He also wrote to others about Bulgaria.

In his moments of prayer Shoghi Effendi will think of you and the other new believers of Bulgaria. He sincerely hopes that each of you will become a flaming light and become a centre of radiation throughout that region. The Balkans have for over a century been a hot-bed of political conflicts and war; may they through your spirit and the teachings of Bahá'u'lláh become the fountain-head of peace and goodwill for all that continent. National hatreds and political and economic strife have almost ruined the civilized world; may you help to turn the steps of the people back to love of God and human brotherhood.[443]

It is needless to say how deeply he was interested in the news you had to give him, especially in the names of those who have accepted the message and those who show enough interest to study it. He sincerely hopes that you will pursue your work and establish a regular Assembly. If you already have five believers it is easy to find the rest. Let every person teach one other soul and immediately you will have the necessary number completed . . .

The Balkan states are in an awful condition. It has been for the last century a centre of constant strife and hatred, and wars that have sprung up there have invariably brought misery to others also. It is therefore very essential that the message of peace be brought to these lands, that swords may be changed into ploughshares and the love of God be inculcated in the heart of the people. Among them are undoubtedly some ready and receptive souls who are fit to act as a leaven of goodness to those regions. Try to win them over and enlist them in the army of God.

186

In his moments of prayer and meditation Shoghi Effendi will surely remember you and ask for you divine guidance and help. Look not to your own ability to present the message; look to the promise of Bahá'u'lláh that He would help every soul who would rise to His service.[444]

... Your splendid services, rendered with such faith, such humility, such perseverance and devotion, have at last been crowned with success. You have achieved a task that will ever live in, nay adorn and enrich, the annals of God's immortal Faith. What is now necessary is to consolidate the work already achieved. I have already cabled you urging a prolongation of your stay which I consider as vital and essential.[445]

He feels deeply thankful and gratified for the wonderful work you and Miss Jack have been doing in Bulgaria. He sincerely hopes that as a result of your work a centre will be created there which will in turn spread the Message through the Balkans. Those countries are in great need of the Divine Message because they have been divided into warring factions that have endangered the life of Europe. Through constant war those countries have come to the verge of ruin. They need the Message of Bahá'u'lláh to bring peace and change the prevailing hatred between the factions into a mutual understanding based upon the love of God and human brotherhood.[446]

Shortly after his departure from Adrianople where He was exiled for five years, Bahá'u'lláh wrote a Tablet in which He states that under every stone He has laid a seed which will soon germinate.[447] This promise refers to the regions around Adrianople which naturally include Bulgaria. His actual words are very promising and who knows but now is the beginning of the day when those promises are to be fulfilled.

187

The Balkan people have for long been suffering from war and social and political strife. It is high time that peace may reign, that differences may be set aside, that strife may cease . . .[448]

Your sojourn in Sofia seems to have been on the whole quite successful and Shoghi Effendi trusts that if you persevere in your work many new souls will be awakened. You should not, however, measure the value of your teaching services by the number of those who actually embrace the Cause. For conversion is not an easy process. It often takes a long, a very long time. What is essential for you to do is to present the Message in a comprehensive and adequate manner and let time do the rest.[449]

Your delightful and highly encouraging letter was a ray of light amidst the anxieties and cares of my arduous work. I was cheered, strengthened and relieved. I believe that the translation of the 'Paris Talks' is an excellent idea. Our Beloved, who watches over your devoted labours from on high, is highly pleased with your perseverance, your efficiency, your high endeavours. Perceive and never, never feel disheartened. The Almighty is guiding you in your great work for so great and sacred a Cause.[450]

My dear & precious sister: Your prolonged stay in Bulgaria, so providential, so timely, has been attended by blessings only future generations can rightly estimate. You should feel thankful & elated. Your work, however, is by no means completed. I am continually praying that the Beloved whom you have served so well may continue to inspire, sustain and guide you. The translation into Bulgarian of Paris Talks is an excellent suggestion & will, I feel, be greatly appreciated. More power to your elbow! Your grateful brother, Shoghi.[451]

188

As the Faith is beginning to expand over the Bulgarian country, it is necessary to bring the people into contact with the Bahá'í literature; indeed this book[452] will give [the opportunity] to obtain extensive knowledge of the teachings and history of the Faith, and will prepare their minds and hearts to accept the claim of Bahá'u'lláh.[453]

Even though Shoghi Effendi would like you to stay in Bulgaria until the group is matured enough to take care of itself, yet he does not mind such short absence. It helps the friends to rely upon their own resources and to learn to become independent of someone to mother them. So there is no harm in prolonging your absence a little more. Shoghi Effendi believes that it would be very nice if you should go with Martha to Belgrade for the Esperanto Congress[454] and proceed to Adrianople for a stay of about two weeks in that city. There you could make some paintings of the Mosque of Sultan Selim that Bahá'u'lláh used to frequent, and also of some of the houses He occupied. It would also be nice to start a group there. In Adrianople you could separate: Martha would go to Greece and you to return to Sofia to your spiritual family.[455]

Your historic work, so nobly initiated in Sofia and so strenuously followed in that capital and the neighbouring cities of Bulgaria, must, I feel, be further consolidated by the early resumption of your activities in that country. I would like you, however, to stay longer with our dearly-beloved Martha, and to visit with her Serbia and Adrianople. May this tour refresh and strengthen you, and enable you to extend still further the scope of your valued activities and exemplary labours in the Divine Vineyard.[456]

Dr and Mrs . . . are now here and give a glowing report of what is being accomplished in Bulgaria and the other countries of Eastern Europe. Shoghi Effendi hopes that these seeds, which these few American ladies[457] are sowing so lovingly, will receive showers of divine blessings and gradually start to germinate. Those countries, more than anywhere else in Europe, should feel the disastrous and ravaging effects of war and conscientiously strive to achieve peace by an orientation of their human interests to what is spiritual and uplifting . . .[458]

Miss Jack and Miss Root will surely highly value your assistance and co-operation and will be only too happy to have you with them. You all three are the shining stars in the dark and gloomy sky of the Balkans. For through the Message you have you are able to heal all those who have been for so long, and under so many different circumstances, victims of the crudest and most deep-seated prejudices.[459]

The Guardian has just received your beautiful message of Sep. 3, 33, written through the kindness of Miss Jack . . .
[Shoghi Effendi's postscript]
Dear co-workers:
    It is such a joy to learn that you have had the pleasure and benefit of the companionship of our dear and distinguished Bahá'í sister, Miss Jack, whose recent exemplary services we all deeply appreciate . . .[460]

The German friends have been greatly suffering as a result [of national fanaticism], during the last two years, and their activities have been largely hampered. The countries where people are relatively more sympathetic to the Teachings are Yugoslavia, Bulgaria and Romania. You should do your best, and in case you find it feasible, to extend your stay in the Balkans and try to establish some new centres there . . .[461]

The Guardian was greatly rejoiced to learn that your historic trip to Adrianople has come to a successful end, and that you are once more back in Sofia and are resuming with the help of Miss Root, your important teaching activities. Your message of Nov. 9th was, indeed, very inspiring and refreshing after a long period of silence during which you were slowly and carefully laying down the foundations for the future development of the Cause in that portion of the Balkans which the Almighty had chosen to be blessed by the presence of Bahá'u'lláh. Your services there will, no doubt bear their fruits in a not distant future, provided you maintain with those few souls you have been able to awaken, continued correspondence. Their interest in the Message, however deep it may have been, cannot last unless it is kept alive by means of direct contact if possible, and if not through writing.[462]

I wish to thank you from the bottom of my heart for the efforts you have exerted in the course of your splendid and historic visit to Adrianople, 'The Land of Mystery'. Despite the increasing difficulties which beset you, notwithstanding ill-health and cares and anxieties which such pioneer work in strange surroundings entails, you have nobly persevered, loyally laboured, and splendidly achieved a work of which future generations will be justly proud. I am so glad to know that precious Martha will collaborate with you for one month in Sofia. I will continue to pray for you both.[463]

Your messages dated November 16th and 22nd, 1933, have filled our Guardian's heart with inexpressible joy, and he wishes me to thank each one of your group for the remarkable devotion, zeal and enthusiasm with which you are spreading the Cause of Bahá'u'lláh in your country. It is the conviction that nothing short of the spread and the application of the divine and salutary teachings which lie embedded in the Bahá'í Message can effectively rescue

191

your country and the world at large, which should spur you on to investigate and whole-heartedly embrace the truth of this Revelation, and to rally yourselves under its glorious banner. The Bahá'í Faith gives you not only a definite plan of world reconstruction, but provides you at the same time with the necessary impetus and means whereby you can carry it into full and fruitful action. In it you will find a goal which is definite, namely the unification of mankind in all its aspects and forms. It asserts that political and economic unity cannot be established on a sound basis without the necessary and indispensable unification in the field of religion. The blending of hearts is the foundation-stone of the Bahá'í social order. It is at once its stronghold and its inherent motivating force. Through it no obstacle can withstand the triumph of the constructive forces of the world. And by its means national and racial prejudices of all sorts melt away and make, thereby, the establishment of an international order not a dream but a living reality.

It is this fundamental truth, that the basis of world unity is essentially spiritual, that makes the strength of the Bahá'í Faith. And it is because our statesmen and leaders have failed to accept such a truth that they find themselves so helpless in the face of the dark forces that are so vehemently assailing the world.

It is Shoghi Effendi's hope that through the pioneering efforts of Miss Root and of Miss Jack your group will develop both in number and in spiritual fervour, and that you will not merely content yourselves with the study of the Teachings but will arise to play your part in their quick and effective dissemination throughout your country.[464]

Dear co-workers:

I was so pleased and gratified to learn that the work in which you are engaged is in full swing and that the prospects are bright and promising. A powerful and efficiently functioning Local Spiritual Assembly, permanently established and truly united, is imperative, and will no doubt act as a magnet that will draw the confirmations of Bahá'u'lláh.[465]

Your letters of April 2nd, 24th and May 21st have been duly received, and their contents have been given careful consideration by the Guardian. The gratifying news of the projected formation of a spiritual assembly in Sofia pleased him particularly, and he trusts that under your guidance and attention this assembly will function with effectiveness and vigour. In view of this new and historic step you have moved to take, Shoghi Effendi feels that your stay in the capital is indispensable, although he approves of your leaving occasionally that centre for a teaching trip in the near surroundings. He does not think it necessary that you should start studying the language of the country, as this will take too much of your time and energy. You may, however, devote your spare time to that purpose, but never should you do so at the expense of your teaching work.[466]

Your patient and strenuous labours in the service of so great a cause and in circumstances that are truly most difficult and trying have endeared you to us all and deserve to rank as high as the great achievements that have signalized the establishment of the Administrative Order of the Faith of Bahá'u'lláh. You should be intensely happy, and profoundly grateful for having rendered such distinguished and never-to-be-forgotten services to the Sacred Threshold.[467]

The Guardian is deeply gratified to learn from your letter of September 5th of the happy news of the successful formation of the Sofia spiritual assembly. He wishes me to hasten in offering to you his heartfelt congratulations and his grateful thanks for this unique and never-to-be-forgotten service which you have been able to render the Faith in Bulgaria. Your pioneering and sustained endeavours for the establishment of the Cause in that country have, undoubtedly, been amply rewarded. You should, therefore, feel happy, and remain assured that the foundations your able hands have so carefully and so patiently laid down will be further consolidated through the united and combined efforts of our Bulgarian friends, and that upon them the edifice of the cause will be gradually raised and firmly established in their country.

As to your return to Sofia, the Guardian leaves it entirely to your discretion. If you feel that the believers in Sofia can conduct their own affairs, and that their assembly is sufficiently strong and united to manage its own work, you need not return, at least for the present, to Bulgaria, and may preferably travel for a few months in Austria where the believers will surely be glad to have you with them, and will, undoubtedly, extend to you every assistance they can for rendering your stay as successful as possible. In any case, the Guardian strongly urges you to keep in close and constant touch with Sofia, and to encourage and guide the believers in spreading the Message, and in extending the scope and in consolidating the foundations of their assembly.[468]

I leave it entirely to your discretion as to whether you should extend your stay in Bulgaria or initiate a new chapter of your historic work in some other country in Europe. I have the utmost confidence in your judgement, your loyalty and disinterested service to the Cause of God. Wherever you labour, with whosoever you collaborate and whatever the nature of your activity my prayers will ever accompany you and my thoughts will continue to be with you. I feel truly proud of the constancy and courage that distinguish your pioneer service.[469]

Now as regards your work in Sofia; Shoghi Effendi trusts that through your efforts the meetings are being regularly held, and that the number of the attendants is on the increase. He too hopes that you have been able to renew the assembly election this year. It is indeed so essential that the friends should enforce, as much as their means and the conditions around them permit, these basic principles and methods of the Administration, so that they may acquire the necessary experience for the conduct of Bahá'í affairs in their community, and thus cease to be in need of any further help from outside.[470]

I am continually reminded of the stupendous work you are achieving for our beloved Faith, though I do not often express it in letters addressed to you. I am keenly aware of the work you are so patiently and almost heroically performing and accomplishing for our beloved Faith. Your services will adorn the annals of God's Faith and inspire the rising generation to tread the path you have so nobly trodden. Persevere therefore and redouble your high endeavours.[471]

. . . when war broke out Shoghi Effendi, concerned over her [Marion Jack's] dangerous position wired her 'Advise return Canada wire whether financially able'. She replied '. . . how about Switzerland' but assured him of her implicit obedience. Shoghi Effendi then wired 'Approve Switzerland' but she still did not want to leave her pioneer post and begged to be allowed to remain in Bulgaria, to which the Guardian replied: 'Advise remain Sofia love.'[472]

The very welcome message you had written the Guardian dated October 21st has just arrived, and he feels indeed most happy to know that you are keeping well in spite of the grave anxieties and uncertainties through which you must have passed during the last two months. At the outbreak of hostilities in Europe which threatened to spread throughout all the Balkans he felt so deeply concerned about your safety that he decided to send you a wire advising you to leave for Switzerland, as he considered that country to be the safest and most suitable place where you could settle. But since the war seems to be localized, at least for the present, he thinks there would be no immediate necessity for you to leave Bulgaria, and has already advised you by wire to this effect.[473]

I have already assured you and the friends by cable, and approved of your remaining at your post in these days of trial and stress. The spirit which you above all the rest so powerfully evince, the progress of the work in which you are so devotedly and determinedly engaged, are a source of extreme and constant joy and inspiration to me in my multitudinous labours and responsibilities. Will continue to pray for you all from the depths of my heart. Be confident and happy always.[474]

11

The Heroine
1941–1954

The political events after 1941 moved ever more swiftly and plunged Bulgaria into the vortex of the Second World War and its totalitarian consequences. Some of the major events that impacted on the life of Marion Jack are listed here.

Chronology of Major Events in Bulgaria

1941

1 March
Bulgaria joins the Tripartite Pact (Germany, Italy, and Japan).

13 December
Bulgaria declares war on the United States and Great Britain. Bulgaria occupies parts of Greece and Yugoslavia.

25 December
Great Britain and the United States declare war on Bulgaria. Very soon afterward the other Allied countries, including Canada, do likewise. All property belonging to Bulgarian nationals and residents of Bulgaria (which includes Marion Jack's bank account) is seized by the Allied governments as enemy property.

1943

August
Death of Tsar Boris III. The heir to the throne, Simeon II, has not come of age and the throne is placed under a regency.

14 November
First air raid over Sofia. (See table below for a list of the other raids.)

1944

2 September
The regency appoints an anti-German coalition.

5 September
The USSR declares war on Bulgaria and the Red Army enters Bulgaria.

9 September
The government of Konstantin Muraviev is overthrown by the Fatherland Front coalition headed by Kimon Georgiev.

1947

June
The communist-dominated Fatherland Front arrests and executes Nikola Petkov, leader of a loose anticommunist coalition, and declares Bulgaria a communist state.

December
A communist-style constitution is adopted.

1949–50

There is severe repression of the Protestant churches.

1950

Diplomatic relations with the United States are severed.

Major Themes in the Life of Marion Jack, 1941–54

The war and post-war years were probably the most difficult for Marion Jack. Material deprivation – lack of food, the bitterly cold winters, poor housing, ailing health, the lack of money and loneliness – that was her lot, her glory. There are very few noteworthy events during this period, especially after Marion returned to Sofia, because she did not do anything, did not go anywhere, did not meet many people. Thus these last years are presented thematically so that the reader will have a greater understanding of and perspective on her heroism.

Bombing Raids, 1943–4

Although a state of war existed between the Allies and Bulgaria from the end of 1941, no military action took place other than Allied assistance to various guerrilla groups. This 'symbolic war' lasted until 14 November 1943, when Sofia was attacked by 130 planes which bombed the area of the central railway station in the north of the city. Civilian casualties numbered 56 dead and 103 injured, while 132 houses were rendered uninhabitable, 24 of them being totally destroyed.

The first air raid caused a great deal of confusion among the civilian population and the authorities. The civil defence services proved totally inefficient. The civilians received no emergency aid.[475]

The policy of the Allied governments of trying to get Bulgaria to quit the war using diplomatic means and by stirring-up and encouraging internal unrest and revolution having failed, they resorted to military means.

Three more air raids occurred during 1943, on 24 November, and 10 and 20 December. The targets this time were the central railway yards and the tobacco warehouses. These air raids terrified the local population. The government's total inaction – first, not preparing and warning the people about the air raids and later, after the air raids, not providing quick and efficient emergency services – demoralized the inhabitants.

The first air raid of 1944 occurred on 4 January when a fleet of a hundred Allied aircraft attempted to bomb Sofia but were driven off. They bombed Dupnitsa, where 46 people were killed, hundreds wounded or injured and many buildings destroyed, including a military hospital. The biggest bombing raid over Sofia occurred at noon on 10 January 1944, in which two Allied air force regiments comprised a total of 250 bombers. Fourteen hundred bombs, each of 250 kilograms, were dropped on the city centre. During the night, while the population of the city was still reeling from the effects of the raids, another hundred planes bombed the city. The heroism of the Bulgarian air force pilots was not enough in the face of the sheer number of attacking aircraft.

Jan. 10 Went to shelter in Kino Rex. My room was bombed. Slept in kitchen.[476]

My only real grief is for the Baha'i literature and your lovely translations, not all can be [lost], but I do hope some may be spared . . .

For the life of me I cannot understand the politics of the Anglo Saxons. I am most awfully impatient to know what they mean in this disgusting treatment of this little country. My heart bleeds for Bulgaria. I am only hoping their actions have some kind of raison d'être behind them, other wise one might almost feel like seeking another nationality. I am exasperated with them.[477]

The consequence of these two attacks were most severe: 750 people killed, 700 wounded, 600 buildings destroyed and electricity, telephone and water supplies broken. The effect was a great panic among the civilian population. The frightened people hurried to leave the badly hit city, blocking railway stations and jamming roads. Taking only their most necessary belongings, they set out in the cold winter to seek shelter and refuge with friends and relatives in the provinces. Within two days the city was completely deserted: 300,000 people had left. Factories, offices and state institutions were abandoned. The government ceased functioning temporarily. The regents fled to Cham Korea (today's mountain resort of Borovets), while the cabinet members scattered all over the country to save themselves. An evacuation of the War Ministry, the Ministry of the Interior and other ministries was begun.[478]

As a result of the bombing raids, part of the cultural heart of Sofia was also destroyed: the National Ethnographic Museum – seriously damaged; the Bulgarian Concert Hall – destroyed completely; and the Sofia City Library – heavily damaged, among others.

Air Raids over Bulgaria 1943–44

Date	Place	No. of aircraft	No. of bombs	Killed	Injured	Target	Note
1943.11.14	Sofia	130	191	56	103	central railway station	
1943.11.24	Sofia	100		7		railway station	Losses: 4 bombers; 1 Bulgarian fighter
1943.12.10	Sofia	120		11	40	railway yards, railway hospital	
1943.12.20	Sofia					tobacco warehouses	Losses: 8 bombers; 2 Bulgarian fighters
1944.01.04	Dup-nitsa	100		46	337	military hospital	
1944.01.10 (1)	Sofia	250	1400	750	700	city centre, 600 build-ings de-stroyed	300,000 left city
1944.01.10 (2)		100					
1944.03.16	Sofia	25				city centre	
1944.03.17	Sofia	40–50	Incendi-ary bombs			city centre	
1944.03.30	Sofia		Incendi-ary bombs	55		city centre	Fresh panic

Source: Rachev, *Anglo-Bulgarian Relations During the Second World War (1939–1944)*; Stefan Semerdjiev, 'Ace in Defense of Bulgaria', *Military History*, pp. 50–6.

During the air raid, Marion Jack with two of her friends took refuge in the Rex cinema. One of the friends was Mrs Alma E. Woodruff 'Woody', an American missionary teaching at the American college at Lovech. The next day Marion discovered that the air raid had destroyed her room at the Station Hotel. She found only tattered remains of her belongings. Also destroyed were 13 years' worth of her paintings. However, for her, even more distressing was that most of the translations of Bahá'í materials that she and other Sofia Bahá'ís had made had been destroyed along with her Bahá'í literature. Fortunately, some of her possessions were scattered among other friends and a suitcase of letters survived. A very severe personal blow to her was to discover that her very close friend Mrs Eugene Belopeteva had been killed when her flat took a direct hit. Also in the flat and totally destroyed was the entire stock of *Bahá'u'lláh and the New Era* in Bulgarian.

Having nowhere else to turn, Marion Jack first went to the Swiss Consulate (it was responsible for looking after British interests in Bulgaria, including British subjects, in the absence of the British Legation) but it was not prepared to assist anyone, being too busy preparing to evacuate. She then turned to Mrs Haskell for help, since she could not contact the Bahá'í friends or they lived too far away. Marion stayed with Mrs Haskell for three nights. The house had its windowpanes blown out, there was no electricity and the only water was melted snow. It was very cold because Mrs Haskell had to conserve the precious fuel.

Evacuation: 16 January 1944

> In spite of the holocaust & its discomforts life has not been without its interests and amusing moments in this poor little unfortunate country. For instance when Miss [sic] Haskell and I wanted to evacuate on Jan 16th after the first really bad blow up, we thought we would have to board an open cattle car, a youth standing near the steps said 'You can't come in here if you are English or American!' We laughed & said O.K. we'll get into the next. Incidentally we were saved from either torture, for it was zero

weather, by the man who was looking after our baggage who found us a second class passenger car. So our lives were probably saved since we have both bronchial tendencies & have had pneumonia. The other funny incident was in the last car. The wife of the President of the English-Speaking League[479] was chatting away happily with us from one end of the appartment [sic] to the other when a well dressed middle aged man opposite her said 'Stop talking that language. I can't stand listening to it' – We shut up pronto presto as we were then under the domination of the superior? race, and couldn't call our souls our own without great risk. But we have often laughed over that little affair. I'd like to see that beau monsieur now when we are 'all the rage' and 9/10s of the country is longing to sing either My Country 'tis of thee or The Maple Leaf forever.[480]

On Sunday Marion Jack and Mrs Haskell left Sofia by train for Pleven, 174 kilometres northeast of Sofia. Pleven was a small administrative district town with a population of about 80,000. It was in Pleven, in the year 1877, that the Russians defeated the Turks and liberated Bulgaria from the Ottoman yoke. Marion and Mrs Haskell stayed in Pleven for two nights and then proceeded to their final destination, Pordim.

Pordim

We were for some weeks in a wee cellar kitchen – stuffy, damp, and not light enough. It was like a prison to me. My only relief was to go upstairs where I had a pupil.[481]

Pordim is a small village 22 kilometres east of Pleven. At Pordim was a peoples' university founded by Mrs Haskell's brother and associated with the agricultural college at

Pleven. The administration and other buildings became home to a large group of refugees from Sofia, a group that constantly grew over the next few weeks. The government gave no assistance to the survivors of Sofia and left their care to individuals and to private institutions. The facilities were wretched: overcrowding, damp, airless. Marion Jack stayed in a cellar room for the remainder of the winter. The room had no windows and it is believed it had an earthen floor. This room she had to share with several other people. She called it her 'mouse hole' but at least it was warm. Not one to complain, however, Marion did write that she passed 'many & many a miserable hour there'. She would go upstairs to the veranda and stay there most of the day. In the spring she was given an upstairs room with windows and a bit more space. At one time she had to share the small room with as many as seven other people. In the building there was a small nursery and Marion would help there by drawing and repairing the clothes of the children and in assisting in other ways. In March several people returned to Sofia only to be met by more bombing raids by the RAF on 16, 17 and 30 March 1944. Greatly dismayed and frightened, more people fled the capital city.

During the spring and summer Marion's most favourite pastime was to lie on the grass in the warm breeze: here she could be alone and free from the overcrowded atmosphere of her temporary home. She read, kept in touch with several of the Bahá'ís left in Sofia and tried to locate the others scattered all over the country. While there, a representative of the Swiss Legation visited her and asked her if she wanted to be repatriated. She said 'NO!' She thought it was her sister Louise who instigated this attempted 'rescue' mission.

In Pordim, during 1944, to pass the time and to avoid complete boredom, Marion Jack and Mrs Haskell read a great deal. Mention is made of Macaulay's *Essays*, Bacon, Shakespeare and *The Lance* by Edward Haskell, a nephew of Mrs Haskell.

On 5 September 1944 the USSR declared war on Bulgaria. Then on 8 September the Red Army received orders to cross the Romanian–Bulgarian border. On the evening of 8/9 September Bulgarian partisan units in cooperation with the Bulgarian army overthrew the government and seized power. The Bulgarian army did not resist the Red Army. The population greeted them as heroes, likening the event to the Russian liberation of Bulgaria from the Turks in 1878. On 13 September the Russians went through Pordim.

Return to Sofia

Marion Jack stayed in Pordim probably until October 1945 and then returned to Sofia. On her way to Sofia from Pordim, her suitcase was stolen from the train. It contained all her possessions.

> Did I tell you that all my things I had in P[ordim] were stolen from the train? It seems wonderful what one can do without . . .[482]

> It is quaint here how the holocaust has drawn people together. After nearly a year's evacuation folks all greet one as if one had been dead & dug up almost. I see faces I have been used to seeing in the shops, restaurants, & who knows where and we mutually drift together & shake fists enquiring about happenings. Half the time I can't for the life of me put a handle to the body's whereabouts let alone the name. So much for the frailties of an octogenarian. We all get there all too soon alas! Que voulez-vous?[483]

206

Praise God there is a lull in the storm. It will be permanent when there is 'Unity in the love of God', and may that day come soon! It is for this purpose, as you know, that I am denying myself the joy of being with you all, i.e. that I may do my little bit to further this aim – small though it be . . .[484]

Back Home in Green Acre

In 1948 Marion Jack received news that her friends were selling the paintings she had left behind in her cottage in Green Acre. Her correspondence on this subject makes it clear that she had no previous knowledge of this fact. She never found out who initiated the distribution and selling of her paintings and she never received a penny for any of them. A very sad episode indeed. In her letters she does not sound bitter but rather disappointed and somewhat hurt:

> I don't want to hurt the feelings of those who are 'making free' with my property – humble as it is. And the funniest part is that the active ones never inform me. Nor even ask if they may sell or give what I might hold dear. It really is a joke.[485]

Poverty

> I have not bought a stitch of clothing here for years, and eat out of tins for the most part, as restaurants are terribly dear, and usually very poor in what they serve . . .
>
> I have to share a big portion of my budget and much of my parcels with the hungry here, there is little left at the end of the month . . .
>
> So dear you see how I stand financially for, as I know the great need for the finishing of the Temple, and how

much depends on it, you must know what a deprivation it is to me not to be able to do my bit . . . This is al entrenous Cherio, but I felt deeply reproached when I read your 'call' last night and realized my helplessness to respond.[486]

Clothing

I have got to the point where I feel that if the Bon Dieu wants me to have glad rags he will provide them, and now I have almost a whole year of looking more or less disreputable & I find it gives one a more friendly & better feeling towards other rag pickers one meets in the streets, and some are really in a pitiable condition. Experience is surely the best teacher.[487]

Letter from Haifa:

Dearest Jacky: It was such a relief to know the shoes reached you but you omitted to tell me the most important fact of all which is whether they are comfortable or not? As I was afraid you would have to pay too much duty on them and also you are not supposed to send things valued more than one Pound out of the country I had one of the Bahá'í girls who is serving in the house wear them for a few days so that I could truthfully say they were not brand new . . .[488]

I was so happy when the shoes fitted you and you would have laughed if you could have seen one of the Bahá'í girls here sitting all day long with your shoes on and refusing to walk in them for fear she spoil them . . .[489]

To this letter Rúḥíyyih Khánum adds a very personal touch:

The mere thought of you makes me feel happy and I only wish I could get my arms around you. Is there as much of you to hug as there used to be?[490]

Back to Marion Jack and post-war Sofia.

How decent it would be to have a decent winter over-coat.
The poor old dear I have shed, dates back to 1937 from
Stuttgart, & is too worn & wan for further use, so that
would be a Godsend. Louie[491] wants to give me hers, but
it may never get here, like the two parcels her daughter
sent from Montreal. Anyhow, one or the other, if both
come, can grace the back of an old believer who has been
most kind. I have her bed-rug, 3 pillows, 2 arm chairs and
towels galore, plates etc. – and last winter she could not
come to town as she had no overshoes! I paid through the
nose & then some for mine – exorbitant.

A decent thick winter dress would be wonderful. The
one I wore last winter was a hand down from the missionaries in Turkey. Or 3 yards of black velveteen cotton to make
a sleeveless jacket, if not the dress. How kind and thought-
ful of you dearest Kitykins! I am not very fussy about
clothes except that I like to look as decent as I can as a
Bahá'í. And last winter we had no social functions anyhow.
I wore my coat from 1 p.m. to 10 p.m. as a rule and sought
warmth in pastry shops, the American Reading Room and
a restaurant during those hours & then came home to my
cold room until March when the daughter of a friend (a
dear dead believer) took me in for some weeks. You see
there is no chimney in this room, & the only stove in the
next room, was never more than half full.[492]

. . . Your dear mother's coat sent in October is not yet seen
or heard of. My old rabbit skin has sadly lost its feathers
and really looks forlorn in big spots, nevertheless it keeps
one warm and that is the chief thing. I could not get it
restored in summer for lack of funds, and my cloth coat
is that of a real hobo – mended until it fairly groans in self-
defence. The two pockets are sending up their dying gasps.

As I usually carry two bags, I hustle and cover the worst spots on the pelt if anyone is coming who seems to matter.[493]

Louise has sent me two winter coats which are still enroute, and may continue the same journey, and my niece sent me a big parcel still careening around God's Kingdom with other parcels people hint of. Dear Miss Douglas & other missionaries have undergarmented me & connections in Canada have sent nice summer wear inside and out also Louise ditto. So what more can I ask for? The Red Cross sent me a fierce looking over coat, lashings too small (fortunately). Talk about a sight for sore eyes! Eyes would have fairly popped out with health at the sight of that Eastend cockney meal sack.

I'll probably get my Tom-cat-rabbit skin fixed over if Louise's latest production fails to hail in sight before long. It's too long anyhow so it can stand losing a bit of its tail to cover the wear and tear of the last ten years.[494]

. . . to my joy the parcel came. The stockings are a great boon and went right on, the pretty dress has also had several outings. Yesterday it went to a Musical tea at the home of a fine German lady who exclaimed at once at the chicness of my robe, in front of the group, all at table, as I was the observance of all observers . . . I was certainly glad to be properly clad to make my debut of the season among other well dressed women . . . Your dear Mother's pretty blue dress has been invited to the next tea . . . .[495]

Leisure

From about 1946/1947 onwards Marion Jack would attend the American Reading Room and the British Council and the English-Speaking League and the occasional tea.

This is the first sizeable tea I have been at [at the home of a German lady] since the Americans and English demolished so many homes and since cakes and tea have been less plentiful. We had several kinds of sandwiches – brown bread ones – little rolled pasties salted, and three cornered sweet pasties. Only two of the dames were Bulgarian – the rest were Armenian, Swiss, Austrian, Hollandaise, German and Canadian – most of them sang and played accompaniments – As I can still tinkle the keys a little, they made use of me too. It was quite a jolly eve as our kind hostess (married to a Czech doctor) is full of life and laughter . . .[496]

Money

At the request of Shoghi Effendi, Marion Jack was sent a regular amount of money from about 1947 or early 1948. The Guardian's secretary wrote about this to Marion on behalf of the Guardian and she quotes from this letter in her letter to the National Spiritual Assembly of the Bahá'ís of the United States:

> He does not feel you should for a moment hesitate to accept assistance from the friends, or call on them for help, your work is historic and very much needed, and you should consider care of yourself as an investment for the Cause and a duty.[497]

There was a lot of confusion over this because the money went directly to the bank and Marion did not always get notice or the notices were late coming and she could not acknowledge receipt. Early in 1948 she must have received a sharp letter from the United States Bahá'í treasury office, for she writes:

211

When you spoke of discontinuing my regular budget, I began to have cold feet.[498]

From December 1947 a sum of $50 was sent to Marion Jack each month. In August 1948 $200 was sent to cover several months of expenses. In October 1948 Marion wrote:

> I think I can get along pretty well with the $50.00 if you dear one would be so very kind as to send an extra $10.00 a month in food parcels . . .[499]

Parcels and Post

The situation in Bulgaria deteriorated over the following years:

> Parcels are now taboo – only 1 of food and 1 of clothing per year.[500]

> I do hope they do not try to send me parcels. I had to refuse the last. The duty was so high.[501]

> The general post office for special airmail letters is too far for me to get at without much muscular pain.[502]

Health

> It is quite a job for me to get about at all, for I am over 80 and have such a cranky back that refuses to go more than a block or two before resting. Apart from that and a fuddy duddy heart I am as spry as a 60 year old gal.[503]

> The heart medicine I have laid aside. It may or may not be of use, but the bottle is lost, so why worry?[504]

I did not know that dear old Saffa[505] was my age. Some old boy. If his glands are still feeble I guess his little tummy has still the same contours. Mine's worse since the hernia begins to be assertive. All these bulges offend my artistic soul, so I am happy angels don't have glands or tummies.[506]

Also I may have told you that the MD wants me to rest an hour after meals, and I must take an hour outing so time I need is quickly gobbled up, and alas I give my correspondence a second place, as beloved Abdu'l-Baha said it the important things give place to the most important, and caring for the souls of people seems to me to belong to that category.[507]

Thanks be to God I am so much better and the M.D.s are quite amazed, but they need not be as the Baha'i family all over have been praying for my health and even our beloved Guardian has been supplicating at the Shrines of the Bab and 'Abdu'l-Baha on Mount Carmel. He is so anxious for me to continue staying on here . . .[508]

The Afterlife

I do hope all of you dear ones – Ivy, the Gregories, the Thompsons, Edith, Dorothy[509] and all are keeping well – and are able to get about – and Marie Hopper, the dear. We will all be together one of these days. Think of the glory of it! It seems too good to be true! And our dear Grace and so many beloved ones are waiting for us there. Think too of again meeting and talking with the Master![510]

Food

. . . however I should worry for though I had to live on spinach and potatoes half the week, there is chicken on tap the other days, although very dear. Milk is very, very scarce and butter horribly dear, real coffee and tea non-existent.[511]

We are still fairly well nourished but rarely see butter, or even oil for cooking and are thankful to have a little meat some days of the week – other days we only have beans, peas or lentils which I cannot digest & poorly cooked cabbage, but we have plenty of bread – no eggs or milk. If it doesn't get worse we may be thankful. We do get a little sugar from time to time. At present a friend gave me 100 saccharines after that I should have to sweeten my drink with jam – or marmalade as they call these poorly sweetened jams. We are indeed fortunate to have what we have when so many are suffering untold misery.[512]

How kind of you to think of sending a food parcel dear Louise. CARE[513] left Sofia months ago, but maybe the Red Cross might attend to the matter. There are plenty of open mouths here who will be glad to share anything sent. A dear pupil sent a fine parcel through the Legation (British). 2 pounds of sugar, tea, dried figs & raisins & a tin of meat. I think something else when he went to England. So kind of him. I like coffee best but only with sugar. The food question here is no joke, and most restaurants are pretty frail. They can't help it no doubt. However, we keep alive most of us.[514]

[Upon receiving a package]
. . . be sure that several grateful hearts will be helped by your bounty including my antediluvian organ, or organs shall we say.[515]

As for turkey, game, ham, & pig one can often get them at the Hallmark Restaurants, but their taste is so disguised that if one were blindfolded one would never guess . . . from which – quaint![516]

Here we have meat once a week, or tail end of goodness knows what perchance in a restaurant. Yesterday we actually had chicken after weeks of doing without.[517]

It will be wonderful to have two parcels a month. You should see the happy faces of the dear ones to share with me! One lovely Baha'i friend often makes her repast on bread and tea – no butter or marmalade to enliven said diet to say nothing of eggs, though from time to time those may be had at a very high price. Fortunately we can get sugar at present. Who knows for how long?[518]

Bedbugs

. . . it seems to me that Alexandrova might be preferable, and especially so since we seem to spend the nights fighting wild animals which make those hours hideous. You no doubt know a pattern in dress goods called 'polka dot'. At this moment both of my bed sheets are rapidly approaching said decoration. My partner is no less a sufferer but she carefully conveys the savages to the bucket. Not I! No such risk on my part for I know how foxy they are in making a get-away! Now you are familiar with such hunting expeditions, that I need go no further, but I will just say that if one building is eaten alive with these bubbly jocks it is likely that others are the same, so much as I dread moving on it seems to be the least of the two evils to choose from.[519]

Housing

I am not keen in having my poor little cubby hole visited. At present its end is a wood-shed up to the high windows sill. I call it the Gypsey callup. It takes almost a third of my income to heat the place small as it is.[520]

215

The Cold

The Americans have opened a fine Reading Room here lately. One can read there in comfort & <u>warmth</u>. How I wish they had some Baha'i Literature in it!

The [English-Speaking] League has no coal so it is not much use for the present.[521]

Last winter I used to have to visit friends who had warm places – but this year I have found this Reading Room, a warm coffee shop, and a couple of warm restaurants, and now I am visiting a kind young woman who has a lovely warm home.[522]

Overcoming Class Bias

. . . I am such a democrat now, and quite ready and happy to have the waiters & servants of the hotels come up and shake hands & pass the time of day. Since the bombardment we all seem more or less equally classed, and I enjoy all kinds and conditions of men except the poor gypsies and I must learn to like them better . . .[523]

Teaching

I like this place [Chaushev Coffee Shop] as I had the chance of speaking to a couple of fine men here, so lately I try to frequent it in the hope of catching a listening ear, and an ear which may not only listen but pass on the Glad Tidings by way of another member of the head ___.

Our dear little Anna Knobloch used to haunt the restaurants of girls in her early days in Europe. God grant that there may be as much success in this corner of the world as she had in hers.

It is much slower here because the spiritual education given from the pulpit does not equal that of the country of her choice – but all in God's good time. I feel that there will be active doings in the Balkans of a spiritual nature as well as elsewhere in Europe.[524]

I told the beloved I was out like Diogenes with a lantern, and no doubt our steps were guided.[525]

Rúḥíyyih Khánum wrote to Marion about the new teaching plans:

No doubt Mrs. Lynch[526] or someone else has told you about the New Seven Year Plan.[527] It was with great reluctance that Shoghi Effendi did not make you an Objective. He certainly would have liked to because you know how much he loves you and admires the work you have done but the Balkans could not be fitted into the picture at this time for various reasons. But I am sure that now that the friends are going to Europe you will receive some help.[528]

From a bulletin published by the Bahá'í International Bureau in Geneva we have this news:

Ernestine Zisman[529] writes to us in Esperanto. 'A friend from Sevlievo informed me that a group of intellectuals in that town wished to study all religions. I told him about the Bahá'í Faith and sent him some pamphlets which he appreciated, and expressed the desire to study the Teachings thoroughly. I possess only one copy of the New Era and three old back-numbers of "La Nova Tago", all of them loaned out. When they are returned I shall send them to him, but I wish I had more Bahá'í literature!' The Goal of a New World Order and the Unfoldment of a World Civilization have been sent, while Some Answered Questions will be sent as soon as it is roneographed (all these in Esperanto).

Ernestine lives in Trojan,[530] but end of December she had the opportunity of travelling to Sofia and visited our dear pioneer there, Miss Marion Jack, known to her near friends as 'Jackie'. 'I must say', she writes, 'that Miss Jack is a real heroine. It is not easy to live in a strange country without knowing either the national or international language, especially when one has to teach. Yet our Jackie has found the solution. With the help of English-speaking friends, she had some Writings translated into Bulgarian. Though well advanced in years, she began learning Esperanto, but could not continue because it is taught here in Bulgarian. She then decided to improve her French as she often meets people who speak that language. Once a week, English-speaking friends gather in her room, once a week French-speaking ones, and once a week those who speak only Bulgarian. There are always some little refreshments on the table. Sometimes other friends invite the people, or, if they have no room to ask them to, they bring refreshments to Miss Jack's. Practically all the expenses are covered by her. She is very generous at Nineteen-Day Feasts, and always offers something even at ordinary meetings. I fear that sometimes her generosity is taken advantage of. At present, Miss Jack is in a very difficult situation. She lives in private lodgings, in a very small room without any comfort. Most of her friends have died, others left the country, and she must have real courage to live as she does at her age (80). She has to do practically everything for herself. Only occasionally she gets a little help. May God assist her.'[531]

A few months later Marion Jack wrote in the bulletin:

So long as I see interest in the blessed Cause by at least a few new ones, I feel happy. I am trying to interest an ex-professor, a very promising person. We are following the same lecture course and our seats are together. He gets

218

a little compilation each week. Now I am going to lend him my only copy of 'Security' by Cobb.[532] You see, the professors of Roberts College, Constantinople, have a great standing here, and Stanwood having been there makes his book doubly interesting to those who glimpsed it. So many Bulgarian folks have graduated from Roberts, and what good English they speak! And how they stand out among their brothers and sisters. Not only material culture is theirs but they have a different outlook on life, many of them are fairly broadminded. Four or five of the women, and some of the men from Roberts seem deeply attracted to the Cause. Time will tell how much. Thanking you for everything, both of you, and praying for an ever greater success by the help of the invisible, your loving Jacky.[533]

Early the following year this article from Bulgaria appeared in the bulletin:

A letter has just arrived from Jackie – Miss Jack, in Sofia. The English-speaking Club which she was able to use for her contacts was closed end of January but reopened in February. Jackie speaks little of her actual work which is becoming increasingly handicapped in that country. She speaks about two of her spiritual sons who left the country some time ago. One of them is Gustav Lowe, who was recently on a business mission in Europe and visited several pioneers. He has become a fervent worker for the Cause. 'When one realizes that this transformation actually began from a little seed dropped at a meal in a hotel dining-room, one ought to feel encouraged to speak out fearlessly.' The other – Hayim Hodara, is now in Johannesburg. 'He called on a friend of mine who became a believer 35 years ago when I was working in London, and I had lost sight of her. And so it goes – our seedlings stretch out their limbs and sow their seeds from one end of the earth to another. "God helps all those who arise to serve Him."'[534]

219

... If only I knew more Bulgarian or they French I could have quantities of garden and park friends. Alas at my advanced age there is no chance of augmenting any language activities ... And yet we get on nicely with a little this and a little that and the other thing ... .[535]

I always feel that where loving work has been expended in His Cause, no matter how gloomy the outlook for the time may be, yet that Garden of God will burst into bloom all in His good time – and what a joy to see it come into this blaze of heavenly light.[536]

... your splendid offspring Eugenie B. is at last devoting herself to teaching. She has four or five or more people who seem to her to be drinking in the teachings ...

A lovely new believer is also teaching her relatives and friends, none of these, and only one of Eugenie's friends know English or French, so you may be sure I am grateful to them for looking after their own friends. Even if we could assemble, where could we meet? I have 3 whole chairs and a couch and could not swing a cat in my palatial chambers. No halls to be had of yore, for the Theosophists from whom we used to hire, don't dare to dare.[537]

It is the telling and in answering of the Message that I get the most thrills and the most happiness.[538]

I must say I quite enjoy copying out the explanations for folks on Revelation, Daniel, Isaiah and other books about the Last Days as the pastors and priests having taken the Bible literally, their parishioners are bewildered. No wonder there are so many agnostics and unbelievers. Fortunately the Bible tells us the books will be sealed until the 'time of the end' or the 'last day', so we know that the latest Messenger Bahá'u'lláh has broken the seals and we can now enjoy the spiritual and symbolic meanings.[539]

At present I am trying to clear some of the minds of the erstwhile Theosophists of 'reincarnation' which is wholly unscientific. Unfortunately the idea is deep seated with some of them –

God's laws like the Millwheel always go in one direction. In no case do they rotate to the left.

People love to think they are 'Cleopatras' or who knows what? . . .[540]

In 1949 Marion Jack reported that a former student, Boris, was proclaiming the Faith.

Restrictions

The friends in the USA are writing for a list of the names of the believers and Assemblies via Jessie Revell, but I think it wiser to leave the matter for the present as the people here have not the perfect freedom of America – and especially in the German domination were very closely watched. I was called to the police and asked to disgorge names – but I politely refused. They had a few, but got no satisfaction from yours truly. Since then I have been caution personified because to accept anything but Orthodoxy (as known here) might mean loss of post and of means of livelihood. Whether this holds good now or not I cannot say, but everyone with but one exception advises patience.[541]

Shoghi Effendi's Thoughts on Marion Jack

You cannot be a hero without action. This is the touchstone. Not movement, coming and going, but in the evidences of your character. Jacky [Marion Jack] is a heroine because of her conduct, the heroic spirit reveals itself in her. Martha [Martha Root] had the heroic action. She went 'til she dropped.[542]

221

ASSURE MARION JACK LOVING, FERVENT PRAYERS HIGH
ADMIRATION HER HEROIC PERSEVERANCE NOBLE COURAGE
EXEMPLARY STEWARDSHIP CAUSE BAHA'U'LLAH . . .[543]

Your most welcome letter of December 18th brought great
joy to the Guardian's heart, and he has instructed me to
answer it on his behalf.

You have very, very often been in his thoughts during
the many dangerous months and years Bulgaria has passed
through, and it was a true happiness for him to see your
letter . . .

How can you feel your offerings are little! You have
remained in the country of your adoption even in spite
of his own urging that you consider your own welfare,
and have demonstrated the quality of your steadfast-
ness and devotion in a way that will never be forgotten,
or effaced from the history of our beloved Faith.

The degree of your devotion and sacrifice cannot but
bear fruit, and the mere act of your remaining there all
these years has laid an irremovable foundation for the
spiritual work there.[544]

Dear and prized co-worker:

I am overjoyed to learn of your safety, your constancy,
your magnificent spirit of devotion, and your exemplary
conduct in the service of our beloved Faith under such
hard and trying circumstances. Future generations not only
in Bulgaria, but in Europe and Canada will recall your
noble stewardship, will extol your superb spirit, will strive
to follow in your footsteps, and will derive inspiration from
the record of your services. I feel so proud of you, so close
to you, so grateful for all that you have done and demonstrated. Be happy and grateful to God for so high a
privilege, so great a bounty, so exalted a station in the
ranks of the followers of His glorious Faith.[545]

Dear and prized co-worker,

I wish to answer you in person of my ever deepening admiration for the exemplary tenacity, devotion & loyalty you have exhibited ever since you have landed on the European continent in the service of our beloved Faith. The example you have set is being followed by the American believers these days and future generations will no doubt extol your magnificent services.

Persevere in your glorious task and be happy. Affectionately. Shoghi.[546]

Advise encourage extend assistance through European Teaching Committee beloved Marion Jack who over decade dauntlessly held fort exemplified spirit worthy emulation entire North American Baha'i community.[547]

He feels that the spirit of Marion Jack, her evident desire to stay with the community she loves so dearly and has fostered through thick and thin, reflects glory not only on the North American community, but on the entire Faith. She should be left free to remain in Bulgaria, and your Assembly should see to it that she receives a sufficient income to end her life in peace and with no more hardships to be endured. She is a heroic soul, the finest example of the pioneer spirit which we have anywhere in the world, and the Guardian feels deeply indebted to her, and loves her very dearly.[548]

It was a Canadian woman, one of the noblest in the ranks of Bahá'í pioneers, who alone and single-handed, forsook her home, settled among an alien people, braved with leonine spirit the risks and dangers of the world conflict that raged around her, and who now, at an advanced age and suffering from infirmities, is still holding the Fort and is setting an example, worthy of emulation by all her fellow pioneers of both the East and the West.[549]

OWING MARION JACKS ILLNESS EXTEND ADDITIONAL FINAN-
CIAL ASSISTANCE. SHOGHI.[550]

. . . Marion Jack, Bulgaria – Americans took the first boat
back when war came. We should follow the example set.
Marion Jack. S.E. urged her to go to Switzerland. She
begged to stay where she was. The Master appreciated her
very much. Not her ability – her spirit and detachment.
Canadians must be proud of her. Even Oriental believers
haven't risen to this height . . .[551]

Marion Jack on Pioneering

The Swiss Legation have had word from headquarters in
Bern asking for my health & whereabouts, and if I wanted
to be repatriated. My dear sister no doubt is anxious &
wants me to come home, but I told them that it would not
at all be convenient at present, so I hope they will get the
idea into their heads, as this is the second time of asking.
As my dear sister is not a Bahai she cannot understand my
preferring warring countries with a possibility to sow a few
Bahai seeds to the safety of 'our own our native land'.[552]
The very thought of being among people who would not
listen to the Cause is depressing, safety or no safety.[553]

As another dear Canadian friend wrote we have been going
through hell in Europe – not so much yours truly by a long
way but some friends and thousands of nameless (to me)
persons. Praise be to God there is a lull in the storm. It
will be permanent when there is 'Unity in the Love of God'.
– And may that day soon come! It is for this purpose, as
you know, that I am denying myself the joy of being with
you all – in that I may do my little bit to further this aim
– small though it may be.[554]

. . . What I am missing at home! The babyhood of your darlings – the pleasure of knowing dear . . .! Thank God I am able to help some people spiritually – and of late a few dear youths. This is my compensation, and if I can only help people to renew their faith in God I shall be more than grateful. Indifference to our Creator is the world's great crime, and there is no worse, for this life is but a preparatory school whereas the great beyond is eternal – so my responsibility is great as a pioneer . . .[555]

I had a letter this week from Haifa, and as I am told to persevere and keep on working I can turn a deaf ear to certain friends who think I should go back to where I came from, just because I had turned 80. I tell them that I never suffer in anticipation of what may come. It is the most foolish of all worries – nor do I feel in any way sure that I may not reach 85 or even more. As I feel that the Guardian senses to a great extent the future, because his heart is pure, I know he would not keep on urging me to be useful here if he felt things would go hard with me. So all aboard in spreading the Gospel of peace and world brotherhood – the joy of my young life.[556]

. . . when the beloved Guardian wrote to me to finish my days here the matter was settled. If only I knew the language how happy I would be, but it is too late to begin at 84.[557]

The Beloved Guardian wrote to me to go to the Second Convention in Brussels[558] this year, but later he wrote that I could spend my remaining years here and to return is a proposition not easy to fulfil so I have to relinquish the joy of that wonderful experience. You may have heard that my permission to attend the first came a month too late. One rejoices in the thought of the Day when we will all be one – no frontiers, no passports, no visas – Glorious![559]

225

Over twenty years – and I came not expecting to stay but a few months with only a suitcase as baggage.[560]

I was quite overwhelmed at your kind thought for me as to the visit to the Stockholm International,[561] and if only my health permits, I ask nothing better than to obey. At present, although up and about (in the house or in a cab), I have been rather under the impression that I am on my 'last legs'. However, your kind thought perks me up, so that even the long journey to Stockholm looms up as a possibility . . .

There is one great obstacle to my obedience to this your latest command beloved Guardian – should I go, how am I to 'finish my days' here with the flock? As you kindly granted that bounty a few years ago. It seems that going is none too easy as regards permission, but coming or rather returning is a horse of another colour. Question? how can I obey both commands? . . .

So there we are, and I must rouse myself from the idea that the transition of death is hovering hereabouts . . .[562]

The Minister's wife could not realize my desire to stick to my post or my love for these dear Bulgarians and my longing to help them, also to long for peace on earth and peace in the heart, and the joy of harmony, she . . . even offered to have me leave with them. Of course they could not realize our scattered condition, or the fact that so many Baha'is had gone away . . . and some how one must stand pat and almost begin to rebuild when permission is given to once more hold meetings . . .[563]

Around 1950 a Bulgarian lady took Marion Jack in. Although not well off, Marion was not in poverty and had a simple room with her own possessions.

The British Legation

Members of the British Legation, under whose responsibility Marion, as a Canadian citizen, fell, often visited her. The vice-consul recollected:

> . . . she did on one occasion agree to come to a Queen's birthday party, where she sat, like Queen Victoria, in a big armchair, and was made much of by everyone, as the sole representative of our community. She was brought to the party in the official Rolls Royce.[564]

> Miss Jack certainly impressed all of us at the legation with her directness and simple determination that she would not be turned away from what she felt was her call to stay in Bulgaria among the Baha'i community there.[565]

A friend from the British Legation who visited Marion in her last illness wrote:

> . . . I feel she is better in herself, but that at 87, she will not have the strength to get up again. She does not say very much, at least when I go to see her – just smiles and likes to hold my hand . . . She does sleep a lot and when awake seems to be already in another world . . .[566]

And so on 25 March 1954 Marion Elizabeth Jack passed way, at the age of 88.

MOURN LOSS IMMORTAL HEROINE MARION JACK GREATLY LOVED AND DEEPLY ADMIRED BY ABDUL BAHA SHINING EXAMPLE PIONEERS PRESENT FUTURE GENERATIONS EAST AND WEST SURPASSED CONSTANCY DEDICATION SELFABNEGATION FEARLESSNESS BY NONE EXCEPT INCOMPARABLE MARTHA ROOT. HER UNREMITTING HIGHLY MERITORIOUS ACTIVITIES

COURSE ALMOST HALF CENTURY BOTH NORTH AMERICA SOUTHEAST EUROPE, ATTAINING CLIMAX DARKEST MOST DANGEROUS PHASE SECOND WORLD WAR SHED IMPERISHABLE LUSTRE CONTEMPORARY BAHAI HISTORY. TRIUMPHANT SOUL NOW GATHERED DISTINGUISHED BAND COWORKERS ABHA KINGDOM MARTHA ROOT, LUA GETSINGER , MAY MAXWELL, HYDE DUNN, SUSAN MOODY, KEITH RANSOM KEHLER, ELLA BAILEY, DOROTHY BAKER WHOSE REMAINS LYING SUCH WIDELY SCATTERED AREAS GLOBE AS HONOLULU, CAIRO, BUENOS AIRES, SYDNEY, TEHERAN, ISFAHAN, TRIPOLI, DEPTHS MEDITERRANEAN ATTEST MAGNIFICENCE PIONEER SERVICES RENDERED NORTH AMERICAN BAHAI COMMUNITY APOSTOLIC FORMATIVE AGES BAHAI DISPENSATION.

ADVISE ARRANGE ASSOCIATION CANADIAN NATIONAL ASSEMBLY EUROPEAN TEACHING COMMITTEE BEFITTING MEMORIAL GATHERING MASHRIQUL ADHKAR. MOVED SHARE WITH UNITED STATES CANADIAN NATIONAL ASSEMBLIES EXPENSES ERECTION SOON AS CIRCUMSTANCES PERMIT WORTHY MONUMENT HER GRAVE DESTINED CONFER ETERNAL BENEDICTION COUNTRY ALREADY HONOURED ITS CLOSE PROXIMITY SACRED CITY ASSOCIATED PROCLAMATION FAITH BAHAULLAH. – SHOGHI.[567]

More of Shoghi Effendi's Thoughts on Marion Jack

He would suggest that, when writing to the European centres, you share with the believers the glorious example of the life of Marion Jack. Young or old could never find a more inspiring pioneer in whose footsteps to walk, than this wonderful soul.

For over thirty years, with an enlarged heart and many other ailments she remained at her post in Bulgaria. Never well-to-do, she often suffered actual poverty and want: want of heat, want of clothing, want of food, when her money failed to reach her because Bulgaria had come under the Soviet zone of influence. She was bombed, lost her possessions, she was evacuated, she lived in drafty, cold dormitories for many, many months in the country, she returned, valiant, to the capital of Bulgaria after the war and continued, on foot, to carry out her teaching work.

The Guardian himself urged her strongly, when the war first began to threaten to cut her off in Bulgaria, to go to Switzerland. She was a Canadian subject and ran great risks by remaining, not to mention the dangers and privations of war. However, she begged the Guardian not to insist and assured him her one desire was to remain with her spiritual children. This she did, up to the last breath of her glorious life. Her tomb will become a national shrine, immensely loved and revered, as the Faith rises in stature in that country.

He thinks that every Bahá'í and most particularly those who have left their homes and gone to serve in foreign fields, should know of, and turn their gaze to, Marion Jack.[568]

. . . To remain at one's post, to undergo sacrifice and hardship, loneliness and, if necessary, persecution, in order to hold aloft the torch of Bahá'u'lláh, is the true function of every pioneer.

Let them remember Marion Jack, who for over twenty years, in a country the language of which she never mastered; during war and bombardment; evacuation and poverty; and at length, serious illness, stuck to her post, and has now blessed the soil of the land she had chosen to serve at such cost with her precious remains, every atom of which was dedicated to Bahá'u'lláh. Perhaps the friends are not aware that the Guardian, himself, during the war on more than one occasion urged her to seek safety in Switzerland rather than remain behind enemy lines and be entirely cut off. Lovingly she pleaded that he would not require her to leave her post, and he acquiesced to her request. Surely the standard of Marion Jack should be borne in mind by every pioneer![569]

The most important thing is to keep the pioneer territories which have been settled open. There must be no lapse. The friends must be urged to remain at their post at all costs. They must remember the glorious example of Marion Jack, who recently passed away in Bulgaria, after almost 30 years of devoting her life to teaching the Faith in that country of her choice. As many of you who knew her personally will recall, her health was very bad, as far back as 1935, when she attended the Esslingen Summer School. It certainly never improved. She was bombed, evacuated, she slept in some drafty, cold room in a school in the country, was often, we have reason to believe, almost hungry, and insufficiently clad after the war, due to difficulties in getting money through to her in a Soviet-dominated territory. She never mastered the language, and was without friends of her own country; and yet, she persevered, and in spite of even the Guardian's pleas that she leave the country during the worst years of the war, remained at her post, and won for herself imperishable fame, her resting-place becoming a shrine in Bulgaria, which the people of that country will increasingly honour and cherish.

It is to this glorious soul that the present generation of pioneers must look for inspiration and example.[570]

He hopes that it has been possible to make arrangements to have Miss Jack's grave built. This is a task which is indeed a precious trust for your Assembly. When the friends realize that her grave will become in the future a place of visitation, they will appreciate the bounty bestowed upon the Canadian Community through being able to claim one of the most distinguished of all pioneers as a member of their community.[571]

It was reported in early 1958[572] that a monument to Marion Jack had been erected at her grave in Sofia. On the gravestone the followings passage taken from the Guardian's memorable cable was inscribed:

MARION JACK
1866 – 1954

IMMORTAL HEROINE . . .
GREATLY LOVED AND DEEPLY ADMIRED BY ABDU'L-BAHA.
A SHINING EXAMPLE TO PIONEERS . . .
HER UNREMITTING, HIGHLY MERITORIOUS ACTIVITIES . . .
SHED IMPERISHABLE SPLENDOUR
ON CONTEMPORARY BAHA'I HISTORY
SHOGHI

Conclusion

A careful look at the endnotes to this book will immediately show how undervalued Marion Jack was by those 'immortalisers of her contemporaries' and even in the memoirs of her contemporaries she is mentioned only in passing, except in a few rare instances. So how did it come about that this 'second fiddle', this one they called 'Jacky', turned out to be an 'immortal heroine'? It is easier to reach for clichés rather than to the Oxford or Webster dictionaries or to mindlessly patter off words seen (but not felt) as they lie on some page 'dearly beloved by 'Abdu'l-Bahá'. If heroes are born on the battlefield, where was hers? Where did she first hear the clash of swords or the whistle of bullets? Was it in the cellars of Sofia or was it rather on the streets of Montparnasse? '. . . highly meritorious activities course almost half century both North America, southeast Europe

...' The one who knew called her 'General'. This must have amused many but didn't she command the 'Concourse on high, each bearing aloft a chalice of pure light'?[573] But perhaps her victory was also of another kind:

> Likewise, reflect upon the perfection of man's creation, and that all these planes and states are folded up and hidden away within him.

> Dost thou reckon thyself only a puny form
> When within thee the universe is folded?

> Then we must labour to destroy the animal condition, till the meaning of humanity shall come to light.[574]

Appendix 1

Talks and Letters of 'Abdu'l-Bahá Associated with Marion Jack

Discourse by 'Abdu'l-Bahá given at the
Unity Meeting of Misses Jack and Herrick.
September 22nd, 1911.[575]

It is a cold and miserable day but as I was anxious to see you I came here. For a man who has love, effort is a rest. He will travel any distance to visit his friends.

Thank God I see you spiritual and at rest; I give you this message from God; that you must be turned toward Him. Praise God that you are near Him! The unworthy things of this world have not deterred you from seeking the world of the Spirit. When in harmony with that world, you care not for the things that perish; your desire is for that which never dies and the Kingdom lies open before you. I hope that the teaching of God will spread throughout the world, and will cause all to be united.

In the time of Jesus Christ there was an outpouring of the Light from the East to West that brought the people under a heavenly banner and illumined them with divine insight. Western lands have been kindled by the Light of the Christ. I pray earnestly that the Light in this advanced age will so illumine the world that all may rally under the banner of Unity and receive Spiritual education.

Then those problems which cause difference among the peoples of the earth will be seen no more, for verily they are not. You are all waves of one sea, mirrors of one reflection.

This day the countries of Europe are at rest; Education has become widespread. The light of liberty is the light of the West, and the intention of government is to work for truth and justice in Western countries. But ever the light of spirituality shines from out of the East. In this age that Light has become dimmed; religion has become a matter of form and ceremony and the desire for God's love has been lost.

In [e]very age of great spiritual darkness, a light is kindled in the East. So once again the light of the teachings of God has come unto you. Even as education and progress travel from West to East, so does the spiritual fire travel from East to West.

I hope that the people of the West may be illumined by the light of God; that the Kingdom may come to them, that they may find eternal Life, that the Spirit of God may spread like a fire among them, that they may be baptized with the Water of Life and may find a new birth.

This is my desire; I hope by the will of God, He will cause you to receive it, and will make you happy.

In the same way that you have education and material progress so may the light of God be your portion.

God keep all of you in safety.

'Abdu'l-Bahá

To the maid-servant of God, Miss Jack, Chicago, Ill. – Upon her be greeting and praise!

He Is God!

O thou who art the well-wisher of mankind!

Thy letter was received and was perused most attentively; its contents were exceedingly pleasing. Thy wish, as well as that of the friends of America, is that I may undertake a voyage to that land; but my heart is there and I am always thinking of them; and as they associate and affiliate in the utmost of love and union therein, my heart and spirit reside. Entertain no doubts whatever for I am linked with you spiritually even though separate in body. We are all under the shade of the unicoloured pavilion of the world of humanity, but heedlessness forms a veil and an obstacle. When it is removed the veil will be rent asunder and we shall see one another gathered up together and present.

Thou hast written of thy wish to use the money of the Mashrekol-azkar to aid some of the dear sisters to get well: If you have gathered the sum from your own money, spend half of it for the sisters, and the other half, spend it for the Mashrekol-azkar; and if the sum is from other people, refer to them (i.e. the contributors) and act according to their wish.

Convey on my behalf greetings and the utmost of respect to the maidservant of God, Mrs. Eva Cooper (of Fruitport, Mich.).

Upon thee be greeting and praise!

(Signed) *Abdul-Baha Abbas*

(Translated by Shoghi Rabbani, Haifa, Palestine, December 27, 1918)[576]

The Maidservant of God, Marion Jack: upon her be the Glory of God the Most Glorious.

He Is God!

O thou respected General Jack!

Thy letter has been received and the contents became the cause of joy. Wherever thou art, take unto thy hands the cup of the wine of the Love of God, give it to the friends and make them intoxicated. Rest assured that sometime thou wilt come to the Holy Land. But now engage thou in teaching. I never forget thee and think always of thee. Convey my utmost kindness to that Irish Lady[577] and also my love and kindness to Mrs Lundberg, Elfie and Eliza. From the bounties of God I implore that they may become confirmed and assisted.

Upon thee be the Glory of the Most Glorious.

(Signed) *Abdul-Baha-Abbas*
Nov. 7, 1921 Haifa Palestine[578]

236

O ye close and dear friends of 'Abdu'l-Bahá!
In the Orient scatter perfumes,
And shed splendours on the West.
Carry light unto the Bulgar,
And the Slav with life invest.

One year after the ascension of Bahá'u'lláh, there came this verse from the lips of the Centre of the Covenant. The Covenant-breakers found it strange indeed, and they treated it with scorn. Yet, praised be God, its effects are now manifest, its power revealed, its import clear; for by God's grace, today both East and West are trembling for joy, and now, from sweet waftings of holiness, the whole earth is scented with musk.

The Blessed Beauty, in unmistakable language, hath made this promise in His Book: 'We behold you from Our realm of glory, and shall aid whosoever will arise for the triumph of Our Cause with the hosts of the Concourse on high and a company of Our favoured angels.'[579]

God be thanked, that promised aid hath been vouchsafed, and is plain for all to see, and it shineth forth as clear as the sun in the heavens.

Wherefore, O ye friends of God, redouble your efforts, strain every nerve, till ye triumph in your servitude to the Ancient Beauty, the Manifest Light, and become the cause of spreading far and wide the rays of the Day-Star of Truth. Breathe ye into the world's worn and wasted body the fresh breath of life, and in the furrows of every region sow ye holy seed. Rise up to champion this Cause; open your lips and teach. In the meeting-place of life be ye a guiding candle; in the skies of this world be dazzling stars; in the gardens of unity be birds of the spirit, singing of inner truths and mysteries.

Expend your every breath of life in this great Cause and dedicate all your days to the service of Bahá, so that in the end, safe from loss and deprivation, ye will inherit the heaped-up treasures of the realms above. For the days of a man are full of peril and he cannot rely on so much as a moment more of life; and still the people, who are even as a wavering mirage of illusions, tell themselves that in the end they shall reach the heights. Alas for them! The men of bygone times hugged these same fancies to their breasts, until a wave flicked over them and they returned to dust, and they found themselves excluded and bereft – all save those souls who had freed themselves from self and had flung away their lives in the pathway of God. Their bright star shone out in the skies of ancient glory, and the handed-down memories of all the ages are the proof of what I say.

Wherefore, rest ye neither day nor night and seek no ease. Tell ye the secrets of servitude, follow the pathway of service, till ye attain the promised succour that cometh from the realms of God.

O friends! Black clouds have shrouded all this earth, and the darkness of hatred and malice, of cruelty and aggression and defilement is spreading far and wide. The people, one and all, live out their lives in a heedless stupor and the chief virtues of man are held to be his rapacity and his thirst for blood. Out of all the mass of humankind God hath chosen the friends, and he hath favoured them with His guidance and boundless grace. His purpose is this, that we, all of us, should strive with our whole hearts to offer ourselves up, guide others to His path, and train the souls of men – until these frenzied beasts change to gazelles in the meadows of oneness, and these wolves to lambs of God, and these brutish creatures to angelic hosts; till the fires of hatred are quenched, and the flame coming out of the sheltered vale of the Holy Shrine doth shed its splendours; till the foul odour of the tyrant's dunghill is blown away, and yieldeth to the pure, sweet scents that stream from the rosebuds of faith and trust. On that day will the weak of intellect draw on the bounty of the divine, Universal Mind, and they whose life is but abomination will seek out these cleansing, holy breaths.

But there needs must be souls who will manifest such bestowals, there needs must be husbandmen to till these fields, gardeners for these gardens, there needs must be fish to swim in this sea, stars to gleam in these heavens. These ailing ones must be tended by spiritual physicians, these who are the lost need gentle guides – so that from such souls the bereft may receive their portion, and the deprived obtain their share, and the poor discover in such as they unmeasured wealth, and the seekers hear from them unanswerable proofs.

O my Lord, my Defender, My Help in peril! Lowly do I entreat Thee, ailing do I come unto Thee to be healed, humbly do I cry out to Thee with my tongue, my soul, my spirit:

O God, my God! The gloom of night hath shrouded every region, and all the earth is shut away behind thick clouds. The peoples of the world are sunk in the black depths of vain illusions, while their tyrants wallow in cruelty and hate. I see nothing but the glare of searing fires that blaze upward from the nethermost abyss, I hear nothing save the thunderous roar that belloweth out from thousands upon thousands of fiery weapons of assault, while every land is crying aloud in its secret tongue: 'My riches avail me nothing, and my sovereignty hath perished!'

O my Lord, the lamps of guidance have gone out. The flames of passion are mounting high, and malevolence is ever gaining on the world. Malice and hate have overspread the face of the whole earth, and I find no souls except Thine own oppressed small band who are raising up this cry:

Make haste to love! Make haste to trust! Make haste to give! To guidance come!

Come ye for harmony! To behold the Star of Day! Come here for kindliness, for ease! Come here for amity and peace!

Come and cast down your weapons of wrath, till unity is won! Come and in the Lord's true path each one help each one.

Verily with exceeding joy, with heart and soul, do these oppressed of Thine offer themselves up for all mankind in every land. Thou seest them, O my Lord, weeping over the tears Thy people shed, mourning the grief of Thy children, condoling with humankind, suffering because of the calamities that beset all the denizens of the earth.

O my Lord, wing them with victory that they may soar upward to salvation, strengthen their loins in service to Thy people, and their backs in servitude to Thy Threshold of Holiness.

Verily Thou art the Generous, verily Thou art the Merciful! There is none other God save Thee, the Clement, the Pitiful, the Ancient of Days![580]

Appendix 2

Exhibitions and Publications

Exhibitions

International Forestry Exhibition, Edinburgh, July 1884[581]
   'Hand painted flowers of forest trees'
   [commendation awarded by jury]

Royal Society of Artists, Birmingham, 72nd Autumn Exhibition, 1898[582]
   The Camber Golf Links, Rye
   A Venetian Byway
   Early Morning, Rye

Royal Society of Artists, Birmingham, 73rd Autumn Exhibition, 1899[583]
   Southwold
   Wheatfield, Southwold
   The Road to Walberswick
   Winding in the Boats, Southwold

Royal Society of Artists, Birmingham, 75th Autumn Exhibition, 1901[584]
   Sunset: Notre Dame, from the Seine
   Grey Day: Notre Dame

Royal Society of Artists, Birmingham, 76th Autumn Exhibition, 1902[585]
   A Garden at Crecy
   Golden Morning at Rye

Paris Salon, Salon des Artistes Indépendants, 1905[586]
Les poiriers
Le petit canal, Venico
Le départ pour la pêche
La cour de ferme
Le souper
Au Luxembourg
Fragment décoratif
Fragment décoratif

Paris Salon, Salon des Artistes Indépendants, 1906[587]
Décorations
Sous le bois
Les arbres d'automne
L'automne
L'effet de nuage
Les bateaux
Les canards
La rivière

Paris Salon, Société Nationale des Beaux-Arts, 1906[588]
Etude de lumière
Panneau décoratif (2)
Projet décoratif (2)

Paris Salon, Société Nationale des Beaux-Arts, 1907[589]
Panneau décoratif (4)

Salon des Humoristes (Paris) (between 1905 and 1907)[590]

Royal Canadian Academy of Arts, 29th Annual Exhibition, Toronto, 1908[591]
Decorative Panels
French Woodland Scene

Art Association of Montreal, Spring Exhibition, 1908[592]
French Woodland Scene

Dominion Exhibition, Saint John, N.B., 1910[593]
Cathedral Bourges
Town Hall and Market Place Stuttgart
The Musee Cluny, Paris
Notre Dame, from the Left Bank of the Seine

Saint John Art Club, Saint John, N.B., 7 October 1910
(solo exhibition)

London Salon, Royal Albert Hall, July 1911 (Allied Artists Association)
The Fields of Kerry
Portrait of Mrs. Hughes, widow of the late George Hughes of the 3rd West Indian
Étude

London Salon, Royal Albert Hall, July 1912 (Allied Artists Association)
Rothesay Park, New Brunswick
Red Maple and Birch Woods, St. John, N.B., Canada
Venetian Gold

Art Association of Montreal, 30th Spring Exhibition, April 1913[594]
Old Cottage at Benfleet, Near the Mouth of the Thames
The Hillside Farm

Royal Canadian Academy of Arts, 36th Annual Exhibition, Toronto, November 1914[595]
The Lecture Pine, Green Acre, Maine

Art Association of Montreal, 31st Spring Exhibition, April 1914[596]
Birches and Maples
Church Interior, Southwold, Sussex
Coming Storm
Spring in England
Bunyan's House, Elstow (watercolour)

Abdul Baha (pastel)
Valley of the Stour (watercolour)
A Bit of English Country (watercolour)

Provincial Exhibition, Saint John, N.B., 1914[597]
Birches and Maples, Rothesay Park, N.B. (oil)
Spring in England (oil)
The Coming Storm, Bedfordshire (oil)
An Irish Cottage (oil)
Garden in Akka, Palestine (pastel)
Head of a Woman (pastel)
Street Scene (watercolour)
Pastelo (pastel)
October Twilight (pastel)
Courtyard and Interior, Palestine (pastel)
Oriental Garden (pastel)
Study of Head (oil)
Fields of Kerry (oil)
Study of Head (oil) [2nd]
Church Interior (oil)

Art Association of Montreal, 32nd Spring Exhibition, 1915[598]
An Autumn Day, Eliot, Me.
Green Acre, Me.
The Harbour, St. Andrews by the Sea (pastel)

Art Association of Montreal, 33rd Spring Exhibition, 1916[599]
The Old Road, Green Acre
Turkish Fortress, Acca, Syria
Etude: Mount Carmel from the Mediterranean (watercolour)

Saint John Art Club, Saint John, N.B., 15 February 1917
Green Acre, Eliot, Maine, Its Beauty and Ideals (solo exhibition
    to accompany lecture)

Saint John Art Club at the Lantern Art Studio, Saint John, N.B.,
13 November 1917[600]
Starving Syrians
(lecture and solo exhibition)

YWCA, Evanston, Illinois, 27 January 1919[601]

Soldier's Club, Dawson City, 2 October 1919[602]
(solo exhibition)

British Columbia Society of Fine Arts, Annual Exhibition,
Vancouver, September 1920[603]
Study of Miss J. Fripp
Savary Island
The Old Favorites

Vancouver Exhibition, Art Section, September 1920[604]
Landscapes in oil
[2nd prize]

Vancouver Sketch Club, Monthly Exhibition, 9 October 1920[605]
2 portrait studies
2 sketches done in Palestine
Landscapes in oil and watercolour

YWCA Benefit Exhibition, Moncton, N.B., 9 November 1922[606]
(solo exhibition)

IODE Benefit Exhibition, Summerside, P.E.I., 1922?[607]
(solo exhibition)

Saint John Art Club, 26 April 1923[608]
Alaska the Wonderland
(lecture and solo exhibition)

Women's Art Institute of Ontario, Toronto, 1924
(solo exhibition)

Green Acre Fine Arts and Crafts Club Exhibition, Rockingham Hotel, Portsmouth, N.H., 1930

Saint John Art Club, 50th Anniversary, 1958[609]
Normandy Poplars by Lake Shore

Exhibition of the Saint John Art Club Collections, Saint John, N.B., 1969[610]
Normandy Poplars by Lake Shore
Birches and Maples
Village Street

Publications

Vancouver Sun, 18 March 1921, published the following sketches:
Garden Acca
The Courtyard Acca
The Prison Home of Abdul Baha at Acca until 1908
The Fortress of St. Jean Acca
Dr Jenabe Fazel Mazandarani

Appendix 3

List of Marion Jack's Known Works[611]

I Works Held at the Bahá'í World Centre, Haifa, Israel

1. *Untitled* (The Prison of Acre)
Oil on canvas, 1908 or 1931
69.5 x 88.5 cm
Signed but not dated
Inscription recto: M-E Jack

2. *Loch Lomond*
Watercolour on grey textured paper, Scotland, c. 1912?
8.5 x 11.5 cm
Not dated
Inscription recto: M.E. Jack

3. *Untitled* (The Mansion of Bahjí)
Pastel on paper, 1914
80 x 63.4 cm
Signed and dated
Inscription recto: M. Jack 1914

4. *Village where John Bunyan was born*
Oil, c. 1914

5. *Varna*
Oil on textured paper, Bulgaria, 1930s
8.9 x 14.5 cm
Inscription recto lower right: M. E. Jack

6. *Untitled* (Village scene with figures)
Oil on textured crème paper, Bulgaria, 1930s
13.3 x 18 cm
 Not signed and not dated
Inscription verso: Samakov

7. *Old Varna* (House with window boxes)
Oil on textured paper, Bulgaria, 1930s
15.5 x 21.7 cm
Not signed and not dated
Inscription on verso: Old Varna

8. *Old Varna* (Farmyard with wagon)
Oil on textured paper, Bulgaria, 1930s
16 x 22 cm
Not signed and not dated
Inscription verso: Old Varna NS

9. *Untitled* (Street with house, probably old Varna)
Oil on textured paper, Bulgaria, 1930s
21.6 x 15.6 cm
Not signed and not dated

10. *Old Varna* (Street with houses and tree)
Oil on textured paper, Bulgaria, 1930s
22 x 16 cm
Not signed and not dated
Inscription verso: Old Varna

11. *Cham Korea*
Oil on canvas, Bulgaria, 1930s
22.7 x 16.1 cm
Not signed and not dated
Inscription verso: Cham Kore

12. *Untitled* (Village scene with figures and spinning wheel)
Oil on canvas, Bulgaria, 1930s
11.1 x 14 cm
Not signed and not dated

13. *Untitled* (The Mansion of Bahjí)
Oil on canvas, Bulgaria, 1930s
59 x 43.5 cm
Not signed and not dated
Inscription verso: Painted by Marion Jack (Brought from Sofia
    Bulgaria)

14. *Untitled* (Bahjí south gardens with Acre in distance – view as
    seen from the balcony of the Mansion)
Oil on canvas, Bahjí, 1931
205 x 104.5 cm
Signed and dated
Inscription recto: Marion Jack General 1931

15. *Untitled* (Shrine of the Báb)
Watercolour or gauche or oil on cotton? Haifa, 1931
155 x 109 cm
Signed and dated
Inscription recto: Marion Jack General March 1931

16. *Untitled* (Shrine of Bahá'u'lláh with surrounding landscape)
Oil on canvas, Bahjí, 1931
415 x 106 cm
Inscription recto: Marion E. Jack (General) Naw Ruz 1931

17. *Doorway*
Oil on canvas, c. 1933
54.7 x 73 cm
Not signed and not dated

18. *Ruins of the House of 'Izzat'u'lláh, Adrianople*
Oil on canvas, 1933
53.2 x 68.8 cm
Inscription recto: M. E. Jack 1933

19. *Murádiyyih Quarter, Adrianople*
Oil on canvas, 1933
54.2 x 72.3 cm
Inscription recto: M. E. Jack 1933

20. *Ruins of the House of Amru'lláh, Adrianople*
Oil on canvas, 1933
53 x 64.7 cm
Inscription recto: M. E. Jack 1933

21. *Ruins of the House of Ridá Big, Adrianople*
Oil on canvas, 1933
55.1 x 72.5 cm
inscription recto: M. E. Jack 1933

22. *Untitled* (Buildings with fields and figures in background,
    Adrianople?)
Oil on canvas, 1933
54.3 x 72 cm
Inscription recto: M. E. Jack 1933

23. *Adrianople. Ruins outside the city*
Oil on textured paper, 1933
9.3 x 15 cm
Not signed and not dated.

24. *Untitled* (Figures seated under trees, Bahá'í summer school,
    Esslingen, Germany)
Oil on canvas, Germany, 1933
8.9 x 13.7 cm
Not signed and not dated

25. *Sea of Galilee*
Oil on canvas, 1933
27.1 x 21.1 cm
Not signed and not dated

26. *Untitled* (Entrance to the Shrine of Bahá'u'lláh)
Oil on canvas
29.5 x 22 cm
Not signed and not dated

27. *Portrait of Elfie Lundberg's Mother*
Oil on canvas
35.6 x 45.5 cm
Not signed and not dated

28. *Untitled* (Shrine of Bahá'u'lláh)
Oil on canvas
69.4 x 69.4 cm
Signed but not dated
Inscription recto: M E Jack

29. *Untitled* (Entrance to the Shrine of Bahá'u'lláh)
Oil on canvas
46.1 x 56.8 cm
Not signed and not dated

30. *Untitled* (Shrine of Bahá'u'lláh and the Mansion of Bahjí)
Oil on canvas
26.5 x 20 cm
Not signed and not dated

II Works Held at the Office of the National Spiritual Assembly of the Bahá'ís of Canada, Thornhill, Ontario

1. *Untitled* (Shrine of Bahá'u'lláh)
Oil on stretched canvas
70.5 x 89.5 cm
Signed but not dated
Inscription recto: M.E. Jack

2. *Portrait of 'Abdu'l-Bahá*
Oil on stretched canvas
61 x 85 cm
Inscription recto: M.E. Jack – 1915–

3. *Untitled* (Farm scene with family and wagon)
Oil on heavy brown textured paper [1930s?]
37.5 x 31.3 cm
Not signed and not dated

4. *Portrait of Elizabeth Greenleaf*
Oil on board
60 x 119 cm
Not signed and not dated
[attributed to Marion Jack]

5. *Portrait of Lua Getsinger*
Oil on board
51 x 41 cm
Not signed and not dated

6. *Portrait of Sarah Farmer*
Oil on board
60 x 45 cm
Signed but not dated
Inscription recto lower left ME Jack; verso in pencil upper right:
    Sara Farmer painted by Marion Jack

7. *The Hall in the Acca Home where 'Abdu'l-Bahá was Living in 1908 when He was Liberated*
Acre, 1908
Oil on board
13.5 x 8.5 cm
Signed but not dated
Inscription recto: ME Jack; title on verso

III Works Held at the Association for Bahá'í Studies, Ottawa

1. *Untitled* (House of 'Abdu'lláh Páshá?)
Oil on canvas
32 x 45 cm
Signed but not dated
Inscription recto: M E Jack; verso: Marion Jack gave this picture to Elizabeth Greenleaf (Lady Betty) who later gave it to Lou and Helen Eggleston

2. *Untitled* (Shrine of Bahá'u'lláh and the Mansion of Bahjí)
Oil on canvas
44 x 58.5 cm
Signed but not dated
Inscription recto: M. E. Jack

3. *Untitled* (Bridge with three figures)
Chalk
26.5 x 24.5 cm
Signed but not dated
Inscription recto: M Jack; verso: chalk by Marion Jack

4. *Gathering Roses*
Oil on canvas. Bulgaria, 1930s
19 x 14 cm
Framed

5. *Waiting at the Gate-House of Akka*
Oil on canvas, c. 1908
66 x 76.5 cm
Inscription recto: 'Abdu'l-Bahá's House, Haifa, Israel

6. *Prison at Akka*
Oil on canvas
49 x 34 cm

IV Works Held at the Bahá'í Shrine (the Maxwell home), Montreal

1. *House of 'Abdu'lláh Pá<u>sh</u>á*

V Works Held at the New Brunswick Museum, Saint John, N.B.

1. *Near the Mouth of the Oromocto – The Approaching Thunder Storm*
Watercolour with opaque white board, New Brunswick, c. 1915
27.8 x 38.2 cm
Inscription recto: lower right, ME Jack

2. *Landscape with blowing trees*
Pastel on heavy dark brown wove paper, c. 1915
27.3 x 25.5 cm
Inscription recto: ME jack

3. *Birches and maples at Rothesay Park*
Oil on canvas, New Brunswick, 1914
76.5 x 40.8 cm
Inscription recto: M Jack

4. *Village Street*
Watercolour on wove paper, 1914
Not signed
[Originally part of St John Art Club collection]

5. *Normandy Poplars by Lakeshore*
Watercolour over graphite on wove paper, 1914
Inscription recto: ME Jack
[Originally part of St John Art Club collection]

6. *Poplars in a Field*
Chalk pastel on brown wove paper, 1914
Inscription recto: M. Jack
[Originally part of St John Art Club collection]

7. *Untitled* (landscape)
Chalk pastel on grey wove paper, c. 1914
Inscription recto: M. Jack
[Originally part of St John Art Club collection]

VI Works Held in the Bahá'í Archives at Eliot, Maine

1. *Portrait of May Maxwell*

2. *Portrait of Helen Ellis Cole*

3. *Portrait of Carter Troop*

4. *Portrait of Elizabeth Greenleaf*
[unfinished]

5. *Portrait of Dr Susan Moody*

6. *Portrait of Miss Fitting*

7. *Portrait of an unidentified woman, seated*

8. *Portrait of Charles Mason Remey*

9. *Portrait of an unidentified woman in Persian dress*
Framed

10. *Portrait of Albert Vail*

11. *Portrait of Kate Ives*

12. *Portrait of James Morton*

13. *Portrait of Mrs [Agnes] Parsons* (?)

14. *Portrait of an unidentified woman*
[unfinished]

15. *Portrait of an unidentified young girl*
Signed

16. *Portrait of Hooper Harris of NY*

VII Works Held by the National Spiritual Assembly of the Bahá'ís of Germany, Hofheim-Langenhain

1. *Bahá'í-Heim, Esslingen*
Oil, 1933
50 x 40 cm
Inscription recto: To my dear friend Dr Grossmann, Marion E. Jack, 1933

VIII Works Held by the National Spiritual Assembly of the Bahá'ís of Austria, Vienna

1. *Bahjí*
Oil
35 x 23 cm
Not signed

IX Works Held in the Archives of the National Spiritual Assembly of the Bahá'ís of the United States

1. *Garden of House of 'Abdu'lláh Páshá,' Akká*
Unframed
30 x 35cm
[Given to Isabella D. Brittingham by Ida A. Finch, c. 1908. From Revell collection of photographs.]

2. *Drawing of Fishermen*
c. 1908
27 x 17 cm
Inscription: 'To E. Cooper souvenir of Jan. 1908 from Jackie'

3. *Bahjí*
31 x 51 cm
Not signed

4. *Laura L. Drum*
57 x 41 cm
Not signed
[donated by George Miller]

5. *The Yukon*
10 x 8 cm
Not signed
Inscription verso: Jackie, *The Yukon*
[Donated by George D. Miller]

6. *Wind Blown Trees on Top of Mount Carmel*
13 x 8 cm
Not signed
Verso: Title
[Donated by George D. Miller]

7. *Green Acre on the Piscataqua*
8 x 14 cm
Not signed
Verso: Title
[Donated by George D. Miller]

8. *'Abdu'l-Bahá's Donkey*

9. *Upper stairs in inner stairway, House of 'Abdúlláh Páshá, 'Akká*
35 x 51 cm
Signed, lower right hand corner
[Donor: National Spiritual Assembly]

10. *Garden of 'Abdu'l-Bahá, 'Akká*
Watercolour
[Donated by Nina Matthisen; given to unidentified individual
by Marion Jack in 1921]

11. *Woman* [possibly Lua Getsinger]
32 x 42 cm
Framed
Not signed

Appendix 4

Personae Gratae

Marion Jack's co-workers, friends, acquaintances and correspondents mentioned in the text or endnotes and the chapters in which they appear.

Abu'l-Faḍl-i-Gulpáygání, Mírzá (1844–1914) Chapter 3
Early Persian Bahá'í; Apostle of Bahá'u'lláh; outstanding scholar.

Publications: *The Brilliant Proof* (1912), *The Bahá'í Proofs* (1914), *The Shining Pearls* (translated into English by Juan Cole under the title *Miracles and Metaphors*, 1981), etc.

See: Adamson and Hainsworth, *Historical Dictionary*, p. 295; Ish'ta'a'l Ebn-Kalantar, 'Mirza Abul-Fazl', in *Star of the West*, vol. 4, no. 19 (2 March 1914), pp. 317–19.

Afruḵẖtih, Youness [Dr Yunis Khan] (–1948) Chapter 7
Early Persian Bahá'í; secretary to 'Abdu'l-Bahá, 1900–9; travelled widely in Europe and America.

See: Adamson and Hainsworth, *Historical Dictionary*, p. 87; Ṭáhirzádeh, 'Dr Youness Afruḵẖtih', *Bahá'í World*, vol. 12, pp. 679–81, illus.

Alexander, Agnes Baldwin (1875–1971) Chapter 3
First Hawaiian Bahá'í, 1901; long-term pioneer in Japan; appointed Hand of the Cause of God, 1957; was in Paris during 1900 and 1901.

See: Harper, *Lights of Fortitude*, pp. 145–55; Marsella, 'Agnes Baldwin Alexander, 1875–1971', *Bahá'í World*, vol. 15, pp. 423–30, illus.

Amatu'l-Bahá Rúhíyyih Khánum Rabbani, née Mary Maxwell (1910–2000) Chapters 7, 11
Early Canadian Bahá'í; married Shoghi Effendi, 1937; appointed Hand of the Cause of God, 1952; daughter of May and William Sutherland Maxwell.

Publications: *Prescription for Living* (1950), *The Priceless Pearl* (1969), *A Manual for Pioneers* (1974), *The Desire of the World* (compiler, 1982), *Poems of the Passing* (1996); etc.

See: Harper, *Lights of Fortitude*, pp. 168–82; Nakhjavani, *A Tribute to Amatu'l-Bahá Rúhíyyih Khánum*.

Bagdadi (Baghdádí), Dr Zia (1884–1937) Chapter 4
Trusted friend of 'Abdu'l-Bahá and His family; lived in the Holy Land and, from 1909, in America.

See: Adamson and Hainsworth, *Historical Dictionary*, p. 111.

Bagdadi, née Tabrízí, Zínat Chapter 4
Wife of Zia Bagdadi; her sister was Fátimíh Nakhjavání, née Tabrízí.

See: 'Zeenat Khanum', *Star of the West*, vol. 5, no. 4, 17 May 1914, pp. 57–8.

Bahíyyih Khánum (1846–1932) Chapters 4, 8
The Greatest Holy Leaf; the daughter of Bahá'u'lláh and sister of 'Abdu'l-Bahá.

See: Adamson and Hainsworth, *Historical Dictionary*, p. 124; *Bahíyyih Khánum, the Greatest Holy Leaf: A Compilation from Bahá'í Sacred Texts and Writings of the Guardian and Bahíyyih Khánum's Own Letters;* Momen, *A Basic Bahá'í Dictionary*, p. 42, illus.

Bailey, Ella (1864–1953) Chapter 11
American Bahá'í; pioneered to Libya, 1953, where she died.

See: Gulick, 'Ella M. Bailey', *Bahá'í World*, vol. 12, pp. 685–8, illus.

Baker, Dorothy Beecher (1898–1954) Chapter 11
Early American Bahá'í; appointed Hand of the Cause of God, 1951; died in plane crash south of Elba.

See: Freeman, *From Copper to Gold: The Life of Dorothy Baker*; Haney, 'Dorothy Beecher Baker', *Bahá'í World*, vol. 12, pp. 670–4, illus.; Harper, *Lights of Fortitude*, pp. 191–201.

Baker, Effie (1880–1968) Chapters 8, 10
Australian Bahá'í and photographer; took most of the photographs for *The Dawn-Breakers*.

See: Heggie, 'Effie Baker, March 25, 1880 – January 1, 1968', *Bahá'í World*, vol. 14, pp. 320–1, illus.

Barney, Alice Pike (1857–1931) Chapter 3
Early American Bahá'í and artist; lived in Paris.

See: Kling, *Alice Pike Barney: Her Life and Art*; 'Mrs Alice Barney', *Bahá'í World*, vol. 5, pp. 419–20.

Basil-Hall, Mary, née Blomfield (d. 1950) Chapters 3, 6
Early English Bahá'í; daughter of Lady Blomfield.

See: Slade, 'Mary Basil-Hall (Parvine)', *Bahá'í Journal* (London), no. 79 (June 1950), pp. 5–6.

Bedikian, Victoria (1879–1955) Chapters 8, 10, 11
Early American Bahá'í and artist; promoted Bahá'í children's classes and nurseries by editing the magazine *World Fellowship for the Children of the Kingdom*; also issued the *Mashriqu'l-Adhkár Leaflet*.

See: Adamson and Hainsworth, *Historical Dictionary*, p. 134; Ebbert and Finke, 'Victoria Bedikian, 1879–1955', *Bahá'í World*, vol. 13, pp. 884–5, illus.

Benke, George Adam (1878–1932) Chapter 9
Russian-born German Bahá'í, 1920, and Esperantist; pioneered to Bulgaria, where he died; named first European martyr by Shoghi Effendi.

See: Adamson and Hainsworth, *Historical Dictionary*, p. 134; 'George Adam Benke', *Bahá'í World*, vol. 5, pp. 416–18.

Benke, Lina (1874–1971) Chapters 9, 10
Early German Bahá'í, 1920; pioneered with her husband to Bulgaria, 1932, later in Leipzig.

See: 'Lina Benke', *Bahá'í Briefe*, heft 45 (juli 1971), p. 1318, illus.

Bishop, Charles Reed (1889–1967) Chapter 10
Early American Bahá'í; husband of Helen Pilkington Bishop.

Bishop, Helen Pilkington Chapter 10
Early American Bahá'í; travelled in Europe in the 1930s with her husband.

See the series of articles by Rassekh, 'A Pearl of the Kingdom', *Portland Bahá'í Bulletin* (Portland, Oregon), September/October 1994 – May/July 1998.

Blomfield, Lady Sara Louisa (1859–1939) Chapters 3, 5, 6
Early Irish Bahá'í, living in England; hosted 'Abdu'l-Bahá in 1911 in London and later Shoghi Effendi; early worker with the Save the Children Fund.

Publication: *The Chosen Highway* (1940)

See: Adamson and Hainsworth, *Historical Dictionary*, pp. 135–7; Whitehead, 'Lady Blomfield', *Some Early Bahá'ís of the West*, pp. 101–10.

Bolles, Jeanne Ruhanguiz [Mrs. Randolph Bolles] Chapter 10
American Bahá'í; sister-in-law of May Bolles Maxwell; sent to Hungary with her daughter by Shoghi Effendi to teach the Faith, c. 1937.

See: Szanto-Felbermann, *Rebirth*, pp. 102–4.

Breakwell, Thomas (1872–1902) Chapter 3
The 'first English believer'; lived in Paris.

See: Adamson and Hainsworth, *Historical Dictionary*, pp. 140–1; Whitehead, 'Thomas Breakwell', *Some Early Bahá'ís of the West*, pp. 65–72.

Brittingham, Isabella D. (1852–1924) Chapter 5
Early American Bahá'í; Disciple of 'Abdu'l-Bahá.

Publication: *The Revelation of Bahä–ulläh in a Sequence of Four Lessons* (1902)

See: Adamson and Hainsworth, *Historical Dictionary*, pp. 141–2.

Brown, Ruth Randall (1887–1969) Chapter 7
American Bahá'í, 1912; pioneered to South Africa, 1953.

See: Brown and Ford, 'Ruth Randall Brown, 1887–1969', *Bahá'í World*, vol. 15, pp. 463–5, illus.

Carpenter, Howard Luxmore (1906–35) Chapter 10
American Bahá'í; husband of Marzieh Carpenter; medical doctor; travelled in the Balkans and Iran.

See: 'Howard Luxmore Carpenter (1906–1935)', *Bahá'í World*, vol. 6, pp. 491–3.

Chamberlain, Isabel Fraser (Soraya) (1871–1939) Chapter 5
Early American Bahá'í of Scottish ancestry.

Publication: *Divine Philosophy*

See: Hatch, 'Soraya Chamberlain (Mrs Isabel Fraser Chamberlain)', *Bahá'í World*, vol. 8, pp. 664–5, illus.

Chute, Jeanne, née Bolles (d. 1997) Chapter 10
American Bahá'í; daughter of Jeanne Ruhanguiz Bolles; active in South America, later in Charlottesville, Virginia.

Cobb, Stanwood (1881–1982) Chapters 7, 9
American Bahá'í and educator; author of many works dealing with the Faith, education, the Middle East and poetry; became a Bahá'í at Green Acre in 1906; lived in Boston and later in Washington DC; founded the Progressive Education Association, 1922.

Publications: *The Real Turk* (1914), *Security for a Failing World* (1934), *Tomorrow and Tomorrow* (1951), *A Saga of Two Centuries* (1979), etc.

See: Dunbar, 'Stanwood Cobb, 1881–1982', *Bahá'í World*, vol. 18, pp. 814–16, illus.; Stockman, *The Bahá'í Faith in America: Early Expansion, 1900–1912*, vol. 2, pp. 218 ff.

Cole, Helen Ellis (d. 1906) Chapter 3
Early American Bahá'í, in Paris c. 1903. Later associated with Green Acre. Bequeathed money and land for the building of Fellowship House to Green Acre School.

Collins, Amelia Engelder 'Milly' (1873–1962) Chapter 10
Early American Bahá'í; appointed Hand of the Cause of God, 1947 (announced 1951); member of the National Spiritual Assembly of the United States and Canada 1924–32 and 1939–50.

See: Ashton, 'Amelia E. Collins, 1873–1962', *Bahá'í World*, vol. 13, pp. 834–41, illus.; Harper, *Lights of Fortitude*, pp. 202–10.

Cooper, Ella Goodall (1870–1951) Chapter 4
Early American Bahá'í in San Francisco, 1899; Disciple of 'Abdu'l-Bahá.

See: Adamson and Hainsworth, *Historical Dictionary*, p. 156; 'Ella Goodall Cooper', *Bahá'í World*, vol. 12, pp. 681–4, illus.; Whitehead, 'Helen Goodall and Ella Cooper', *Some Early Bahá'ís of the West*, pp. 21–34.

Cress, Dorothy Culver Chapter 3
Daughter of Henry S. Culver, early American Bahá'í; met Marion Jack in Paris c. 1908; served on the Spiritual Assembly of Eliot, Maine, 1933–4.

Culver, Henry S. (1854–1936) Chapter 5
Together with his wife, Mary Diana Culver (1856–1937), early American Bahá'í in Canada and Ireland; US consul; lived in Saint John, New Brunswick.

See: Armstrong-Ingram, 'Early Irish Bahá'ís', *Research Notes in Shaykhí, Bábí and Bahá'í Studies*, vol. 2, no. 4 (July 1998). Internet document: http://www.h-net2.msu.edu/~bahai/notes/vol2/irish.htm

Culver, Julia (1861–1950) Chapters 5, 10
Early American Bahá'í; served at the International Bahá'í Bureau in Geneva, 1928–33.

See: Adamson and Hainsworth, *Historical Dictionary*, p. 159; Warde, 'Julia Culver, February 8, 1861–January 22, 1950', *Bahá'í World*, vol. 11, pp. 507–9, illus.

Davis, Laura Rumney Chapter 7
Early Canadian Bahá'í in Toronto.

Dealy, Mrs Chapter 7
Early Canadian Bahá'í in Saint John, New Brunswick; corresponded with 'Abdu'l-Bahá.

de Bons, Edith, née McKay (1878–1959) Chapter 3
Early Bahá'í in Paris, later in Cairo and Switzerland.

See: de Bons, 'Edith de Bons, 1878–1959 & Joseph de Bons, 1871–1959', *Bahá'í World*, vol. 13, pp. 878–81, illus.

Diestelhorst, Thilde Chapters 8, 10
Early German Bahá'í, living in Berlin; met Marion Jack on pilgrimage, 1931; later travelled to Bulgaria.

Dreyfus-Barney, Hippolyte (1873–1928) Chapters 3, 5
The first French Bahá'í, 1901; Disciple of 'Abdu'l-Bahá; French scholar; translated many of the Bahá'í writings into French.

Publications: *Essai sur le Béhaïsme* (translated as *The Universal Religion: Bahaism*, 1909); many translations of Bahá'í books into French.

See: Adamson and Hainsworth, *Historical Dictionary*, pp. 167–8; Shoghi Effendi, 'Hippolyte Dreyfus-Barney: An Appreciation', *Bahá'í World*, vol. 3, pp. 210–14.

Dreyfus-Barney, Laura Clifford (1879–1974) Chapter 3
Early American Bahá'í settled in Paris; became a Bahá'í in Paris c. 1900; wife of Hippolyte Dreyfus-Barney; translated and collected *Some Answered Questions*, by 'Abdu'l-Bahá; active in women's organizations associated with the League of Nations and later the United Nations.

See: Adamson and Hainsworth, *Historical Dictionary*, pp. 168–70; Giachery, 'Laura Clifford Dreyfus-Barney', *Bahá'í World*, vol. 16, pp. 535–8.

Drum, Laura L., née David (d. 1938) Chapter 7
Early American Bahá'í from Washington DC and Baltimore, Maryland; first met Marion Jack at Green Acre 1914 or 1915.

Edwards, Ivy Drew (d. 1955) Chapters 7, 11
American Bahá'í in Jacksonville, Florida and Green Acre,
c. 1920s–1930s; Assistant Secretary of the Spiritual Assembly of Eliot, Maine, 1933–4.

Esslemont, John Ebenezer (1874–1925) Chapters 6, 10
Scottish Bahá'í, active in England, who worked closely with
Shoghi Effendi; named Hand of the Cause of God posthumously.

Publication: *Bahá'u'lláh and the New Era* (1923)

See: Harper, *Lights of Fortitude*, pp. 72–84; Momen, *Dr John
Ebenezer Esslemont, M.B., Ch.B., SBEA, Hand of the Cause
of God*.

Fáḍil-i Mázandarání [Mírzá Asadu'lláh Fáḍil] (1880(?)–1957)
Chapter 7
Persian Bahá'í and scholar.

See: 'Jináb-i-Fáḍil, 1880(?)–1957', *Bahá'í World*, vol. 14,
pp. 334–6, illus.

Farmer, Sarah J. (1847–1916) Chapter 5
Early American Bahá'í, 1896; Disciple of 'Abdu'l-Bahá;
founder of the Green Acre Conferences.

See: Adamson and Hainsworth, *Historical Dictionary*, p. 183.

Fitting, Barbara Appendix 3
American Bahá'í; chairman of the Finance Committee of
the Green Acre Festival, c. 1915.

Fozdar, Khodadad M. (1898–1958) Chapter 10
Indian Bahá'í of Parsi origin; medical doctor and educationist; visited Europe in 1935; together with his wife,

Shirin, pioneered to Singapore, 1935, and to the Andaman Islands, 1953.

See: 'Dr K. M. Fozdar, 1898–1958', *Bahá'í World*, vol. 13, pp. 892–3, illus.

Ford, Mary Hanford (1856–1937) Chapter 3
Early American Bahá'í, 1902; associated with Paris and Green Acre.

See: Rúháníyyih (Madame 'Alí-Kuli) Khánum, 'Mary Hanford Ford', *Bahá'í World*, vol. 7, pp. 541–2.

Forel, Auguste (1848–1931) Chapter 10
Early Swiss Bahá'í, 1921; neurologist, psychiatrist and entomologist; professor at university in Zurich.

See: Vader, *For the Good of Mankind: August Forel and the Bahá'í Faith*.

Fujita, Saichiro (1886–1976) Chapter 8
Japanese Bahá'í; served at the Bahá'í World Centre for many years.

See: True, 'Saichiro Fujita, 1886–1976', *Bahá'í World*, vol. 17, pp. 406–8, illus.

Gail, Marzieh Nabil Carpenter (1908–93) Chapter 10
Early American Bahá'í; scholar and translator.

Publications: *Persia and the Victorians* (1951), *The Sheltering Branch* (1959), *Avignon in Flower* (1965), *The Three Popes* (1969), *Dawn over Mount Hira and Other Essays* (1976), *Other People, Other Places* (1982), *Summon Up Remembrance* (1987), *Arches of the Years* (1991), etc.

Translations: *The Seven Valleys and The Four Valleys*, *The Secret of Divine Civilization*, *Memorials of the Faithful*, *Selections from the Writings of 'Abdu'l-Bahá*, *My Memoirs of Bahá'u'lláh*.

See: Chen, 'Marzieh Nabil Carpenter Gail, Translator and Author, "Patron Saint" of Women Bahá'í Scholars (1 April 1908 – 16 October 1993)', *Bahá'í Studies Review* (London), vol. 6 (1996).

Gamble, Annie (1848–1947) Chapter 5
Early English Bahá'í in London.

George, Florence 'Mother' (1859–1950) Chapter 5
Early English Bahá'í.

See: Sugar, 'Florence George', *Bahá'í Journal* (London), December 1950, p. 6; reprinted in *Bahá'í World*, vol. 12, pp. 697–8, illus.

Getsinger, Edward Christopher (1866–1935) Chapter 3
Early American Bahá'í, 1897; medical doctor; married Lua Getsinger, 1897; recorded 'Abdu'l-Bahá's voice, 1898; among the first Western pilgrims to meet 'Abdu'l-Bahá.

See: Adamson and Hainsworth, *Historical Dictionary*, pp. 192–3; Hatch, 'Edward Christopher Getsinger', *Bahá'í World*, vol. 6, pp. 493–6.

Getsinger, Louisa Aurora Moore (Lua) (1871–1916) Chapters 3, 11
Early American Bahá'í, 1897; Disciple of 'Abdu'l-Bahá; introduced the Bahá'í Faith to May Ellis Bolles, née Maxwell; married Edward Getsinger 1897; among the first Western pilgrims to visit 'Abdu'l-Bahá; had an audience with the Sháh; died in Egypt during a teaching trip.

See: Adamson and Hainsworth, *Historical Dictionary*, p.193; Metelmann, *Lua Getsinger: Herald of the Covenant*; Sears and Quigley, *The Flame*.

Goodall, Helen Mirrell (1864–1922) Chapters 4, 7
Early American Bahá'í in San Francisco, 1898; Disciple of 'Abdu'l-Bahá.

See: Adamson and Hainsworth, *Historical Dictionary*, pp. 204–5; Whitehead, 'Helen Goodall and Ella Cooper', *Some Early Bahá'ís of the West*, pp. 21–34.

Greenleaf, Elizabeth (1863–1941) Chapter 7
Early American Bahá'í; spent some summers at Green Acre.

See: Sala, 'The Greenleafs: An Eternal Union', *Bahá'í News* (Wilmette), no. 510 (September 1973), pp. 8–9, 23.

Greeven, Inez Marshall Cook (1889–1983) Chapters 8, 10
Early American Bahá'í; pioneered to Germany, 1930, and later to the Netherlands; moved to US, 1940.

See: Adamson and Hainsworth, *Historical Dictionary*, p. 207.

Greeven, Max (1869–1961) Chapter 10
Early American Bahá'í, 1927; pioneered to Hamburg, Germany, 1930; published Bahá'í books in Dutch.

See: Greeven, 'Max Greeven, 1869–1961', *Bahá'í World*, vol. 13, pp. 909–11, illus.

Gregory, Louis G. (1874–1951) Chapters 3, 5, 7, 9, 11
Early American Black Bahá'í, c. 1908; travelled widely in USA and Canada teaching the Bahá'í Faith; married Louisa Mathews; named Hand of the Cause of God posthumously.

See: Harper, *Lights of Fortitude*, pp. 85–98; Morrison, *To Move the World: Louis G. Gregory and the Advancement of Racial Unity in America*; Ober, 'Louis G. Gregory', *Bahá'í World*, vol. 12, pp. 666–70, illus.

Gregory, Louisa Mathew (1866–1956) Chapters 3, 7, 8, 9, 10, 11
Early British Bahá'í, c. late 1890s in Paris; pioneered to Bulgaria; married Louis Gregory.

See: Earl, 'Louisa Mathew Gregory, 1866–1956', *Bahá'í World*, vol. 13, pp. 876–8, illus.

Grossmann, Hermann (1899–1968) Chapters 9, 10
Early German Bahá'í, 1920, born in Argentina; frequent lecturer at German summer schools, 1930s; appointed Hand of the Cause of God, 1951.

See: Harper, *Lights of Fortitude*, pp. 243–52; Mühlschlegel, 'Hermann Grossmann, 1899–1968', *Bahá'í World*, vol. 15, pp. 416–21, illus.

Ḥakím, Luṭfu'lláh (1888–1968) Chapters 5, 8
Persian Bahá'í; medical doctor; member Universal House of Justice 1963–8; knew Marion Jack when a student in London.

See: Faizi, 'Dr Luṭfu'lláh Ḥakím, 1888–1968', *Bahá'í World*, vol. 15, pp. 430–4, illus.

Haney, Mariam (1872–1965) Chapter 7
Early American Bahá'í, 1900; mother of Paul Haney; secretary of National Teaching Committee of the United States and Canada.

See: Martin, 'Mariam Haney, 1872–1965', *Bahá'í World*, vol. 14, pp. 343–6, illus.

Haney, Paul Edmund (1909–82) Chapter 7
American Bahá'í and economist; appointed Hand of the
Cause of God, 1954.

See: Adamson and Hainsworth, *Historical Dictionary*,
pp. 217–19; Harper, *Lights of Fortitude*, pp.156–63.

Harris, W. Hooper Appendix 3
Early American Bahá'í; served on the Chicago House of
Spirituality in 1905; listed as the vice-chairman of the
Spiritual Assembly of New York, 1933–4.

Haydar-'Alí, Ḥájí Mírzá (c. 1830–1920) Chapter 4
Early Persian Bahá'í in Haifa; known to western Bahá'ís
as the 'Angel of Carmel'.

See: *Stories from the Delight of Hearts: The Memoirs of Ḥájí
Mírzá Haydar-'Alí.*

Hoagg, Henrietta Emogene Marten (1869–1945) Chapters 3, 7,
8, 10
Early American Bahá'í from Oakland, California; Marion
Jack's companion in Alaska; in Acre in 1921; pioneered
to Italy; served in the International Bahá'í Bureau, Geneva.

See: De Mille, 'Emogene Hoagg: An Exemplary Pioneer',
Bahá'í News (Wilmette), no. 511 (October 1973), pp. 6–11;
Cooper, 'Henrietta Emogene Martin Hoagg, 1869–1945',
Bahá'í World, vol. 10, pp. 520–6, illus.

Holley, Horace Hotchkiss (1887–1960) Chapter 3
Early American Bahá'í, in Paris, then in USA; member
(1923–59) and secretary (1924–30; 1932–59) of the
National Spiritual Assembly of the United States and
Canada; editor *World Unity Magazine*, *Bahá'í News* and
Bahá'í World; appointed Hand of the Cause of God, 1951.

Publications: *The Social Principle* (1915), *Bahai, the Spirit of the Age* (1921), *Religion for Mankind* (1956), etc.

See: Amatu'l-Bahá Rúḥíyyih Khánum, 'Horace Hotchkiss Holley, April 7, 1887 – July 12, 1960', *Bahá'í World*, vol. 13, pp. 849–58, illus.; Harper, *Lights of Fortitude*, pp. 253–64.

Hopper, Marie, née Squires (–1953) Chapter 3
American Bahá'í; lived in Urbana, Illinois and Greenwich, Connecticut.

Hyde-Dunn, John Henry (1855–1941) Chapter 11
British-born American Bahá'í; pioneered to Australia, 1919. Named Hand of the Cause of God posthumously.

See: Adamson and Hainsworth, *Historical Dictionary*, pp. 234–5; Harper, *Lights of Fortitude*, pp. 60–71.

Ilich, Draga Chapter 10
Serbian Bahá'í, c. 1920s and 1930s; translated *Bahá'u'lláh and the New Era* and the *Hidden Words* into Serbian.

See: Root, 'Appreciations from Yugoslavia', *Bahá'í Magazine*, 24 (October 1933), p. 209, illus.

Isfandíyár Chapter 8
Burmese Bahá'í; served as 'Abdu'l-Bahá's coachman in the Holy Land.

Ives, Kate Cowan (1863–1927) Chapters 5, 7
First woman in the Occident to accept the Bahá'í Faith; travelled in the Maritime provinces, Canada; helped develop Green Acre School.

See: van den Hoonaard, *The Origins of the Bahá'í Community of Canada, 1898–1948*, pp. 17ff.

Kennedy, Charles Nelson (1875–1950) Chapter 10
American Bahá'í; settled in Paris.

See: Sanderson, 'Charles Nelson Kennedy', *Bahá'í World*, vol. 12, pp. 711–12, illus.

Kinney, Edward Beadle 'Saffa' (1863–1950) Chapter 11
Early Bahá'í in America.

See: Thompson, 'Edward B. Kinney', *Bahá'í World*, vol. 12, pp. 677–9, illus.; Whitehead, *Some Early Bahá'ís of the West*, pp. 43–53.

Klebs, Margaret (1862–1939) Chapter 7
Early American Bahá'í and first Bahá'í in Augusta, Georgia; vocal teacher at Green Acre.

See: Haney, 'Margaret Klebs', *Bahá'í World*, vol. 8, pp. 670–2.

Knobloch, Alma (1864–1943) Chapters 3, 4, 5
Early American Bahá'í who pioneered to Germany in 1907.

See: Schwartz, 'Alma Knobloch', *Bahá'í World*, vol. 9, pp. 641–3.

Köstlin, Anna (1884–1972) Chapter 10
Early German Bahá'í; taught children's classes in Esslingen at the time of 'Abdu'l-Bahá's visit.

See: Bender, 'Anna Koestlin, 1884–1972', *Bahá'í World*, vol. 15, pp. 511–13, illus.

Latimer, George Orr (1889–1948) Chapter 7
Early American Bahá'í from Portland, Oregon; associated
with Marion Jack in Vancouver in 1921; later served on
the National Spiritual Assembly of the United States and
Canada and the Spiritual Assembly of Toledo, Ohio.

Publication: *The Light of the World* (1920)

See: Holley, 'George Orr Latimer', *Bahá'í World*, vol. 11,
pp. 511–12, illus.

Lea, Elsie (d. 1935) Chapter 10
English Bahá'í; associated with Annie Gamble in London;
for many years member and treasurer of the Spiritual
Assembly of London; attended the German summer school
in Esslingen, 1933.

Lentz, Margaret (1879–1965) Chapter 10
Early German Bahá'í; served at the International Bahá'í
Bureau in Geneva; after World War II, pioneered to
Vienna; translated *Thief in the Night* into German.

See: Mühlschlegel, 'Margaret Lentz, 1879–1965', *Bahá'í
World*, vol. 14, pp. 354–5, illus.

Lowe, Gustave Chapter 10
Austrian; became a Bahá'í in Sofia; went to California
before World War II.

Lundberg, Elfie (b. 1896) Chapter 7
Along with her mother, Emma, an early American Bahá'í
in the Urbana, Illinois area.

See: 'Elfie Lundberg: Memories of the Master's Presence',
The American Bahá'í, January 1982, p. 17.

Luther, Laura Chapter 7
Early American Bahá'í from Seattle; active in Vancouver, British Columbia, in the 1920s.

Lynch, Anne Slastiona (1892–1966) Chapters 7, 10, 11
Russian-born Bahá'í; became a Bahá'í in Italy, 1926; served for many years at the International Bahá'í Bureau in Geneva until 1957.

See: 'Anne Slastiona Lynch, 1892–1966', *Bahá'í World*, vol. 14, pp. 355–6, illus.

MacNutt, Howard (–1926) Chapter 7
Early American Bahá'í, 1898; Disciple of 'Abdu'l-Bahá; compiled *The Promulgation of Universal Peace*.

See: Adamson and Hainsworth, *Historical Dictionary*, p. 278.

Magee, Esther Chapter 5
Early Canadian Bahá'í, 1893; lived in London, Ontario, later moved to New York City.

See: '1893: The First Canadian Bahá'í', *Bahá'í Canada* (Toronto), September 1966, p. 6.

Maxwell, May Ellis Bolles (1870–1940) Chapters 3, 5, 7, 11
Early American Bahá'í; lived in Paris and later settled in Montreal; established Bahá'í community of Canada; hostess to 'Abdu'l-Bahá in Montreal; mother of Mary, Amatu'l-Bahá Rúḥíyyih Khánum; among the first western pilgrims to visit 'Abdu'l-Bahá; died in Argentina; named a martyr by Shoghi Effendi.

Publication: *An Early Pilgrimage*

277

See: Holley, 'May Ellis Maxwell', *Bahá'í World*, vol. 8, pp. 631–42.

Maxwell, William Sutherland (1874–1952) Chapters 3, 5, 7, 8
Early Canadian Bahá'í; architect; appointed Hand of the Cause of God, 1951.

See: Harper, *Lights of Fortitude*, pp. 276–86; 'William Sutherland Maxwell, 1874–1952', *Bahá'í World*, vol. 12, pp. 640–5.

Mills, Mary Olga Katherine (1882–1974) Chapters 8, 10
American Bahá'í, born in Germany, lived in Leipzig, then in the British Isles; pioneered to Malta, 1953, for which she was named Knight of Bahá'u'lláh by Shoghi Effendi.

See: Hainsworth, 'Mary Olga Katherine Mills, 1882–1974, Knight of Bahá'u'lláh', *Bahá'í World*, vol. 16, pp. 531–4, illus.

Moody, Susan I. (1851–1934) Chapters 7, 11
Early American Bahá'í, 1903; medical doctor; spent her summers at Green Acre; served in Iran from 1908 to 1924 and from 1928 to 1934.

See: Adamson and Hainsworth, *Historical Dictionary*, pp. 300–1.

Morton, James, Jr. Appendix 3
Early American Bahá'í from the New York area; curator of the Museum of Natural History, Paterson, New Jersey; served on the National Esperanto Committee in the 1930s and 1940s.

Muḥammad Taqí Afnán, Ḥájí Mírzá, Vakílu'd-Dawlih (c.1830/31–1911) Chapter 4

Persian Bahá'í; Apostle of Bahá'u'lláh; responsible for the erection of the first House of Worship in Ashkhabad; was in Haifa after 1907.

See: 'Ḥájí Mírzá Muḥammad-Taqí, the Afnán', in 'Abdu'l-Bahá, *Memorials of the Faithful*, pp. 126–9.

Mühlschlegel, Adelbert (1897–1977) Chapter 10
German Bahá'í; medical doctor; appointed Hand of the Cause of God, 1952.

See: Adamson and Hainsworth, *Historical Dictionary*, pp. 306–7; Harper, *Lights of Fortitude*, pp. 372–83.

Mühlschlegel, Herma (1902–64) Chapter 10
German Bahá'í; wife of Hand of the Cause of God Adelbert Mühlschlegel.

See: Mühlschlegel, 'Herma Mühlschlegel, 1902–1964', *Bahá'í World*, vol. 14, pp. 367–8, illus.

Munírih Khánum (1848–1938) Chapters 4, 8
Wife of 'Abdu'l-Bahá.

See: Adamson and Hainsworth, *Historical Dictionary*, pp. 310–11.

Ober, Grace Robarts (d. 1938) Chapters 7, 9
Early American Bahá'í and educator; born in Thorold, Ontario, Canada; served on the Spiritual Assembly of Eliot, Maine, 1933–4.

See: Ives, 'Grace Robarts Ober', *Bahá'í World*, vol. 8, pp. 656–60, illus.

Ober, Harlan Foster (1881–1962) Chapter 9
Early American Bahá'í; travelled widely in the US, India, Germany and later in South Africa; member of the Bahá'í Temple Unity 1918–20 and of the National Spiritual Assembly of the United States and Canada 1938–41; would have met Marion Jack at Green Acre, Boston and probably in Illinois.

See: Adamson and Hainsworth, *Historical Dictionary*, pp. 317–18; Ober, Bullock and Irwin, 'Harlan Foster Ober, 1881–1962', *Bahá'í World*, vol. 13, pp. 866–71, illus.

Parsons, Agnes S. (1861–1934) Appendix 3
Early American Bahá'í, c. 1908; hosted 'Abdu'l-Bahá in Washington DC; organized the First Racial Amity Convention, 1921.

See: Adamson and Hainsworth, *Historical Dictionary*, pp. 323–4; Haney, 'Mrs Agnes Parsons', *Bahá'í World*, vol. 5, pp. 410, 412–14.

Pinson, Josephine 'Josie' Chapter 7
Early American Bahá'í in Sumter, South Carolina.

Pöllinger, Franz (1895–1979) Chapter 10
Early Austrian Bahá'í, 1914; member first Assembly of Vienna, 1926, and the first National Spiritual Assembly of Austria, 1959.
See: Adamson and Hainsworth, *Historical Dictionary*, pp. 337–8.

Pomeroy, Mary B. Chapters 5, 7, 10
Early Canadian Bahá'í and artist in Montreal.

Ransom-Kehler, Keith (1878–1933) Chapter 11
American Bahá'í; died in Iran; personal emissary of Shoghi
Effendi to Iran; named Hand of the Cause of God pos-
thumously.

See: Adamson and Hainsworth, *Historical Dictionary*, p. 350;
Harper, *Lights of Fortitude*, pp. 99–109; 'The Unity of East
and West', *Bahá'í World*, vol. 5, pp. 389–410.

Remey, Charles Mason (1874–1974) Chapters 3, 4, 5, 10
Early American Bahá'í in Paris and America; architect;
appointed Hand of the Cause of God, 1951; declared a
Covenant-breaker, 1960.

See: Adamson and Hainsworth, *Historical Dictionary*,
pp. 354–5; Harper, *Lights of Fortitude*, pp. 287–306.

Revell, Jessie (1891–1966) Chapter 11
Early American Bahá'í, 1906; member first International
Bahá'í Council, 1950.

See: Adamson and Hainsworth, *Historical Dictionary*, p. 358.

Robarts, John Aldham (1901–91) Chapter 7
Early Canadian Bahá'í; appointed Hand of the Cause of
God, 1957.

See: Adamson and Hainsworth, *Historical Dictionary*,
pp. 360–2; Harper, *Lights of Fortitude*, pp. 473–95.

Root, Martha L. (1872–1939) Chapters 9, 10, 11
American Bahá'í and journalist; born in USA, died in
Hawaii; travelled widely for the Bahá'í Faith and circled
the globe four times; appointed Hand of the Cause of God
posthumously.

See: Garis, *Martha Root: Lioness at the Threshold*; Harper, *Lights of Fortitude*, pp. 112–22.

Rosenberg, Ethel Jenner (1858–1930) Chapter 3
Early English Bahá'í and painter; close associate of Marion Jack in Paris and London.

See: Weinberg, *Ethel Jenner Rosenberg: The Life and Times of England's Outstanding Bahá'í Pioneer Worker*; Whitehead, 'Ethel Rosenberg', *Some Early Bahá'ís of the West*, pp. 55–64.

Sala, Emeric (1906–90) Chapter 10
Canadian Bahá'í; pioneered with his wife to Venezuela (1939), South Africa (1954–67) and after 1971 lived in Mexico.

Publication: *This Earth One Country* (1945)

Ṣamímí, Aḥmad, OBE (1893–1976) Chapter 10
Persian Bahá'í employed as the Secretary of the British Embassy in Tehran.

See: National Spiritual Assembly of the Bahá'ís of Persia, 'Ahmad Samímí, 1893–1976', *Bahá'í World*, vol. 17, pp. 411–12, illus.

Sanderson, Edith Roohie (d. 1955) Chapters 3, 4
Early American Bahá'í, 1901; settled in Paris.

See: Barney, 'Edith Sanderson', *Bahá'í World*, vol. 13, pp. 889–90, illus.

Schmidt, Eugen (1901–82) Chapter 10
Early German Bahá'í; publisher of several Bahá'í periodicals in German; lecturer at German summer school;

member of National Spiritual Assembly of Germany and Austria.

See: Adamson and Hainsworth, *Historical Dictionary*, p. 372.

Schopflocher, Florence (Kitty, Lorol) (1886–1970) Chapters 7, 10
Early Canadian Bahá'í, c. 1920; wife of Siegfried Schopflocher; travelled widely teaching the Bahá'í Faith.

Publication: *Sunburst* (1937)

See: Adamson and Hainsworth, *Historical Dictionary*, p. 372; 'Florence Evaline (Lorol) Schopflocher, 1886–1970', *Bahá'í World*, vol. 15, pp. 488–9, illus.

Schopflocher, Siegfried (Fred) (1877–1953) Chapters 7, 11
Canadian Bahá'í; appointed Hand of the Cause of God, 1952.

See: Adamson and Hainsworth, *Historical Dictionary*, pp. 372–3; Harper, *Lights of Fortitude*, pp. 384–90; 'Siegfried Schopflocher', *Bahá'í World*, vol. 12, pp. 664–6, illus.

Schwarz-Solivo, Alice (1875–1965) Chapter 10
Early German Bahá'í in Stuttgart; founded the review *Sonne der Wahreit*.

See: Schwarz, 'Alice Schwartz-Solivo, 1875–1965', *Bahá'í World*, vol. 14, pp. 377–8, illus.

Schweizer, Annemarie (1884–1957) Chapter 10
Early German Bahá'í in Stuttgart; met 'Abdu'l-Bahá in 1911 in Paris and was His hostess in Stuttgart in 1913; imprisoned by the Gestapo during World War II.

See: Adamson and Hainsworth, *Historical Dictionary*, pp. 373–4; 'Annemarie Schweizer', *Bahá'í World*, vol. 13, pp. 890–1, illus.

Scott, Edwin (1862–1929) Chapter 3
English Bahá'í and artist; settled in Paris.

See: 'Mr Edwin Scott', *Bahá'í World*, vol. 5, pp. 418–19; *Paintings by Edwin Scott*.

Scott, Joséphine (d. 1955) Chapters 3, 10
English Bahá'í settled in Paris; wife of Edwin Scott.

See: Barney, 'Joséphine Scott', *Bahá'í World*, vol. 13, pp. 899–900, illus.

Shoghi Effendi (Rabbani) (1897–1957) Chapters 4, 8, 9, 10, 11
Named the Guardian of the Bahá'í Faith in the Will and Testament of 'Abdu'l-Bahá; succeeded 'Abdu'l-Bahá as head of the Bahá'í Faith on the passing of 'Abdu'l-Bahá in 1921.

See: Rabbaní, *The Priceless Pearl*.

Sohrab, Ahmad (c. 1893–1958) Chapters 7, 8
Persian Bahá'í active in America; served as one of 'Abdu'l-Bahá's translators; did not accept Shoghi Effendi as the Guardian of the Faith.

Sprague, Philip Goddard (1899–1951) Chapter 10
Early American Bahá'í; elected a member of the National Spiritual Assembly of the United States and Canada, 1944.

See: Campbell, 'Philip Goddard Sprague', *Bahá'í World*, vol. 12, pp. 698–9, illus.

Stannard, Jean E. (1865–1944) Chapters 3, 4, 5
English Bahá'í, lived in India, c. 1914; highly praised by
'Abdu'l-Bahá; established the International Bahá'í Bureau
in Geneva, 1922.

Suhráb, 'Ináyatu'lláh (d. 1968) Chapter 10
Persian Bahá'í, one of the first members of the Spiritual
Assembly of Iṣfáhán.

See: "Ináyatu'lláh Suhráb', *Bahá'í World*, vol. 14,
pp. 381–2, illus.

Szanto-Felbermann, Renée (1900–84) Chapter 10
Early Hungarian Bahá'í,1936, in Budapest; moved to
England, 1956, and then to Germany, 1981.

Publication: *Rebirth: The Memoirs of Renée Szanto-Felbermann*
(1980)

See: Adamson and Hainsworth, *Historical Dictionary*, p. 395.

Thompson, Emma (d. 1951) Chapters 8, 11
Thompson, Louise Chapters 8, 11
American Bahá'ís, sisters, associated with Green Acre
where they had a cottage; on pilgrimage, 1931; both
served on the Spiritual Assembly of Eliot, Maine, 1933–4,
when Louise was secretary.

Thompson, Juliet (1873–1956) Chapter 3
Early American Bahá'í and painter; Disciple of 'Abdu'l-
Bahá; encountered the Faith, c. 1901, in Paris; lived in
New York City.

See: 'Juliet Thompson', *Bahá'í World*, vol. 13, pp. 862–4,
illus.; Whitehead, 'Juliet Thompson', *Some Early Bahá'ís
of the West*, pp. 73–85.

Thornburgh-Cropper, Mary Virginia (Maryam) (d. 1938) Chapter 3
American Bahá'í living in London; first resident Bahá'í in the British Isles, c. 1898; among the first western pilgrims to visit 'Abdu'l-Bahá; served on the first National Spiritual Assembly of the British Isles, 1923–5.

See: 'Mrs Thornburgh-Cropper', *Bahá'í World*, vol. 8, pp. 649–51; Whitehead, 'Mary Virginia Thornburgh-Cropper', *Some Bahá'ís to Remember*, pp. 17–30.

Townshend, George (1876–1957) Chapters 4, 7
Irish Bahá'í and theologian; appointed Hand of the Cause of God, 1951.

Publications: *The Promise of All Ages* (1934), *The Heart of the Gospel* (1939), *The Mission of Bahá'u'lláh and Other Literary Pieces* (1952), *Christ and Bahá'u'lláh* (1957), etc.

See: Harper, *Lights of Fortitude*, pp. 317–28; Hofman, *George Townshend*.

Troop, J. S. Carter Appendix 3
Professor; President of the New York Lecture Association; lectured at Green Acre on literature.

True, Corinne Knight (1861–1961) Chapter 10
Early American Bahá'í; associated with the building of the Temple in Wilmette; appointed a Hand of the Cause of God, 1952.

See: Harper, *Lights of Fortitude*, pp. 391–407; Linfoot, 'Corinne Knight True', *Bahá'í World*, vol. 13, pp. 846–9, illus.

Tweedie, Anna Chapter 8
Russian refugee; married Charles Tweedie who was
English; became a Bahá'í in Sofia, c. early 1930s; during
the Second World War she was in Hong Kong and possibly
in the Philippines; registered as a Bahá'í in Brisbane,
Australia, 1951, where she passed away a few years later.

Vail, Albert Ross (b. 1880) Appendix 3
Early American Bahá'í, c. 1918; former Unitarian minister
in Chicago; served on the Green Acre School Committee.

Wilhelm, Roy C. (1875–1951) Chapters 7, 10
Early American Bahá'í; member of the Bahá'í Temple
Unity and then the National Spiritual Assembly of the
United States and Canada for 37 years; appointed Hand
of the Cause of God posthumously.

See: Adamson and Hainsworth, *Historical Dictionary*,
pp. 427–8; Harper, *Lights of Fortitude*, pp. 129–41; Holley,
'Roy C. Wilhelm', *Bahá'í World*, vol. 12, pp. 662–4. illus.

Windust, Albert Robert (1874–1956) Chapter 7
Early American Bahá'í; Disciple of 'Abdu'l-Bahá; member
first Spiritual Assembly of Chicago; co-founder of first
Bahá'í publishing agency.

See: 'Albert R. Windust, 1874–1956', *Bahá'í World*, vol. 13,
pp. 873–4, illus.

Yordanov, Petar Chapters 9, 10
Bulgarian Bahá'í, c. 1934; very active Esperantist.

See: Sarafov, *Skizo de la Historio de Bulgara Esperanto-
Movado*, pp. 22, 23.

Bibliography

Manuscript Collections

Audio-Visual Archives, Bahá'í World Centre Archives

Canadian Bahá'í National Archives, Thornhill, Ontario

German Bahá'í National Archives, Hofheim-Langenhain

Logie Collection (private collection), Canada

Marion Jack Collection, Bahá'í World Centre Archives

A collection of letters, diaries and notes by and to Marion Jack. Contains many letters written by Marion Jack but never sent; also copies of letters both sent and received. The author came across the collection while in Sofia, Bulgaria. The collection is now in the Bahá'í World Centre Archives.

New Brunswick Museum Archives

United States National Bahá'í Archives

Periodicals Consulted

American Bahá'í (Wilmette, IL)

Bahá'í Briefe (Langenhain)

Bahá'í Canada (Toronto, ON)

Bahá'í Journal (London)

Bahá'í Magazine (Washington DC)

Bahá'í-Nachrichten (Stuttgart)

Bahá'í News (Wilmette, IL)

Bahá'í News Letter (Green Acre, South Eliot, ME)

Bahá'í Newsletter (Haifa)

Bahá'í Studies Review (London)

Hamilton Spectator (Hamilton, ON)

International Bahá'í Bureau. *Bulletin* (Geneva)

The International Studio

Saint John Globe (Saint John, NB)

Saint John Standard (Saint John, NB)

Sonne der Wahrheit (Stuttgart)

Star of the West (Chicago, IL)

Teaching Committee of Nineteen. *Bulletin* (Washington DC)

Times (Moncton, NB)

Transcript (Moncton, NB)

Vancouver Sun (Vancouver, BC)

The Weekly Star (Whitehorse, Yukon)

Western Woman's Weekly (Vancouver, BC)

World Fellowship (Montclair, NJ)

Bahá'í Literature

'1893: The First Canadian Bahá'í'. *Bahá'í Canada* (Toronto), (September 1964), p. 6.

'Abdu'l-Bahá. *Memorials of the Faithful*. Wilmette, IL: Bahá'í Publishing Trust, 1971.

— *Paris Talks*. London: Bahá'í Publishing Trust, 1969.

— *Selections from the Writings of 'Abdu'l-Bahá*. Haifa: Bahá'í World Centre, 1978.

— *Tablets of Abdul-Baha Abbas*. Chicago: Bahai Publishing Society; vol. 1, 1909; vol. 2, 1915; vol. 3, 1916.

— *Tablets of the Divine Plan*. Wilmette, IL: Bahá'í Publishing Trust, 1993.

— *The Will and Testament of 'Abdu'l-Bahá*. Wilmette, IL: Bahá'í Publishing Trust, 1971.

'Abdu'l-Bahá in London. London: Bahá'í Publishing Trust, 1987. Compiled by Eric Hammond. First published in 1912 in London by Longmans Green & Co., and in East Sheen, Surrey by the Unity Press.

Adamson, Hugh C. and Philip Hainsworth. *Historical Dictionary of the Bahá'í Faith*. Lanham, MD: Scarecrow Press, 1998.

Afnan, Nooshfar. 'An Introduction to the Life and Work of Marion Elizabeth Jack 1866–1954'. Directed reading paper, Carleton University, Ottawa, 1999.

'Albert R. Windust, 1874–1956'. *Bahá'í World*, vol. 13, pp. 873–4, illus.

'Anne Slastiona Lynch, 1892–1966'. *Bahá'í World*, vol. 14, pp. 355–6, illus.

Armstrong-Ingram, R. Jackson. 'Early Irish Bahá'ís: Issues of Religious, Cultural, and National Identity', in *Research Notes in Shaykhí, Bábí and Bahá'í Studies*, vol. 2, no. 4 (July 1998). Internet document: http://www.h-net2.msu.edu/~bahai/notes/vol2/irish.htm

Ashton, Beatrice. 'Amelia E. Collins, 1873–1962'. *Bahá'í World*, vol. 13, pp. 834–41, illus.

The Bahá'í Centenary 1844–1944. Wilmette, IL: Bahá'í Publishing Committee, 1944.

The Bahá'í Faith in Bulgaria: Short History and Information About the Activities of the Community. [Bulgaria, s.n., n.d.]. Internet document: http://www.bahai-bulgaria.org/english/faith_in_bulgaria.htm

The Bahá'í Faith in Newfoundland and Labrador. [s.l., s.n.], 1998. Internet document: http://www.infonet.st-johns.nf.ca/providers/bahai/nf-hist.html

'Bahai News', *Star of the West*, vol. 13, no. 5 (August 1922), pp. 122–3.

Bahá'í Prayers: A Selection of Prayers revealed by Bahá'u'lláh, the Báb and 'Abdu'l-Bahá. Wilmette, IL: Bahá'í Publishing Trust, 1991.

Bahai Temple Unity. *Eleventh Annual Mashrekol-Azkar Convention and Bahai Congress.* New York: Bahai Temple Unity, 1919.

Bahá'í World, The. vols. 1–12, 1925–54. rpt. Wilmette, IL: Bahá'í Publishing Trust, 1980.

Bahá'í World, The. vol. 13. Haifa: The Universal House of Justice, 1970.

Bahá'í World, The. vol. 14. Haifa: The Universal House of Justice, 1974.

Bahá'í World, The. vol. 15. Haifa: Bahá'í World Centre, 1976.

Bahá'í World, The. vol. 16. Haifa: Bahá'í World Centre, 1978.

Bahá'í World, The. vol. 17. Haifa: Bahá'í World Centre, 1981.

Bahá'í World, The. vol. 18. Haifa: Bahá'í World Centre, 1986.

Bahá'u'lláh. *The Book of Assurance (The Book of Ighan).* Trans. Ali Kuli Khan, assisted by Howard MacNutt, New York, 1924; 2nd edn. 1929.

— *Gleanings from the Writings of Bahá'u'lláh.* Wilmette, IL: Bahá'í Publishing Trust, 1983.

— *The Kitáb-i-Aqdas.* Haifa: Bahá'í World Centre, 1992.

— *The Seven Valleys and the Four Valleys*. Wilmette, IL: Bahá'í Publishing Trust, 1991.

Bahíyyih Khánum, the Greatest Holy Leaf: A Compilation from Bahá'í Sacred Texts and Writings of the Guardian of the Faith and Bahíyyih Khánum's Own Letters. Haifa: Bahá'í World Centre, 1982.

Balyuzi, H. M. *'Abdu'l-Bahá: The Centre of the Covenant of Bahá'u'lláh*. Oxford: George Ronald, 2nd edn. with minor corr. 1987.

'Basic Principles of the Bahai Movement: Miss Jack Gives Her Impression of Founder of Universal Religion', *The Hamilton Spectator* (Hamilton, Ont.), 25 May 1922.

Bender, Gerhard. 'Anna Koestlin, 1884–1972'. *Bahá'í World*, vol. 15, pp. 511–13, illus.

Benke, Adam. 'Eidrücke eines Bahá'í von bulgarischen Esperanto-Kongress 1931', *Sonne der Wahrheit* (Stuttgart) heft 7 (Sept. 1931), pp. 83–4.

Blomfield, Lady [Sara Louise]. *The Chosen Highway*. Wilmette, IL: Bahá'í Publishing Trust, 1967.

Bramson-Lerche, Loni. 'Some Aspects of the Development of the Bahá'í Administrative Order in America, 1922–1936', in Momen, ed. *Studies in Bábí and Bahá'í History*, vol. 1. Los Angeles: Kalimát Press, 1982, pp. 255–300.

'Brief Notes from Other Lands', *Bahá'í News*, no. 193 (March 1947), p. 12.

Brown, Bishop and Margaret Bahíyyih Randall Ford. 'Ruth Randall Brown, 1887–1969'. *Bahá'í World*, vol. 15, pp. 463–5, illus.

'Bulgaria', *Bahá'í News*, no. 177 (November 1945), p. 18.

'Bulgaria', *Bulletin* (Geneva: International Bahá'í Bureau), 10 (2 Feb. 1932).

'Bulgaria', *Bulletin* (Geneva: International Bahá'í Bureau), 12 (1 March 1933).

'Bulgaria', *Bulletin* (Geneva: International Bahá'í Bureau), 13 (25 May 1933), p. 3.

'Bulgaria', *Bulletin* (Geneva: International Bahá'í Bureau), 15 (9 May 1934), p. 3.

'Bulgaria', *Bulletin* (Geneva: International Bahá'í Bureau), 16 (June 1934).

'Bulgaria', *Geneva Bureau News Exchange* (Geneva: International Bahá'í Bureau), (Nov. – Dec. 1946), p. 3.

'Bulgaria', *Geneva Bureau News Exchange* (Geneva: International Bahá'í Bureau), (March 1947), pp. 1–2.

'Bulgaria', *Geneva Bureau News Exchange* (Geneva: International Bahá'í Bureau), (June 1947), p. 2.

'Bulgaria', *Geneva Bureau News Exchange* (Geneva: International Bahá'í Bureau), (November 1947 – March 1948), p. 1.

'Bulgarien', *Bahá'í-Nachrichten* (Stuttgart), no. 17 (Oktober 1931), p. 4.

Cameron, Glenn, with Wendi Momen. *A Basic Bahá'í Chronology*. Oxford: George Ronald, 1996.

Campbell, Helen. 'Philip Goddard Sprague'. *Bahá'í World*, vol. 12, pp. 698–9, illus.

Chapman, Anita Ioas. *Leroy Ioas: Hand of the Cause of God*. Oxford: George Ronald, 1998.

Chen, Constance M. 'Marzieh Nabil Carpenter Gail, Translator and Author, "Patron Saint" of Women Bahá'í Scholars (1 April 1908 – 16 October 1993)', in *The Bahá'í Studies Review* (London) 6 (1996).

Cobb, Stanwood. *Security for a Failing World*. Washington DC: Avalon Press, 1934.

Collins, William P. *Bibliography of English-Language Works on the Bábí and Bahá'í Faiths, 1844–1985*. Oxford: George Ronald, 1990.

Compilation of the Holy Utterances of Baha'o'llah and Abdu Baha Concerning the Most Great Peace, War and Duty of the Bahais Towards Their Government. Boston: Tudor Press, 2nd edn. 1918.

Cooper, Ella Goodall. 'Henrietta Emogene Martin Hoagg, 1869–1945'. *Bahá'í World*, vol. 10, pp. 520–5, illus.

'Corrections in Cable from the Guardian', *Bahá'í News*, no. 281 (July 1954), p. 4 (contains a photograph of Marion Jack).

Cuthbert, Arthur. 'London, England, News Notes', *Star of the West*, vol. 2, no. 2 (9 April 1911), p. 2.

De Bons, Mona Haenni. 'Edith de Bons, 1878–1959 and Joseph de Bons, 1871–1959'. *Bahá'í World*, vol. 13, pp. 878–81.

'Dr K. M. Fozdar, 1898–1958'. *Bahá'í World*, vol. 13, pp. 892–3, illus.

Dunbar, Ruth L. 'Stanwood Cobb, 1881–1982'. *Bahá'í World*, vol. 18, pp. 814–15, illus.

Dunn, J. L. 'Occultism to Hold Sway for Devotees of Bahai', *Vancouver Sunday Sun* (Vancouver, BC), 30 January 1921, p. 32.

Earl, Joy Hill. 'Louisa Mathew Gregory, 1866–1956'. *Bahá'í World*, vol. 13, pp. 876–8, illus.

'Eastern Europe and the Soviet Union: A Compilation from the Bahá'í Writings', compiled by the Research Department of the Universal House of Justice, in *The Bahá'í Studies Review*, vol. 3.1 (1993), pp. 96–117.

Ebbert, Doris and Olga Finke. 'Victoria Bedikian, 1879–1955'. *Bahá'í World*, vol. 13, pp. 884–5, illus.

'Elfie Lundberg: Memories of the Master's Presence', *The American Bahá'í* (Jan. 1982), p. 17.

'Ella Goodall Cooper'. *Bahá'í World*, vol. 12, pp. 681–4, illus.

'Elsa Maria Grossmann, 1896–1977, Knight of Bahá'u'lláh'. *Bahá'í World*, vol. 17 , pp. 440–1, illus.

Esslemont, J. E. *Bahá'u'lláh and the New Era*. London: Bahá'í Publishing Trust, 1974.

'European Conference Will Constitute a Landmark', *Bahá'í News*, no. 206 (April 1948), p. 1.

Fáḍil-i Mázandarání, Asadu'lláh. Lectures Giving the Solution of the World's Problems from a Universal Standpoint. Series 1–5.Trans. Ahmad Sohrab. Seattle: Bahai Literature Center, [1921].

'Florence Evaline (Lorol) Schopflocher, 1886–1970'. *Bahá'í World*, vol. 15, pp. 488–9, illus.

Freeman, Dorothy. *From Copper to Gold: The Life of Dorothy Baker*. Oxford: George Ronald, 1984.

Gail, Marzieh. 'Mírzá Ali-Kuli Khan, 1879(?) – April 7, 1966'. *Bahá'í World*, vol. 14, pp. 351–3, illus.

Garis, M. R. *Martha Root: Lioness at the Threshold*. Wilmette, IL: Bahá'í Publishing Trust, 1983.

'George Adam Benke'. *Bahá'í World*, vol. 5, pp. 416–18.

Giachery, Ugo R. 'Laura Clifford Dreyfus-Barney, 1879–1974'. *Bahá'í World*, vol. 16, pp. 535–8, illus.

Goodall, Helen S. and Cooper, Ella Goodall. *Daily Lessons Received at 'Akká*. Wilmette, IL: Bahá'í Publishing Trust, 1979. [Originally published in 1908.]

Green Acre on the Piscataqua. Eliot, Maine: Green Acre Bahá'í School Council, 1991.

Greeven, Inez. 'Max Greeven, 1869–1961'. *Bahá'í World,* vol. 13, pp. 909–11, illus.

Gregory, Louis G. 'The Thirteenth Mashreq'ul-Azkar Convention and Bahai Congress', *Star of the West*, vol. 12, no. 4 (17 May 1921), pp. 86, 90.

Grundy, Julia M. *Ten Days in the Light of Acca*. Chicago: Bahai Publishing Society, 1907.

Gulick, Jr., Robert L. 'Ella M. Bailey'. *Bahá'í World*, pp. 685–8, illus.

Hainsworth, Philip. 'Mary Olga Katherine Mills, 1882–1974, Knight of Bahá'u'lláh'. *Bahá'í World*, vol. 16, pp. 531–4, illus.

Hall, E. T. *Early Days of the Bahá'í Faith in Manchester*. Manchester: Bahá'í Assembly, 1925.

Haney, Mariam. 'Dorothy Beecher Baker'. *Bahá'í World*, vol. 12, pp. 670–4, illus.

— 'Travelling and Teaching in Alaska', *The Bahá'í Magazine*, vol. 15, no. 7 (October 1924), pp. 210–11.

Hatch, William P. 'Edward Christopher Getsinger'. *Bahá'í World*, vol. 6, pp. 403–6, illus.

Harmon, W. W. *Divine Illumination*. Boston: Bahai Movement, 1915.

Harper, Barron. *Lights of Fortitude: Glimpses into the Lives of the Hands of the Cause of God*. Oxford: George Ronald, 1997.

Ḥaydar-'Alí, Ḥájí Mírzá. *Stories from the Delight of Hearts: The Memoirs of Ḥájí Mírzá Ḥaydar-'Alí*. Trans. A. Q. Faizi. Los Angeles: Kalimát Press, 1980.

Heggie, James. 'Effie Baker, March 25, 1880 – January 1, 1968'. *Bahá'í World*, vol. 14 , pp. 300–3, illus.

Herrick, Elizabeth. *Unity Triumphant: The Call of the Kingdom*. London: Kegan Paul Trench Trubner and Company, 1923.

Hoagg, Emogene. '1919 Alaska'. Typescript. Ella Robarts Papers, United States National Bahá'í Archives.

Holley, Horace. 'Roy C. Wilhelm'. *Bahá'í World*, vol. 12, pp. 662–4. illus.

Holley, Marion. 'Margaret Klebs'. *Bahá'í World,* vol. 8, pp. 670–2.

— 'May Ellis Maxwell'. *Bahá'í World, vol.* 8, pp. 631–42, illus.

Hoonaard, Will. C. van den. *The Origins of the Bahá'í Community of Canada, 1989–1948.* Waterloo, Ontario: Wilfrid Laurier University Press, 1996.

— and Lynn Echevarria-Howe. *Black Roses in Canada's Mosaic: Four Decades of Black History.* [s.l., s.n.], 1994. Internet document: http://bahai-library.org/unpubl.articles/black.roses.html

Hudson, Ray and Kolstoe, John. 'Alaska: Planting the Seeds of Victory', *Bahá'í News*, no. 603 (August 1981), pp. 6–9.

'Hungary'. *Bulletin* (Geneva: International Bahá'í Bureau), 15 (9 May 1934), p. 4.

"Ináyatu'lláh Suhráb'. *Bahá'í World,* vol. 14, pp. 381–2, illus.

Ish'ta'a'l Ebn-Kalantar. 'Mirza Abul-Fazl'. *Star of the West*, vol. 4, no. 19 (2 March 1914), pp. 317–19.

Ives, Mabel Rice-Wray. 'Grace Robarts Ober'. *Bahá'í World,* vol. 8, pp. 656–60, illus.

Jack, Marion. 'Akka – 1908', MSS, n.d. Marion Jack Collection, Bahá'í World Centre Archives.

— 'A Few Notes on My Own Prison Experiences', MSS (n.d., probably 1930s). Marion Jack Collection, Bahá'í World Centre Archives.

— 'A Few Suffrage Experiences in London', n.d., Marion Jack Collection, Bahá'í World Centre Archives.

[Jasion, Jan Teofil]. *Marion Jack: Immortal Heroine*. Thornhill: Bahá'í Canada Publications, 1985. Translated into French as *Marion Jack: Héroïne Immortelle*. Thornhill: Publications Bahá'í Canada, 1987. Translated into Bulgarian as 'Марион Джак', in *Бахайски Вести* [Bahaiski vesti] (Sofia), no. 50 (May–June 1999), pp. 10–15.

— 'Marion Jack in Bulgaria: A Discussion'. Cumberland Twp. [Ont.]: 1979.

'Jináb-i-Fádil, 1880(?)–1957'. *Bahá'í World*, vol. 14, pp. 334–6, illus.

'Juliet Thompson'. *Bahá'í World*, vol. 13, pp. 889–90, illus.

Khursheed, Anjam. *The Seven Candles of Unity*. London: Bahá'í Publishing Trust, 1991.

'Lina Benke'. *Bahá'í Briefe* (Langenhain), heft 45 (juli 1971), p. 1318, illus.

Linfoot, Charlotte. 'Corinne Knight True'. *Bahá'í World*, vol. 13, pp. 846–9, illus.

Lunt, Alfred E. 'Sixth Annual Convention of Bahai Temple Unity, Chicago, April 25–18, 1914'. *Star of the West*, vol. 5, no. 4 (17 May 1914), pp. 51–8; no. 5 (5 June 1914), pp. 69–71.

MacNutt, Howard. *Unity Through Love*. Chicago: Bahai Publishing Society, 2nd edn. 1908.

McNamara, Brendan. 'The Culvers: Earliest Recorded Bahá'ís in Ireland'. *Ré Nua (New Day)* (Dublin), vol. 151 (July 1998), pp. 2–5, illus.

'Marion Jack'. *Bahá'í World*, vol. 12, pp. 674–7, illus.

'Marion Jack in Bulgaria'. *Bahá'í News*, no. 182 (April 1946), p. 8.

'Marion Jack in Sofia'. *Bahá'í News*, no. 90 (March 1935), p. 10.

'Marion Jack Teaching in Bulgaria'. *Bahá'í News*, no. 195 (May 1947), p.12.

Marion Jack – Immortal Heroine. [Toronto]: Canadian Bahá'í News Committee, April 1955.

Marion Jack – Immortal Heroine. reprinted. [Toronto]: National Pioneer Committee, July 1975.

Marsella, Elena Maria. 'Agnes Baldwin Alexander, 1875–1977'. *Bahá'í World,* vol. 15, pp. 423–30, illus.

'Martha L. Root's International Services'. *Bahá'í World,* vol. 5, pp. 45–59.

Martin, Lydia Jane. 'Mariam Haney, 1872–1965'. *Bahá'í World,* vol. 14, pp. 343–6, illus.

Masson, Jean. *Mashrak-el-Azkar and the Bahai Movement.* (Reprinted from *The Lake Shore News,* 19 October 1916.)

'Memoirs of the Pioneers: Marion Jack: Immortal Heroine'. *Bahá'í News Letter* (New Delhi), no. 79 (June–July 1955), pp. 11–12.

'Memorial in Honor of Marion Jack'. *Bahá'í News,* no. 280 (June 1954), p. 6.

'Memorial in Temple in Tribute to Marion Jack'. *Bahá'í News,* no. 282 (August 1954), pp. 4–6.

Metelmann, Velda Piff. *Lua Getsinger: Herald of the Covenant.* Oxford: George Ronald, 1997.

Momen, Moojan. *The Bábí and Bahá'í Religions, 1844–1944: Some Contemporary Western Accounts.* Oxford: George Ronald, 1981.

— *Dr. John Ebenezer Esslemont.* London: Bahá'í Publishing Trust, 1975.

— ed. *Studies in Bábí and Bahá'í History,* vol. 1. Los Angeles: Kalimát Press, 1982.

Momen, Wendi. *A Basic Bahá'í Dictionary.* Oxford: George Ronald, 1989.

'Monument Erected in Sofia to Immortal Bahá'í Heroine'. *Bahá'í News,* no. 324 (Feb. 1958), p. 6, illus.

Morrison, Gayle. *To Move the World*. Wilmette, IL: Bahá'í Publishing Trust, 1982.

Mu'ayyad, Habíb. *Khátirát-i-Habíb*. Tehran, [1961].

Mühlschlegel, Adelbert. 'Hermann Grossmann, 1899–1968'. *Bahá'í World*, vol. 15, pp. 416–21, illus.

Mühlschlegel, Ursula. 'Margaret Lentz, 1879–1965'. *Bahá'í World*, vol. 14, pp. 354–5, illus.

Nabíl-i-A'zam. *The Dawn-Breakers: Nabíl's Narrative of the Early Days of the Bahá'í Revelation*. Wilmette, IL: Bahá'í Publishing Trust, 1970.

National Bahá'í Memorial in Tribute to Marion Jack. Wilmette, IL: National Spiritual Assemblies of the Bahá'ís of the United States and Canada, 1954.

National Spiritual Assembly of the Bahá'ís of Persia. 'Ahmad Samímí, 1893–1976'. *Bahá'í World*, vol. 17 , pp. 411–12, illus.

'News from Other Lands'. *Bahá'í News*, no. 199 (Sept. 1947), p.15.

'News of the Cause'. *Bahá'í News Letter* (Green Acre, South Eliot, Maine), no. 10 (February 1926), p. 5.

Ober, Elizabeth Kidder, Matthew W. Bullock and Beatrice Irwin. 'Harlan Foster Ober, 1881–1962'. *Bahá'í World*, vol. 13, pp. 889–90, illus.

Ober, Harlan F. 'Louis G. Gregory'. *Bahá'í World*, vol. 12, pp. 665–70, illus.

— 'Report of the Tenth Annual Convention of Bahai Temple Unity . . . :Monday Afternoon Session'. *Star of the West*, vol. 9, no. 4 (17 May 1918), pp. 50–2.

'Our Dawnbreakers: George Orr Latimer'. *Canadian Bahá'í News*, no. 206, March 1967, p. 4.

'Our Dawnbreakers: Miss Marion Jack'. *Canadian Bahá'í News*, no. 198, July 1966, p. 4; no. 199, August 1966, p. 4.

Phelps, Myron H. *Abbas Effendi: His Life and Teachings*. New York: G. P. Putnam's Son, 1903.

Quickeners of Mankind: Pioneering in a World Community. Wilmette, IL: Bahá'í Publishing Trust, 1998.

Rabbaní, Rúḥíyyih. 'Horace Hotchkiss Holley, April 7, 1887 – July 12, 1960'. *Bahá'í World*, vol. 13, pp. 849–58.

— *The Priceless Pearl*. London: Bahá'í Publishing Trust, 1969.

Rassekh, Nasratolláh. 'A Pearl of the Kingdom'. *Portland Bahá'í Bulletin* (Portland, Oregon), series of articles published between September/October 1994 and May/July 1998.

Remey, Charles Mason. *Bahá'í Reminiscences, Diary Letters and Other Documents*. 56 vol. Washington DC: 1938.

— 'Green Acre, Maine'. *Star of the West*, vol. 1, no. 9 (20 August 1910), p. 13.

— *Reminiscences of Green Acre*. [Washington DC]: Remey, 1949.

Root, Martha L. 'Appreciations from Yugoslavia'. *Bahá'í Magazine*, vol. 24 (Oct. 1933), p. 209, illus.

— 'Seeing Adrianople with New York Eyes'. *Bahá'í Magazine*, vol. 25, no. 3 (June 1934), pp. 74–7, illus.

— *Ṭáhirih the Pure*. Los Angeles: Kalimát Press, rev. edn. 1981.

— 'A Visit to Adrianople'. *Bahá'í World*, vol. 5, pp. 581–93, illus.

Sala, Emeric. 'The Greenleafs: An Eternal Union'. *Bahá'í News*, no. 510 (September 1973), pp. 8–9, 23.

Sanderson, Edith R. 'Charles Nelson Kennedy'. *Bahá'í World*, vol. 12, pp. 711–12, illus.

Schwartz, Rosa. 'Alma Knobloch'. *Bahá'í World*, vol. 9, pp. 641–3.

Sears, Marguerite. 'Marguerite Sears' Pilgrim Notes Taken during March 1953 at Haifa'. Photocopy of typescript. Author's papers.

Sears, William and Robert Quigley. *The Flame: The Story of Lua*. Oxford: George Ronald, 1972.

Shoghi Effendi. *Citadel of Faith: Messages to America 1947–1957*. Wilmette, IL: Bahá'í Publishing Trust, 1965.

— *God Passes By*. Wilmette, IL: Bahá'í Publishing Trust, rev. edn. 1995.

— 'Hippolyte Dreyfus-Barney: An Appreciation'. *Bahá'í World*, vol. 3, pp. 210–11, 214.

— 'Immortal Heroine'. *Bahá'í News*, no. 278 (April 1954), pp. 1–2.

— *The Light of Divine Guidance: The Messages from the Guardian of the Bahá'í Faith to the Bahá'ís of Germany and Austria*. 2 vols. Hofheim-Langenhain: Bahá'í-Verlag, 1982.

— 'Marion Jack'. *Bahá'í News*, no. 216 (February 1949), p. 1.

— *Messages to Canada*. [Toronto]: National Spiritual Assembly of the Bahá'ís of Canada, 1965.

— 'Messages to the National Spiritual Assembly'. *Bahá'í News*, no. 143 (May 1941), p. 1.

— *The Unfolding Destiny of the British Bahá'í Community: The Messages of the Guardian of the Bahá'í Faith to the Bahá'ís of the British Isles*. London: Bahá'í Publishing Trust, 1981.

'Siegfried Schopflocher'. *Bahá'í World*, vol. 12, pp. 664–6, illus.

Smith, Peter. 'The American Bahá'í Community, 1894–1917: A Preliminary Survey', in Momen, ed. *Studies in Bábí and Bahá'í History*, vol. 1. Los Angeles: Kalimát Press, 1982, pp. 85–223.

Sohrab, Ahmad. *Unveiling of the Divine Plan*. New York, 1919. Later published as 'Abdu'l-Bahá. *Tablets of the Divine Plan*.

— 'With Abdul Baha in London: Extracts from Letters'. *Star of the West*, vol. 3, no. 19 (2 March 1913), p. 4.

'Some of New Teachings of Baha'o'llah Called the Twelve Basic Principles'. *The Weekly Star* (Whitehorse, Yukon) (17 October 1919).

Stockman, Robert H. *The Bahá'í Faith in America, Early Expansion, 1900–1912*, vol. 2. Oxford: George Ronald, 1995.

Sugar, Alfred. 'Florence George'. *Bahá'í Journal* (London) (December 1950), p. 6. Reprinted in *Bahá'í World*, vol. 12, pp. 667–8, illus.

Sur les pas de 'Abdu'l-Bahá à Paris. Paris : Librarie Bahá'íe, 1998.

Szanto-Felbermann, Renée. *Rebirth: The Memoirs of Renée Szanto-Felbermann*. London: Bahá'í Publishing Trust, 1980.

Taherzadeh, Adib. *The Covenant of Bahá'u'lláh*. Oxford: George Ronald, 1992.

Táhirzádeh, Habíb. 'Dr. Youness Afrakhtih'. *Bahá'í World*, vol. 12, pp. 679–81, illus.

Teaching Committee of Nineteen. *Bulletin* (Washington DC), no. 2 (19 July 1920).

Thompson, Juliet. 'Edward B. Kinney'. *Bahá'í World*, vol. 12, pp. 677–9, illus.

True, Edna. 'Saichiro Fujita, 1886–1976'. *Bahá'í World*, vol. 17, pp. 406–8, illus.

Vail, Albert R. [A.R.V] 'The Bahai Movement: Its Spiritual Dynamic'. Reprinted from *Harvard Theological Review*, 1914.

— 'The Teaching Campaign'. *Star of the West*, vol. 9, no. 16 (31 December 1918), p. 181.

— 'The Teaching Campaign'. *Star of the West*, vol. 10, no. 1 (21 March 1919), p. 5.

'Vancouver to Welcome Persian Philosopher This Week: Local Organizations Will Hear Dr. Jenabe Mazandarani'. *Vancouver Sunday Sun* (Vancouver BC) (30 January 1921), p. 32.

Weinberg, Robert. *Ethel Jenner Rosenberg: The Life and Times of England's Outstanding Bahá'í Pioneer Woman*. Oxford: George Ronald, 1995.

White, Roger. 'The Pioneer'. *Another Song, Another Season: Poems and Portrayals*. Oxford: George Ronald, 1979.

— *A Sudden Music*. Oxford: George Ronald, 1983.

Whitehead, O. Z. *Some Bahá'ís to Remember*. Oxford: George Ronald, 1983.

— *Some Early Bahá'ís of the West*. Oxford: George Ronald, 1976.

'William Sutherland Maxwell, 1874–1952'. *Bahá'í World*, vol. 12, pp. 657–62, illus.

Winkler, Bahíyyih Randall, in collaboration with M. R. Garis. *William Henry Randall: Disciple of 'Abdu'l-Bahá*. Oxford: Oneworld, [2000].

Wisdom Talks of Abdul-Baha (Abbas Effendi) at Chicago, Illinois, April 30th to May 5th, 1912. Chicago: Publishing Committee, 1912.

World Fellowship (Montclair, NJ), vol. 1, no. 9/10 (August 1924).

'Zeenat Khanum'. *Star of the West*, vol. 5, no. 4 (17 May 1914), pp. 57–8.

Literature on the Arts

Exhibition Catalogues

The Art Association of Montreal. *Catalogue of the Thirtieth Spring Exhibition, 1913*. Montreal, 1913.

— *Catalogue of the Thirty-first Spring Exhibition, 1914*. Montreal, 1914.

— *Catalogue of the Thirty-second Spring Exhibition, 1915*. Montreal, 1915.

— *Catalogue of the Thirty-third Spring Exhibition,1916*. Montreal, 1916.

Birmingham Royal Society of Artists. *Autumn Exhibition Catalogue*, 1898.

— *Autumn Exhibition Catalogue*, 1899.

— *Autumn Exhibition Catalogue*, 1901.

— *Autumn Exhibition Catalogue*, 1902.

British Columbia Society of Fine Arts. *Annual Exhibition . . . September 18th to 25th, 1920*. Vancouver, 1920.

Dominion Exhibition. *Catalogue: Loan Exhibit of Oil and Water Colour Paintings, Miniatures, etc.* Saint John: The Saint John Art Club, 1910.

Provincial Exhibition. St. John, N.B., Sept. 5 to 12, 1914. Art Exhibition. Saint John: The Saint John Art Club, 1914.

'Records of the Saint John Art Club', Scrap Book No. 2, 15 February 1917. New Brunswick Museum Archives, Saint John, NB.

Royal Canadian Academy of Arts. *Catalogue 1908: Twenty-ninth Annual Exhibition*. Toronto, 1908.

— *Catalogue of the Thirty-sixth Annual Exhibition*. Toronto, 1914.

Saint John Art Club. *Programme 1917–1918*. Saint John, 1918.

— *Saint John Art Club 50th Anniversary*. Saint John, 1958.

Articles

'An Artist's Trip Through Alaska'. *The Standard* (Saint John, NB), 26 April 1923.

'Exhibit of Art the Work of N.B. Lady Artist'. *Times* (Moncton) (9 November 1922).

'Fine Art Exhibition Shown in Y.W.C.A. Home: Miss Marion Jack's Work Compares with that of Noted Painters'. *Transcript* (Moncton, NB) (9 November 1922).

'Great Day at the Exhibition: The Art Gallery'. *Standard* (Saint John, NB), 7 May 1914.

'The Group of Seven and Their Contemporaries', McMichael Canadian Art Collection, 2001. Internet document: http://www.mcmichael.on.ca/group.htm

Shadbolt, Jack. 'A Personal Recollection'. *Vancouver: Art and Artists, 1931–1983*. Vancouver: Vancouver Art Gallery, 1983.

Taylor, E. A. 'American Colony of Artists in Paris'. *The International Studio*, vol. 44 (July 1911), pp. 103–18.

'Vancouver Sketch Club'. *Western Women's Weekly* (Vancouver, BC), vol. 3, no. 44 (9 October 1920), p. 7.

'Vancouver Sketch Club Takes Part in Exhibit'. *Western Women's Weekly* (Vancouver, BC) 3, no. 41 (18 September 1920), p. 3.

Monographs

Harper, J. Russell. *Painting in Canada: A History*. Toronto: University of Toronto Press, 2nd edn. 1977.

John Hammond, R.C.A., 1843–1939: Retrospective Exhibition. March 25 – April, 1967. Sackville: Sackville Art Association, Owens Art Gallery, Mount Allison University, 1967.

Johnson, J. and A. Greeutzner, comps. *The Dictionary of British Artists 1880 – 1940*. Woodbridge, Sussex: Antique Collectors Club, 1976.

McMann, Evelyn de R. *Montreal Museum of Fine Arts, formerly Art Association of Montreal. Spring Exhibitions 1880–1970*. Toronto: University of Toronto Press, 1988.

— *Royal Canadian Academy of Arts/Académie royale des arts du Canada: Exhibitions and Members 1880–1979*. Toronto: University of Toronto Press, 1981.

Reid, Denis. *A Concise History of Canadian Painting*. Toronto: Oxford University Press, 1973.

Tweedie, R. A., Fred Cogswell and W. Stewart MacNutt. *Arts in New Brunswick*. Fredericton: Brunswick Press, 1967.

Literature about Bulgaria

Capienko, Michaił. *Sofia, Tyrnowo, Płowdiw*. Warsaw: Wydawnictwa Artystyczne i Filmowe, 1983.

Dellin, L. A. D., ed. *Bulgaria*. New York: Frederick A. Praeger, for Mid-European Studies Center of the Free Europe Committee, 1957.

Dymitrowa, Iłczo, ed. *Bułgaria: Zarys Dziejów*. Warsaw: Książka i Wiedza, 1986.

Pesher, Marin, ed. *History of the Bulgarian Trade Unions*. Sofia: Sofia Press, 1977.

Rachev, Stoyan. *Anglo-Bulgarian Relations during the Second World War (1939–1944)*. Sofia: Sofia Press, 1981.

Semerdjiev, Stefan. 'Ace in Defense of Bulgaria'. *Military History* 16, no. 3 (August 1999), pp. 50–6.

Other Works Consulted

Biographical Review . . . Province of New Brunswick. Boston: Biographical Review, 1900.

Cameron, Kenneth William. *Transcendentalists in Transition: Popularization of Emerson, Thoreau and the Concord School of Philosophy in the Greenacre Conferences and the Monsalvat School (1894–1909)*.Hartford, CN: Transcendental Books, 1980.

Danchov, N.G. and I. G. Danchov. *Българска Енциклопедия* [Bulgarska entsiklopediia]. Sofia: St Atanasov, 1936.

'Death of Mr. D. R. Jack', *Saint John Globe*, 2 December 1913.

Fulford, Roger. *Votes for Women: The Story of a Struggle*. London: Faber and Faber, 1957.

'Henry Jack (1824–1884)', in 'Markham Scrapbook – New Brunswick Biographies', typescript. New Brunswick Museum Archives.

Kessler, Deirdre. *A Century on Spring Street: Wanda Lefurgey Wyatt of Summerside, Prince Edward Island (1895–1998)*. Charlotte-town: Indigo Press, 1999.

Leonard, John William, ed. *Woman's Who's Who of America: A Biographical Dictionary of Contemporary Women of the United States and Canada*. New York: American Commonwealth Company, 1914–15.

Morgan, Henry James, ed. *The Canadian Men and Women of the Times*. Toronto: William Briggs, 2nd edn. 1912.

— *The Dominion Annual Register and Review for the Eighteenth Year of Canadian Union 1884*. Toronto, 1885.

Pankhurst, Christabel. *Unshackled: The Story of How We Won the Vote*. London: Hutchinson, 1959.

Pankhurst, E. Sylvia. *The Suffragette Movement: An Intimate Account of Persons and Ideals*. London: Longman, 1931.

Pope-Hennessay, James. *Queen Mary 1867–1953*. London: George Allen & Unwin, 1959.

Raeburn, Antonia. *The Militant Suffragettes*. London: Michael Joseph, 1973.

Sarafov, Ivan. *Skizo de la Historio de Bulgara Esperanto-Movado*. Sofia: Bulgara Esperantista Asocio, 1971.

Stewart, George. *The Story of the Great Fire in St. John, N.B.: June 20, 1877*. Woodstock, NB: Non-Entity Press, 1980.

Wallace, W. S. *Macmillan Dictionary of Canadian Biography*. Toronto: Macmillan, 1963.

Bahá'í Literature in Bulgarian (published before 1954)

Afnan, Ruhi. *Бахаистката Религия* [Bahaistkata Religiia], (S.D.G. Biuro) [n.d.]

[Translation of *The Baha'i Religion*; translated by L. Dobrovsky]

Bahá'u'lláh. *Скритиђ слова на Баха'у'лахь* [Skritit Slova na Baha'u'lah]. Sofia, 1937.
[Translation of *The Hidden Words of Bahá'u'lláh*].

Esslemont, John E. *Баха-у-ллах и новата ера* [Baha-u-llah i novata era]. Sofia; Genève: Bureau International Bahá'í, 1932.
[Translation of *Bahá'u'lláh and the New Era*, translated by Konstantin B. Dinkov.]

Що е Бахаизьмь? [Shto e Bahaizum] [n.d.].
[Translation of *What is the Baha'i Movement?*]

Що е Бахаизьмь? [Shto e Bahaizum]. [n.d.], 1 p.
[Translation of *What is the Baha'i Movement?*, publication arranged by Martha Root.]

Notes and References

1. The military definition of a pioneer: *Collins Dictionary of the English Language*: 'member of an infantry group that digs entrenchments, builds roads, etc.' *The Concise Oxford Dictionary*: 'member of infantry group serving to prepare road for main body of troops'.
2. Loyalists were those Americans who supported Britain during the War of American Independence. Many of them emigrated to Canada.
3. Marion Jack, to an unknown Bahá'í from Yugoslavia living in New Zealand, undated, probably late 1930s. Marion Jack Collection, Bahá'í World Centre Archives.
4. Marion Jack to Marion Logie, 19 March 1951. Logie Collection.
5. Unfortunately it has not been possible to verify any of this information.
6. Jack, 'David William Jack . . .' in *Biographical Review*, p. 433.
7. ibid. p. 434.
8. Marion Jack, to an unknown Bahá'í from Yugoslavia living in New Zealand, undated, probably late 1930s. Marion Jack Collection, Bahá'í World Centre Archives.
9. Marion Jack to Marion Logie, 16(?) September 1948. Logie Collection.
10. Marion Jack to Marion Logie, 16 January 1951. Marion Jack Collection, Bahá'í World Centre Archives.
11. ibid.
12. Jack, 'David William Jack . . .' in *Biographical Review*, p. 433.

13. Marion Jack to Fred Hubbard, November – December (probably late 1940s). Marion Jack Collection, Bahá'í World Centre Archives.

14. Marion Jack to Marion Logie, 26 January 1951. Marion Jack Collection, Bahá'í World Centre Archives.

15. Stewart, *The Story of the Great Fire in St John*, pp. 19–20.

16. Letter of Marion Jack to Neneva Rozeva, 15 and 16 April 1944. Marion Jack Collection, Bahá'í World Centre Archives.

17. 'Henry Jack (1824–1884)', in *Markham Scrapbook*. New Brunswick Museum Archives.

18. Letter of Don Morris to the author, 16 June 1983.

19. Morgan, ed. *The Canadian Men and Women of the Times* and Leonard, ed. *Woman's Who's Who of America*.

20. 'Death of Mr. D. R. Jack', *Saint John Globe*, 2 December 1913; and 'Jack, David Russell', in Wallace, *Macmillan Dictionary of Canadian Biography*.

21. Morgan, ed. *Canadian Men and Women of the Times*, p. 572.

22. Letter of Louisa Hubbard to Marion Jack, 9 May [1948?]. Marion Jack Collection, Bahá'í World Centre Archives.

23. David Russell Jack to Marion Jack, 6 October 1884. Copy in author's collection.

24. Morgan, *Dominion Annual Register*, p. 194.

25. For more information on Hammond see *John Hammond, R.C.A., 1843–1939: Retrospective Exhibition*.

26. Leonard, ed. *Woman's Who's Who of America*, p. 425.

27. Harper, *Painting in Canada*, p. 207.

28. Leonard, *Woman's Who's Who of America*, p. 425.

29. Taylor, 'American Colony of Artists in Paris', *International Studio*, vol. 44, July 1911, pp. 110–12.

30. Allaire, 'Les Artistes Canadiens aux Salons de Paris de 1870 á 1914', quoted in Afnan, 'An Introduction to the Life and Work of Marion Elizabeth Jack 1866–1954'.

   See Appendix 3 for a list of Marion Jack's exhibited paintings.

31. Morgan, ed. *Canadian Men and Women of the Times*, p. 572.

32. Letter of Marion Jack to Marion Logie, 8 April 1951. Marion Jack Collection, Bahá'í World Centre Archives. 'On the line' refers to paintings hung at eye level. The walls of the galleries of the Paris Salon were covered with paintings from ceiling to the floor. Having one's paintings hung 'on the line' was a sign of approval.

33. A list of Marion's major exhibitions can be found in Appendix 2 and a list of her exhibited paintings in Appendix 3.

34. Letter of Marion Jack to Miss Jeanne Kauz, 9 May 1937. Marion Jack Collection, Bahá'í World Centre Archives.

35. Remey, quoted in 'Memorial in Temple in Tribute to Marion Jack', *Bahá'í News*, August 1954, no. 282, pp. 4–6.

36. Remey, 'Paris, 1901' [unpublished diary], quoted in White, *A Sudden Music*, p. ix.

37. Remey, *Reminiscences of Green Acre*, vol. 2, p. 132.

38. Letter of Marion Jack to Miss Jeanne Kauz, 9 May 1937. Marion Jack Collection, Bahá'í World Centre Archives.

39. Remey, 'In Paris and London the Summer of 1907', in *Bahá'í Reminiscences, Diary Letters and Other Documents*, vol. 1, p. 4.

40. Phelps, *Abbas Effendi: His Life and Teachings*.

41. American Bahá'í who pioneered to Germany in 1907.

42. Letter of Marion Jack to Rúḥíyyih Khánum, 18 May 1946. Marion Jack Collection, Bahá'í World Centre Archives.

43. Letter of Marion Jack to unknown Bahá'í in New York, Christmas (c. 1935?). Marion Jack Collection, Bahá'í World Centre Archives.

44. Laura Clifford Dreyfus-Barney, American Bahá'í settled in Paris.

45. Edith R. Sanderson, American Bahá'í settled in Paris.

46. Joséphine Scott, wife of Edwin Scott, an English Bahá'í settled in Paris.

47. Jean E. Stannard, English Bahá'í, lived in India, c. 1914 and in 1922 established the International Bahá'í Bureau in Geneva.

48. Letter of Marion Jack to C. N. Kennedy, c. 1930s. Marion Jack Collection, Bahá'í World Centre Archives.

49. Letter of Marion Jack to an unknown Bahá'í from Yugoslavia living in New Zealand, late 1930s. Marion Jack Collection, Bahá'í World Centre Archives.

50. Lua Getsinger, stalwart American Bahá'í.

51. Letter of Marion Jack to an unknown Bahá'í in Paris, c. 1930s. Marion Jack Collection, Bahá'í World Centre Archives.

52. Letter of Marion Jack to Ella [Ella Robarts?], 8 March 1948. Marion Jack Collection, Bahá'í World Centre Archives.

53. May Maxwell, early American Bahá'í teacher, named a martyr when she died in Buenos Aires.

54. Edith de Bons, née McKay, 1878–1959.

55. Holley, 'May Ellis Maxwell', *Bahá'í World*, vol. 8, p. 634.

56. Remey, 'In Paris and London the Summer of 1907', in *Bahá'í Reminiscences, Diary Letters and Other Documents*, vol. 1.

57. Green Acre Bahá'í School, near Eliot, Maine. See chapter 7.

58. Letter of Dorothy C. Cress to 'Dear Frau', 3 March 1969.

59. Anna Watson, an American Bahá'í and artist living in Paris.

60. Marion Jack later recalled how she had to be persuaded by one of her friends, a Miss Wyman who came to Marion's flat, sat on the floor and stated: 'I'll sit here until the letter of acceptance is written!' Letter of Marion Jack to Rúḥíyyih Khánum, 13 May 1946. Marion Jack Collection, Bahá'í World Centre Archives.

61. 4 January 1908.

62. Helen S. Goodall and her daughter Ella Goodall Cooper.

63. Jack, 'A Few Notes on My Own Prison Experiences', MSS (n.d., probably 1930s). Marion Jack Collection, Bahá'í World Centre Archives.

64. Goodall and Cooper, *Daily Lessons*, pp. 10–11.

65. Rhua Khanum = Rúḥá Khánum, daughter of 'Abdu'l-Bahá.

66. House of 'Abdu'lláh Páshá, residence of 'Abdu'l-Bahá and His family from 1896 to 1910. Now a Bahá'í Holy Place.

67. Greatest Holy Leaf, Bahíyyih <u>Kh</u>ánum (1846–1932), daughter of Bahá'u'lláh and sister of 'Abdu'l-Bahá.

68. The fortress prison, or citadel, of Acre, now an Israeli museum. The cell which Bahá'u'lláh occupied is a Bahá'í Holy Place.

69. Ṭúbá <u>Kh</u>ánum, daughter of 'Abdu'l-Bahá.

70. Jack, 'A Few Notes on My Own Prison Experiences', MSS (n.d., probably 1930s). Marion Jack Collection, Bahá'í World Centre Archives.

71. Remey, 'My Trip to Persia in the Summer of 1908', in *Bahá'í Reminiscences, Diary Letters and Other Documents*, vol. 3, p. 38.

72. Jack, 'A Few Notes on My Own Prison Experiences', MSS (n.d., probably 1930s). Marion Jack Collection, Bahá'í World Centre Archives.

73. Letter of Marion Jack to an unknown Bahá'í, n.d. Marion Jack Collection, Bahá'í World Centre Archives.

74. The governor (or more properly mutasarif) of Acre in 1908 was Ismá'íl Raḥmí Bey. See Momen, *Bábí and Bahá'í Religions*, p. 488.

75. Munavvar <u>Kh</u>ánum, daughter of 'Abdu'l-Bahá.

76. Jack, 'Akka – 1908', MSS, n.d. Marion Jack Collection, Bahá'í World Centre Archives.

77. Shoghi Effendi (Rabbani), the grandson of 'Abdu'l-Bahá, was named Guardian of the Bahá'í Faith in the Will and Testament of 'Abdu'l-Bahá.

78. Collège des Frères, Haifa.

79. Shoghi Effendi's mother was Ḍiyá'iyyih <u>Kh</u>ánum, eldest daughter of 'Abdu'l-Bahá.

80. Probably Ḥasan <u>Sh</u>ahíd. See Taherzadeh, *The Covenant*, p. 358.

81. Jack, 'A Few Notes on My Own Prison Experiences', MSS (n.d., probably 1930s). Marion Jack Collection, Bahá'í World Centre Archives.

82. Marion Jack, to an unknown Bahá'í in Iran, 2 October 1948. Marion Jack Collection, Bahá'í World Centre Archives.

83. The Shrine of Bahá'u'lláh at Bahjí, north of Acre.
84. Isfandíyár, a Burmese Bahá'í serving the Holy Household as a coachman.
85. Jack, 'A Few Notes on My Own Prison Experiences', MSS (n.d., probably 1930s). Marion Jack Collection, Bahá'í World Centre Archives.
86. Tripoli or Tripolitania, a province and region of North Africa, now part of Libya.
87. Dr Zia Bagdadi (or Baghdádí) (d. 1937), trusted friend of 'Abdu'l-Bahá and His family, lived in the Holy Land and from 1909 in America. His wife was Zínat Bagdadi, née Tabrízí, and her sister was Fátimih Nakhjavání, née Tabrízí. See 'Zeenat Khanum', *Star of the West*, vol. 5, no. 4, pp. 57–8.
88. Jack, 'A Few Notes on My Own Prison Experiences', MSS (n.d., probably 1930s). Marion Jack Collection, Bahá'í World Centre Archives. For more information on this episode in 'Abdu'l-Bahá's life see Balyuzi, *'Abdu'l-Bahá*, p. 122; and Shoghi Effendi, *God Passes By*, p. 269.
89. Jack, 'A Few Notes on My Own Prison Experiences', MSS (n.d., probably 1930s). Marion Jack Collection, Bahá'í World Centre Archives. It is possible that this official was Pietro Abeli (d. 1911), the dragoman of the British Vice-Consulate in Haifa and also Lloyd's agent.
90. Remey, 'My Trip to Persia in the Summer of 1908', in *Bahá'í Reminiscences, Diary Letters and Other Documents*.
91. A short mystical work written in Persian and Arabic. The first English translation was published in 1900 and by 1907 there were at least five or six various editions available.
92. First Universal Races Congress, London, 26–9 July 1931.
93. Jack, 'A Few Notes on My Own Prison Experiences', MSS (n.d., probably 1930s). Marion Jack Collection, Bahá'í World Centre Archives.
94. Letter of Marion Jack to Margaret Lentz, September 1946. Marion Jack Collection, Bahá'í World Centre Archives.
95. This was most likely rosewater.

96. Letter of Marion Jack to an unknown Bahá'í in Iran, 2 October 1948. Marion Jack Collection, Bahá'í World Centre Archives.

97. Letter of Marion Jack to George Townshend, 31 July 1949. Marion Jack Collection, Bahá'í World Centre Archives.

98. Alma Knobloch (1864–1943). An early American believer who pioneered to Germany at the request of 'Abdu'l-Bahá.

99. Her *Town Hall and Market Place Stuttgart* was exhibited at the Dominion Exhibition, Saint John, New Brunswick in 1910. See also Appendix 2.

100. Undated letter of Marion Jack to an unknown Bahá'í. Marion Jack Collection, Bahá'í World Centre Archives.

101. Royal Canadian Academy of Arts. *Catalogue 1908: Twenty-ninth Annual Exhibition.* Toronto, 1908, p. 14.

102. Persian believer in America, a teacher of Persian and one of the translators of *Tablets of Abdul Baha Abbas.*

103. Early American believer. The only information available states that she had a summer home in Eliot and that she wintered in the south.

104. Early American believer. She edited *Magazine of the Kingdom* with Victoria Bedikian and in the 1930s pioneered to Barbados. She died in 1950.

105. Early Canadian-born believer. He studied art at the Ecole des Beaux-Arts, Paris, and exhibited in France and in the United States. See van den Hoonaard, *Origins of the Bahá'í Community of Canada*, pp. 30–1.

106. Remey, 'Green Acre, Maine', *Star of the West*, vol. 1, no. 9, pp. 13–14.

107. Elizabeth Herrick (d. 1929), milliner and early English Bahá'í, originally from Liverpool, then in London, author of *Unity Triumphant: The Call of the Kingdom.*

108. Letter of Marion Jack to Annie Gamble, 3 July 1935. Marion Jack Collection, Bahá'í World Centre Archives.

109. Blomfield, *Chosen Highway*, pp. 149–50.

110. For the full text, see Appendix 1.

111. For 'Abdu'l-Bahá's talks in Paris see *Paris Talks.*

112. Mirza Ahmad Sohrab, 'With Abdul-Baha in London', *Star of the West*, vol. 3, no. 19, p. 4.

113. A very readable account of both of His visits is recorded by Hasan M. Balyuzi in his biography *'Abdu'l-Bahá: The Centre of the Covenant of Bahá'u'lláh*, pp. 140–58, 343–71.

114. Letter of Marion Jack to Marion Logie, 31 January 1951. Marion Jack Collection, Bahá'í World Centre Archives.

115. Isabel Fraser Chamberlain (Soraya) (1871–1939), early American believer of Scottish ancestry.

116. Khursheed, *Seven Candles of Unity*, p. 117.

117. Annie Gamble (1831–1931), staunch early English Bahá'í in London.

118. Mrs Florence 'Mother' George.

119. Arthur Cuthbert, very active early English Bahá'í in London.

120. Luṭfu'lláh Ḥakím (1881–1968). Persian physiotherapist who lived in England, Haifa and Persia. Elected to the first Universal House of Justice in 1963.

121. Letter of Marion Jack to a member of the British Isles Bahá'í Youth Committee, c. 1947. Marion Jack Collection, Bahá'í World Centre Archives.

122. 'Abdu'l-Bahá in a Tablet to Luṭfu'lláh Ḥakím in Mu'ayyad, *Khátirát-i-Habíb*, p. 421. The author thanks Mariam Rabbani for this translation.

123. See Appendix 2 for a list of these paintings.

124. Armstrong-Ingram, 'Early Irish Bahá'ís', in *Research Notes in Shaykhí, Bábí and Bahá'í Studies*, vol. 2, no. 4. Internet document: http://www.h-net2.msu.edu/~bahai/notes/vol2/irish.htm

125. See *'Abdu'l-Bahá in London*, p. 102.

126. Qurratu'l-'Ayn, Ṭáhirih. For her life see Root, *Ṭáhirih the Pure*.

127. John Ebenezer Esslemont (1874–1925). Scottish doctor and author of *Bahá'u'lláh and the New Era*.

128. 18 June 1910.

129. William Wymark Jacobs (1863–1943). English writer.

130. David Lloyd George (1863–1945), Welsh Liberal politician, chancellor of the exchequer 1908–15; Herbert Henry Asquith (1852–1928), British Liberal politician, prime minister 1908–16.

131. Jack, 'A Few Suffrage Experiences in London', n.d. Marion Jack Collection, Bahá'í World Centre Archives.

132. Leonard, ed. *Woman's Who's Who of America*, p. 425.

133. Mary Basil-Hall, née Blomfield.

134. This refers to the brutal methods used in the prisons to break the hunger-strikes of the suffragettes.

135. This incident was widely reported in the press. Particularly of note are the reports in *The Times* and *Daily Mirror* and in at least four books on the Suffragette movement: Pankhurst, *The Suffragette Movement: An Intimate Account of Persons and Ideals*, pp. 296–7; Fulford, *Votes for Women: The Story of a Struggle*, p. 277; Pankhurst, *Unshackled: The Story of How We Won the Vote*, p. 554; Raeburn, *The Militant Suffragettes*, p. 234; and also in Pope-Hennessay, *Queen Mary 1867–1953*, p. 468.

136. 'Jack, Miss Marion Elizabeth' in Morgan, ed. *Canadian Men and Women of the Times*, p. 572. This refers to the 1907 Paris Salon of the Societé Nationale des Beaux-Arts.

137. Chapman, *Leroy Ioas*, p. 15.

138. Harper, *Painting in Canada*, 1977.

139. Bahai Temple Unity, formed in Chicago in March 1909, was the first national Bahá'í institution. Its main purpose was the construction of the Bahá'í House of Worship in Wilmette, Illinois but it soon started to act as the local Bahá'í administration of the area and to provide guidance for the propagation of the Bahá'í Faith. It was elected annually by delegates from the various communities in North America and elsewhere. Standard procedures for electing delegates and the body itself were established later, under the guidance of Shoghi Effendi. In 1925 it was replaced by the National Spiritual Assembly of the Bahá'ís of the United States and Canada. For a history of this development see Smith, 'The American Bahá'í Com-

munity', pp. 85–223; and Bramson-Lerche, 'Some Aspects of the Development of the Bahá'í Administrative Order in America', pp. 255–300, both in Momen, *Studies in Bábí and Bahá'í History*, vol. 1.

140. The Bahá'í House of Worship.

141. Alfred E. Lunt, 'Sixth Annual Convention of Bahai Temple Unity, Chicago, April 25–28, 1914', *Star of the West*, vol. 5, no. 4, pp. 51–5, 58; and no. 5, pp. 69–71.

142. First woman in the Western world to declare her belief in the Bahá'í Faith.

143. American Bahá'í and educator.

144. Cameron, *Transcendentalists in Transition*, p. 210.

145. 'Great Day at the Exhibition: The Art Gallery', *The Standard*, 17 May 1914.

146. 'Records of the Saint John Art Club', New Brunswick Museum Archives, Saint John, N.B., box 4, p. 237.

147. Cameron, *Transcendentalists in Transition*, pp. 213, 216.

148. *Green Acre on the Piscataqua*, p 32.

149. Fragment of a letter written by Bahiyyih Ford, from Durban, South Africa, December? (copy in the author's collection).

150. For the later controversy around Harmon and his teachings see Smith, 'The American Bahá'í Community', pp. 169, 189, 190, 192, 218n in Momen, *Studies in Bábí and Bahá'í History*, vol. 1.

151. Letter of Marion Jack to Helen Goodall, 11, 13 December 1915.

152. See Appendix 1, no. 2.

153. Letter of Marion Jack to Anne Lynch, 24 July 1947. Marion Jack Collection, Bahá'í World Centre Archives.

154. Cora E. Gray, believer from Urbana, Illinois, associated with the Green Acre School Committee.

155. Letter of Eleanor S. Hutchens to the author, 18 November 1981.

156. May Maxwell

157. Chautauqua Institution. This is a system of summer school and correspondence school education founded at Lake

Chautauqua, in northwestern New York state in 1874. It is described as 'a dynamic centre of cultural, educational, and religious thought, where thousands gathered over the summer months'. Garis, *Martha Root: Lioness at the Threshold*, p. 116. It is not know whether Marion Jack went there or whether the Bahá'ís were active there, although Harry Randall and Jináb-i Fáḍil-i Mázandarání spoke there in 1920.

158. Letter to 'My dear Spiritual Brother' [Alfred Lunt?], 17 May 1916. Helen Goodall Papers, United States National Bahá'í Archives.

159. Letter of Marion Jack to Mrs Gregory, 23 December 1916. Canadian National Bahá'í Archives.

160. Letter of John A. Robarts to Marion Jack, 31 October 1951. Canadian National Bahá'í Archives.

161. Edna McKinney, early Chicago Bahá'í (1908), was the chairman of the Green Acre Festival in 1915.

162. An early type of slide projector.

163. 'Records of the Saint John Art Club', Scrap Book no. 2, 15 February 1917, p. 70. [Unidentified newspaper clipping]. New Brunswick Museum Archives, Saint John, N.B.

164. Mary Diana Culver and Henry S. Culver, early American believers in Ireland and New Brunswick. See Armstrong-Ingram, 'Early Irish Bahá'ís', in *Research Notes in Shaykhí, Bábí and Bahá'í Studies*, vol. 2, no. 4, p. 4; and McNamara, 'The Culvers', *Ré Nua (New Day)* (Dublin), vol. 151, July 1998, pp. 2–5. Henry S. Culver also took part in the cultural life of Saint John. The 1917–1918 *Programme* of the Saint John Art Club announced that he was to present a special illustrated lecture entitled 'The Beauty Spots in the Green Isle'.

165. Letter of Marion Jack to an unknown person, March [193–?]. See also letter of Marion Jack to George Townshend, 31 July 1949. Marion Jack Collection, Bahá'í World Centre Archives.

166. Letter of Marion Jack to George Townshend, 31 July 1949. Marion Jack Collection, Bahá'í World Centre Archives.
167. ibid.
168. van den Hoonaard, *Origins of the Bahá'í Community of Canada*, p. 109.
169. This could refer to the Sign O' the Lantern Tea Rooms operated by Miss Mary Louise Culver and Miss Mary Robinson Warner, both Bahá'ís. See van den Hoonaard, *Origins of the Bahá'í Community of Canada*, p. 115.
170. Letter of Marion Jack to Corinne True, 27 February 1919. United States National Bahá'í Archives. For the Harmon incident, see Smith, 'The American Bahá'í Community', in Momen, *Studies in Bábí and Bahá'í History*, vol. 1, pp. 169, 189, 190, 192, 218n.
171. Ober, 'Report of the Tenth Annual Convention of Bahai Temple Unity', *Star of the West*, vol. 9, no. 4, pp. 50–2.
172. Vail, 'The Teaching Campaign', *Star of the West*, vol. 9, no. 16, p. 181. This is mentioned again in Vail, 'The Teaching Campaign', ibid. vol. 10, no. 1, p. 5.
173. van den Hoonaard, *Origins of the Bahá'í Community of Canada*, p. 110.
174. Afnan, 'An Introduction to the Life and Work of Marion Elizabeth Jack 1866–1954', pp. 11, 31.
175. Wyatt, in Kessler, *A Century on Spring Street*, p. 189.
176. Bahai Temple Unity. *Eleventh Annual Mashrekol-Azkar Convention and Bahai Congress*. New York: Bahai Temple Unity, 1919, p. 16.
177. These were first published in Sohrab, *Unveiling of the Divine Plan*; they were later published as *Tablets of the Divine Plan*.
178. 'Abdu'l-Bahá, *Tablets of the Divine Plan*, pp. 31–2.
179. Letter of Marion Jack to May Maxwell, July 1919. Bahai Temple Unity Records, United States National Bahá'í Archives. This is an unsigned typed copy and the original orthography has been maintained.
180. Haney, 'Travelling and Teaching in Alaska', *The Bahá'í Magazine*, vol. 15, no. 7, pp. 210–11.

181. See also Hudson and Kolstoe, 'Alaska: Planting the Seeds of Victory', *Bahá'í News*, August 1981, p. 7.

182. Letter of Marion Jack to 'Very dear brother in the service' [n.d., c. 1951]. Marion Jack Collection, Bahá'í World Centre Archives.

183. Vail, 'The Bahai Movement: Its Spiritual Dynamic'; *Wisdom Talks of Abdul-Baha (Abbas Effendi) at Chicago, Illinois, April 30th to May 5th, 1912*; Masson, *Mashrak-el-Azkar and the Bahai Movement*.

184. MacNutt, *Unity Through Love*; Grundy, *Ten Days in the Light of Acca*.

185. Probably *Compilation of the Holy Utterances of Baha'o'llah and Abdul Baha Concerning the Most Great Peace, War and Duty of the Bahais Towards Their Government*.

186. Alaska Native Brotherhood, an organization of native peoples founded in 1912 in Sitka.

187. 'Big Ben' was the colloquial name of a small, very popular introductory booklet on the Bahá'í Faith developed by Roy Wilhelm in 1917 and later translated into many languages. See Garis, *Martha Root*, pp. 77, 289; photograph p. 78.

188. Letter of Marion Jack to May Maxwell, July 1919. Bahai Temple Unity Records, United States National Bahá'í Archives.

189. Emogene Hoagg, '1919 Alaska', typescript. Ella Robarts Papers. United States National Bahá'í Archives. All the following entries are from this document unless otherwise noted.

190. Church of Christ, Scientist.

191. Charles Mason Remey

192. Ethel Rosenberg

193. Great War Veterans Association

194. Letter from Emogene Hoagg to 'Dear Friend', 15 July 1919, on board the *Julia B.*, Yukon River. Ella Robarts Papers. United States National Bahá'í Archives.

195. Loyal Order of Moose, a fraternal order that sponsors civic and philanthropic endeavours.

196. 'Some New Teachings of Baha'o'llah. Called the Twelve Basic Principles', *The Weekly Star* (Whitehorse), 17 October 1919.

197. The Benevolent and Protective Order of Elks, a charitable and fraternal organization.

198. Wife of the famous Juneau lawyer and US Marshall. Herbert Faulkner established the legal firm of Faulkner Banfield, P.C. in Juneau in 1914.

199. See Hudson and Kolstoe, 'Alaska: Planting the Seeds of Victory', *Bahá'í News*, August 1981, p. 7.

200. A believer from San Francisco also served on the Berkeley Spiritual Assembly.

201. Territorial Governor Thomas Christian Riggs, Jr. (1873–1945).

202. For an account of this trip see Cooper, 'Henrietta Emogene Martin Hoagg, 1869–1945', *Bahá'í World*, vol. 10, pp. 522–3.

203. Wife of the 'Gold Commissioner' of the Yukon, George Patton Mackenzie.

204. Letter of Emogene Hoagg to 'My dear', 14 January 1943. Ella Robarts Papers. United States National Bahá'í Archives.

205. Hudson Stuck (1863–1920), London-born Episcopalian missionary. In 1905 he became the archdeacon of the Yukon. Best known for the first ascent of Mount McKinley with two companions in 1913.

206. 'An Artist's Trip Through Alaska', *The Standard* (Saint John, N.B.), 26 April 1923.

207. Letter of Marion Jack to 'Very dear brother in the service' [n.d., c. 1951]. Marion Jack Collection, Bahá'í World Centre Archives.

208. Presumably the daughter of one of two well-known painters in Vancouver: Charles Edwin Fripp (1854–1936) or his brother Thomas William Fripp (1864–1931), who was also the founder of the British Columbia Society of Fine Arts, in 1908.

209. One of the Gulf Islands in the Strait of Georgia near Powell River, British Columbia, used as an artists' colony and holiday resort.

210. 'Vancouver Sketch Club Takeş Part in Exhibit', *Western Woman's Weekly* (Vancouver), 18 September 1920, vol. 3, no. 41, p. 3.

211. 'Vancouver Sketch Club', *Western Woman's Weekly* (Vancouver), 9 October 1920, vol. 3, no. 44, p. 7.

212. Jináb-i Fáḍil-i Mázandarání

213. Teaching Committee of Nineteen, *Bulletin*, no. 2, pp. 11–12.

214. Teaching Committee of Nineteen, *Bulletin*, no. 3, p. 11.

215. ibid. no. A, p. 14.

216. For the life of this remarkable man, see 'Jináb-i-Fáḍil, 1880(?)–1957', in *Bahá'í World*, vol. 14, pp. 334–6, illus.

217. His lectures were later published as *Lectures Giving the Solution of the World's Problems from a Universal Standpoint*.

218. *Vancouver Sun*, 30 January 1921, p. 32.

219. Teaching Committee of Nineteen, *Bulletin*, no. D, p. 1.

220. Early American Bahá'í

221. A North American organization of men's clubs founded in 1915 to promote community service.

222. Teaching Committee of Nineteen, *Bulletin*, no. D, pp. 6–7.

223. The national Bahá'í directory of 1933–4 lists Austin Collin as the chairman and Rhoda A. Harvey as secretary of the Vancouver Spiritual Assembly. *Bahá'í News*, Supplement November 1933, p. 3.

224. Mrs Christine Monroe passed away in Seattle, Washington, on 26 October 1954.

225. *The Bahá'í Centenary, 1844–1944*, p. 176.

226. Charlotte M. Linfoot, memo to National Bahá'í Archives Committee, 15 June 1964. United States National Bahá'í Archives.

227. Gregory, 'The Thirteenth Mashreq'ul-Azkar Convention and Bahai Congress', *Star of the West*, vol. 12, no. 4, pp. 86 and 90.

228. 'Elfie Lundberg: Memories of the Master's Presence', *The American Bahá'í*, January 1982, p. 17.

229. Letter of Marion Jack to Ella Cooper, 2 April 1922, Royal Alexandria, Winnipeg. United States National Bahá'í Archives.

230. Letter of Marion Jack to Marion Logie, 20 March [194?]. Logie Collection.

231. Letter of R. Jackson Armstrong-Ingram to the author, 8 May 1984.

232. 'Basic Principles of the Bahai Movement: Miss Jack Gives Her Impression of Founder of Universal Religion', *The Hamilton Spectator*, 25 May 1922.

233. 'Bahai News', *Star of the West*, vol. 13, no. 5, pp. 122–3.

234. Wanda Lafurgey Wyatt (1895–1998). Canadian diarist from Prince Edward Island.

235. The Imperial Order Daughters of the Empire was founded in 1900 by Margaret Polson Murray. IODE, as the organization is now known, is a Canadian women's volunteer organization, with a particular focus on children.

236. Kessler, *A Century on Spring Street*, pp. 189–90.

237. 'Fine Art Exhibition Shown in Y.W.C.A. Home: Miss Marion Jack's Work Compares with that of Noted Painters', *Transcript*, 9 November 1922. The same article appeared as 'Exhibit of Art the Work of N.B. Lady Artist', in *Moncton Times*, 9 November 1922.

238. 'An Artist's Trip Through Alaska', *The Standard*, 26 April 1923.

239. 'Records of the Saint John Art Club', Scrap Book no. 2, 15 February 1917, p. 74. New Brunswick Museum Archives, Saint John, N.B.

240. *Green Acre on the Piscataqua*, p. 111; location map on p. 103.

241. Letter of William Sutherland Maxwell to Marion Jack, 21 January 1945. Marion Jack Collection, Bahá'í World Centre Archives. This refers to the paintings that Marion Jack did of some of the Bahá'í Holy Places and which Shoghi Effendi had hung in the main gallery of the Mansion of Bahjí.

242. Quoted in 'Marion Jack', in *Bahá'í World*, vol. 12, p. 659.
243. This was Rev. Cecil (or Claude) Stewart, who later moved to Hamilton, Ontario.
244. van den Hoonaard and Echevarria-Howe, *Black Roses in Canada's Mosaic*, 16 February 1994, p. 7. Internet document: http://bahai-library-org/unpbl.articles/black.roses.html based on letters from Jean E. Nixon in United States National Bahá'í Archives.
245. Letter of Marion Jack to Marion Logie 16(?) September 1948. Logie Collection.
246. *World Fellowship*, vol. 1, no. 9/10, p. 6. This was a loosely-knit Bahá'í international association of children's classes and some children's homes. The international correspondence was maintained by the founder, 'Auntie' Victoria Bedikian.
247. Kessler, *A Century on Spring Street*, p. 191.
248. 'The Group of Seven and Their Contemporaries', McMichael Canadian Art Collection, 2001. Internet document: http://www.mcmichel.on.ca./group.htm
249. Shadbolt, 'A Personal Recollection', *Vancouver: Art and Artists*, quoted in van de Hoonaard, *Origins of the Bahá'í Community of Canada*, pp. 243, 248 n.20. Van den Hoonaard states that he could not find any evidence in the Vancouver Bahá'í Archives to support this assertion.
250. Letter of the secretary [of the National Spiritual Assembly of Canada] to Horace Holley, 13 June 1954. Canadian National Bahá'í Archives.
251. Early Canadian believer, known as the 'mother' of the Toronto Bahá'í community. See van den Hoonaard, *Origin of the Bahá'í Community of Canada*, pp. 101–7.
252. Letter of Laura Rumney Davis to Marion Jack, 8 June 1950. Canadian National Bahá'í Archives.
253. 'Our Dawnbreakers: Miss Marion Jack', *Canadian Bahá'í News*, no. 198, July 1966, p. 4.
254. Bahiyyih (Margaret) Randall-Winckler, daughter of William Henry and Ruth Randall. Pioneered to South

Africa in 1953. In 1968 she was appointed to the Continental Board of Counsellors for Africa.

255. Mrs Louise D. Boyle, early believer active in teaching the Faith in the southern states of the Unites States, c. 1925.

256. Roshan (Amy) Wilkinson, early believer, secretary to William Henry Randall. Also served as secretary of the Boston Assembly.

257. Yúnis Afrukhtih, secretary to 'Abdu'l-Bahá when Marion Jack was in Acre in 1908.

258. *Green Acre on the Piscataqua*, p. 17; photograph p. 69.

259. Laura L. Drum (d. 1938), wife of George Drum. The couple were active believers in the Washington DC community.

260. *Green Acre on the Piscataqua*, p. 17.

261. 'News of the Cause', *Bahá'í News Letter*, no. 10, p. 5.

262. Kessler, *A Century on Spring Street*, p. 190.

263. Bahá'í World Centre Audio-Visual Department, Haifa.

264. Correspondence between George D. Miller and Francis M. Guy, December 1942. United States National Bahá'í Archives.

265. Women's Christian Temperance Union

266. Lorol Schopflocher

267. Margaret Klebs

268. Letter of Marion Jack to Julia Culver, 10 November 1931. Julia Culver Papers, United States National Bahá'í Archives.

269. Letter of Marion Jack to Mrs Charles Tweedie, 11 June 1949. Marion Jack Collection, Bahá'í World Centre Archives.

270. Saichiro Fujita (1886–1976). Japanese Bahá'í.

271. Effie Baker (1880–1968). Australian photographer and early Bahá'í.

272. Letter of Marion Jack to Emma and Louise [Thompson], 21 February 1931. Marion Jack Collection, Bahá'í World Centre Archives.

273. *The Bahá'í Newsletter* (Haifa), March 1931, p. 2. Marion Jack refers to the Bahá'í archives that were housed in a new room built by Shoghi Effendi at the back of the Shrine

of the Báb. Shoghi Effendi later had a special building constructed on Mount Carmel to house these relics.

274. Louise Drake Wright, 'Diary' – 23 February 1931. Louise Drake Wright Papers, United States National Bahá'í Archives.

275. Fourth daughter of 'Abdu'l-Bahá.

276. Shoghi Effendi's cousin. Her mother was Rúḥá Khánum, 'Abdu'l-Bahá's third daughter.

277. Shoghi Effendi's cousin. Her mother was Ṭubá Khánum, 'Abdu'l-Bahá's second daughter.

278. Shoghi Effendi's sister

279. This is a list from Louise Drake Wright's 'Diary' – 26 February 1931. Louise Drake Wright Papers, United States National Bahá'í Archives.

280. *The Bahá'í Newsletter*, March 1931, p. 2.

281. Letter of Marion Jack to Lorol Schopflocher, March 1931. Marion Jack Collection, Bahá'í World Centre Archives.

282. Zahrá Khánum Shahíd

283. Isfandíyár, a Burmese Bahá'í serving in Haifa.

284. Emma and Louise Thompson

285. Mrs Esther Gordon Harding. Early believer from Urbana, Illinois. Served at various times on the National Index, Reviewing and Editorial Committees.

286. Possibly Mary Barton (d. 1957), American believer, later active in South America.

287. Naw-Rúz, the Bahá'í New Year, celebrated 21 March.

288. For a description and history of Shoghi Effendi's family see Taherzadeh, *Covenant of Bahá'u'lláh*, pp. 351–69.

289. Garden of Riḍván, a garden and orchard which was visited frequently by Bahá'u'lláh, about a kilometre from Acre and where several Bahá'í families lived. For a description see Momen, *Basic Bahá'í Dictionary*, pp. 196–8.

290. Letter of Marion Jack to Auntie Victoria [Bedikian], 23 March 1931. United States National Bahá'í Archives. Note that spelling is as in original letter.

291. *The Book of Assurance* (*The Book of Ighan*) by Bahá'u'lláh, translated by Ali Kuli Khan, assisted by Howard MacNutt,

New York, 1924 and 2nd ed. 1929. This was replaced in 1931 by Shoghi Effendi's translation under the title of *The Kitáb-i-Íqán, the Book of Certitude*.

292. Louise Drake Wright, 'Diary'. Louise Drake Wright Papers, United States National Bahá'í Archives.

293. A small grouping of former Bahá'ís associated with Ahmad Sohrab who challenged and worked against the authority of Shoghi Effendi as described in 'Abdu'l-Bahá's Will and Testament.

294. The *Kitáb-i-Aqdas*, Bahá'u'lláh's Most Holy Book.

295. Conference for Inter-Racial Amity, first held in Washington DC as the Convention for Amity between the Colored and White Races in 1921 and later in Green Acre, Maine.

296. Louis and Louisa Gregory, an inter-racial couple. See Morrison, *To Move the World*.

297. Letter of Marion Jack to Emma and Louise [Thompson], n.d. [1931]. Marion Jack Collection, Bahá'í World Centre Archives.

298. Luṭfu'lláh Ḥakím

299. Possibly Mrs Mary Barton.

300. *The Bahá'í Newsletter*, March 1931

301. Letter of Marion Jack to Emma and Louise [Thompson], 21 February 1931, Marion Jack Collection, Bahá'í World Centre Archives.

302. Letter of Marion Jack to Louisa Gregory, 1 March 1931. Marion Jack Collection, Bahá'í World Centre Archives.

303. An agent of the Thomas Cook travel agency.

304. Letter of Marion Jack to Lorol Schopflocher, 10 April 1931, Sofia. Marion Jack Collection, Bahá'í World Centre Archives.

305. 'Abdu'l-Bahá, *Selections*, p. 270.

306. For the whole Tablet see Appendix 1.

307. Shoghi Effendi, *God Passes By*, pp. 252–3. The author wishes to thank the Research Department of the Universal House of Justice for bringing this quotation to his attention.

308. Austria-Hungary in 1916 took in what is today Austria, Hungary, Czech Republic, Slovakia, Slovenia, Bosnia-

Hercegovina, Croatia and parts of Poland, Italy, Romania and Ukraine.

309. 'Abdu'l-Bahá, *Tablets of the Divine Plan*, p. 41. From this list of European countries, Marion Jack travelled to the following either before or after World War I: the British Isles, France, Germany, Austria-Hungary, Italy, Belgium, Switzerland, Serbia and Bulgaria. In addition she travelled to these places in North America, mentioned in other Tablets in the *Tablets of the Divine Plan*: Alaska, Maine, New Hampshire, South Carolina, Massachusetts, New York, Florida, Illinois, Washington, Newfoundland, Prince Edward Island, Nova Scotia, New Brunswick, Quebec, Ontario, Manitoba, British Columbia, Yukon and also to Madeira Islands. For details of the North American areas in which Marion Jack was active as a Bahá'í in response to these Tablets, see chapter 7 above.

310. Stanwood Cobb

311. 'Abdu'l-Bahá

312. Letter of Louisa Gregory to Marion Jack, 28 November 1932, Varna. Marion Jack Collection, Bahá'í World Centre Archives.

313. Pesher, *History of the Bulgarian Trade Unions*.

314. Information on Martha Root's activities in Bulgaria are taken from the biography by Garis, *Martha Root: Lioness at the Threshold* and from Marion Jack's letters, notes and diary entries.

315. Shoghi Effendi, *God Passes By*, p. 386.

316. Sarafov, *Skizo de la Historio de Bulgara Esperanto-Movado*, p. 25. Green is the Esperanto colour.

317. Що е Бахаизьмь? [*Shto e Bahaiz'm?*] София: С & Ж. Карас, [n.d.]. 1 p.

318. Martha Root, quoted in Garis, *Martha Root*, pp. 291–2. The footnote states, 'The paper to which Martha Root referred was the *Tolstoi Journal*, December 1927.'

319. Letter of Marion Jack to Horace Holley, 11 March 1934. Marion Jack Collection, Bahá'í World Centre Archives.

320. Marion Jack Collection, Bahá'í World Centre Archives.

321. Letter of Marion Jack to Horace Holley, 11 March 1934. Marion Jack Collection, Bahá'í World Centre Archives.
322. Hall, *Continuation of 'The Baha'i Dawn: Manchester'*, p. 1.
323. Garis, *Martha Root*, p. 257.
324. Letter of Louisa Gregory to Marion Jack, 6 April 1931. Marion Jack Collection, Bahá'í World Centre Archives.
325. Burgas, a seaside resort on the Black Sea.
326. Louisa Gregory, 'Louise's Report' (c. 1936). Marion Jack Collection, Bahá'í World Centre Archives.
327. Letter of Marion Jack to Louisa Gregory, 19 April 1937. Marion Jack Collection, Bahá'í World Centre Archives. Underscoring hers.
328. Letter of Marion Jack to Ella Robarts, 31 May 1949. Ella Robarts Papers, United States National Bahá'í Archives.
329. Information drawn largely from 'Lina Benke: In Memoriam', *Bahá'í Briefe*, juli 1971, heft 45, p. 1318, illus.; and 'George Adam Benke', *Bahá'í World*, vol. 5, pp. 416–18, illus.
330. Adelbert Mühlschlegel, 'Hermann Grossmann', *Bahá'í World*, vol. 15, p. 417.
331. For Adam Benke's recollections of the Congress see Benke, 'Eidrücke eines Bahá'í von bulgarischen Esperanto-Kongress 1931', in *Sonne der Wahrheit*, September 1931, heft 7, pp. 83–4.
332. Marion Jack Collection.
333. Letter of Marion Jack to Shoghi Effendi, 22 May 1932. Marion Jack Collection, Bahá'í World Centre Archives.
334. Letter of Marion Jack to Thilde Diestelhorst, 6 December 1932. German National Bahá'í Archives.
335. Shoghi Effendi, *Light of Divine Guidance*, vol. 1, p. 263.
336. Letter written on behalf of Shoghi Effendi to Adam and Lina Benke, 17 November 1931. Bahá'í World Centre Archives.
337. The author is only too aware that these notes on the Benkes are fragmentary, incomplete and do not do justice to this exemplary, self-sacrificing couple.

338. Marion Jack, 'Report of Bulgarian Progress' [n.d., 1934?].
Marion Jack Collection, Bahá'í World Centre Archives.

339. Mary Olga Katherine Mills

340. Letter of Marion Jack to Shoghi Effendi, 8 May [1931].
Marion Jack Collection, Bahá'í World Centre Archives.

341. Missionary teacher at the American school in Lovech.
During World War II she went to Turkey and could not
return to Bulgaria.

342. Letter from Marion Jack to Mrs Alyn, 26 December 1937.
Marion Jack Collection, Bahá'í World Centre Archives.

343. The Alexander Nevsky Cathedral, built in the late 1800s
to celebrate the liberation of Bulgaria from the Turks.

344. Letter of Marion Jack to Lorol Schopflocher, 10 April
1931. Marion Jack Collection, Bahá'í World Centre
Archives.

345. Letter of Shoghi Effendi to Marion Jack, 11 July 1931.
Hand-written copy in Marion Jack Collection, Bahá'í
World Centre Archives.

346. International Bahá'í Bureau, Geneva. Established in 1925
by Jean Stannard on the instructions of Shoghi Effendi.
Forerunner of the office of the Bahá'í International
Community.

347. Letter of Marion Jack to Julia Culver, 10 November 1931.
United States National Bahá'í Archives.

348. Letter of Marion Jack to an unknown Bahá'í in South
America, August [194?]. Marion Jack Collection, Bahá'í
World Centre Archives.

349. In the journal *Възраждане* [Vuzrazhdane] (Sofia), 21 March
(12.1931), p. 96. The article consisted of quotations from
the writings of Bahá'u'lláh and 'Abdu'l-Bahá, apparently
translated from the French, and a long article appeared
in the daily paper *Заря* [*Zaria*] (Sofia) on 12 December.

350. This is a chapter from the book *Bahá'u'lláh and the New Era*
by John E. Esslemont.

351. Letter of Marion Jack to Shoghi Effendi, 10 December
1931. Marion Jack Collection, Bahá'í World Centre
Archives.

352. Letter of Marion Jack to Julia Culver, 10 November 1931. United States National Bahá'í Archives.

353. Letter of Effie Baker to Marion Jack, 14 December 1931. Marion Jack Collection, Bahá'í World Centre Archives.

354. Letter of Marion Jack to Julia [Culver?], 8 March [1932]. Marion Jack Collection, Bahá'í World Centre Archives.

355. Letter of Marion Jack to Shoghi Effendi, 17 March 1932. Marion Jack Collection, Bahá'í World Centre Archives.

356. Esslemont, *Баха-у-ллах и новата ера* [*Baha-u-llah i novata era*].

357. Letter written on behalf of Shoghi Effendi to Alexander Lyaptcheov [Lepchev], 27 April 1932. Copy in Marion Jack Collection, Bahá'í World Centre Archives.

358. The small, very popular introductory booklet on the Bahá'í Faith developed by Roy Wilhelm in 1917.

359. Letter of Marion Jack to unknown Bahá'í, c. 1932. Marion Jack Collection, Bahá'í World Centre Archives.

360. For example, there are four letters written during May 1932 to Shoghi Effendi in the Marion Jack Collection, Bahá'í World Centre Archives which were never sent.

361. Letter of Marion Jack to Shoghi Effendi, 30 May 1932. Marion Jack Collection, Bahá'í World Centre Archives.

362. Letter of Marion Jack to Mrs [Thilde] Diestelhorst, 7 November 1932. German National Bahá'í Archives.

363. Victoria Bedikian, Montclair, NJ, circular letter, 16 November 1932. Louise Wright Papers, United States National Bahá'í Archives.

364. Letter of Marion Jack to Ella [Robarts?], 26 February [1933 or 1934]. Marion Jack Collection, Bahá'í World Centre Archives.

365. Marion Jack Collection.

366. This refers to the publishing of the Armenian translation of *Bahá'u'lláh and the New Era*, which was printed in Varna.

367. Letter of Emogene Hoagg to Marion Jack, [1933]. Marion Jack Collection, Bahá'í World Centre Archives.

368. Letter of Marion Jack to Shoghi Effendi, 16 January [1932]. Marion Jack Collection, Bahá'í World Centre Archives.

369. Szanto-Felbermann, *Rebirth*, pp. 82–3.

370. Auguste Forel (1848–1931), early Swiss believer and world-famous scientist.

371. Letter of Marion Jack to Miss Ferry Mawi, 22 August [1933?]. Marion Jack Collection, Bahá'í World Centre Archives.

372. Marion Jack, quoted in 'Hungary', *Bulletin International Bahá'í Bureau*, circular 15 (9 May 1934), p. 3.

373. Letter of Marion Jack to Martha Root, 11 June [1933]. Marion Jack Collection, Bahá'í World Centre Archives.

374. Root, in *Bahá'í World*, vol. 5, pp. 581–3.

375. Garis, *Martha Root*, p. 394.

376. Root, 'A Visit to Adrianople', *Bahá'í World*, vol. 5, p. 593.

377. Root, 'Seeing Adrianople with New York Eyes', *Bahá'í Magazine*, vol. 25, no. 3, pp. 74–5.

378. ibid. p. 75.

379. *Bahá'í Newsletter*, December 1931, p. 3.

380. The Russo-Turkish War of 1877–8.

381. Letter of Marion Jack to Dr and Mrs Fozdar, 10 October 1936. Marion Jack Collection, Bahá'í World Centre Archives.

382. Should read Turnovo, a shorted form of Veliko Turnovo.

383. Ruse

384. Kemal Atatürk, President of the Republic of Turkey.

385. Letter of Marion Jack to Charles Mason Remey; in Remey, *Baha'i Reminiscences*, vol. 48.

386. Persian believer, secretary of the Unity Committee of the East and West of the Tehran Spiritual Assembly. Travelled widely in Europe and America in the 1930s.

387. Letter of Marion Jack to 'Dearest Friends in El Abha', 6 April [1934]; the postscript is dated 30 May. Marion Jack Collection, Bahá'í World Centre Archives.

388. Letter of Marion Jack to Marzieh Carpenter [Gail], 10 April 1934. Marion Jack Collection, Bahá'í World Centre Archives.

389. Letter of Marion Jack to Horace Holley, 11 March 1934. Marion Jack Collection, Bahá'í World Centre Archives.

390. Letter of Marion Jack to Philip Sprague, 21 March 1934. Marion Jack Collection, Bahá'í World Centre Archives.

391. Letter of Marion Jack to Horace Holley, 11 March 1934. Marion Jack Collection, Bahá'í World Centre Archives.

392. Letter of Louisa Gregory to Marion Jack, 15 June 1934. Marion Jack Collection, Bahá'í World Centre Archives.

393. 'Abdu'l-Ḥusayn Khán Na'ímí

394. 'Bulgaria', *International Bahá'í Bureau Bulletin*, no. 16 (June 1934).

395. ibid.

396. Letter of Marion Jack to Martha Root, 11 June [1934]. Marion Jack Collection, Bahá'í World Centre Archives.

397. Letter of Marion Jack to an unknown German believer (c. 1934). Marion Jack Collection, Bahá'í World Centre Archives.

398. Letter of Marion Jack to Shoghi Effendi, (1935?). Marion Jack Collection, Bahá'í World Centre Archives.

399. Jack, 'Report of Bulgarian Progress'. Marion Jack Collection, Bahá'í World Centre Archives.

400. From a letter written on behalf of Shoghi Effendi, 30 September 1934. Shoghi Effendi, in *Unfolding Destiny*, p. 98.

401. Anna Koestlin

402. Petar Yordanov

403. Austrian believer (d. 1935) in Salzburg. She was taught the Faith by Louisa Gregory.

404. Mme Hess translated *Paris Talks* into French.

405. Joséphine Scott

406. Margaret Lentz

407. Alice Schwartz-Solivo

408. Letter of Marion Jack to Charles Mason Remey, 29 August [1934] in Remey, *Baha'i Reminiscences*, vol. 49.

409. Letter of Emogene Hoagg to Charles Mason Remey, 4 September 1934, in ibid.

410. Letter of Marion Jack to Kennedy, [1935]. Marion Jack Collection, Bahá'í World Centre Archives.

411. Jeanne Bolles Chute (d. 1997), American believer. Later active in Argentina and Virginia. Passed away in Denmark.

412. Letter of Marion Jack to C. N. Kennedy, (1 May 193?). Marion Jack Collection, Bahá'í World Centre Archives.

413. This would have been the Romanian translation of *Bahá'u-'lláh and the New Era*.

414. Princess Ileana, daughter of Queen Marie of Romania. See Garis, *Martha Root*, pp. 288–9, illustration.

415. Diary of Marion Jack. Marion Jack Collection, Bahá'í World Centre Archives.

416. Diary of Marion Jack. Marion Jack Collection, Bahá'í World Centre Archives.

417. Diary of Marion Jack. Marion Jack Collection, Bahá'í World Centre Archives.

418. Letter of Marion Jack to Anne Lynch, n.d. [late 1940s?]. Marion Jack Collection, Bahá'í World Centre Archives.

419. 'Babism' and 'Bab', in Danchov and Danchov, *Българска Енциклопедия* [Bulgarska entsiklopediia], p. 94.

420. Letter of Marion Jack to Nellie French, 18 July 1937. Marion Jack Collection, Bahá'í World Centre Archives.

421. Letter of Marion Jack [to a friend in Green Acre], 5 October 1937. Marion Jack Collection, Bahá'í World Centre Archives.

422. Letter of Marion Jack to Emogene Hoagg, 5 October 1937. Marion Jack Collection, Bahá'í World Centre Archives.

423. Letter of Marion Jack to Nellie French, 18 July 1937. Marion Jack Collection, Bahá'í World Centre Archives.

424. Letter of Marion Jack to Marta Weys, 9 November 1937. Marion Jack Collection, Bahá'í World Centre Archives.

425. Letter of Marion Jack to Shoghi Effendi, [1938]. Marion Jack Collection, Bahá'í World Centre Archives.

426. Fragment of a letter from Marion Jack, written c. 1937. Marion Jack Collection, Bahá'í World Centre Archives.

427. Letter of Marion Jack to Jeanne Bolles, 6 June 1937. Marion Jack Collection, Bahá'í World Centre Archives.

428. Bahá'u'lláh. Скритиђ слова на Баха'у'лахь [*Skritit Slova na Baha'u'lah*]. Translation of *The Hidden Words of Bahá'u-'lláh*.

429. Letter of Marion Jack to Marion Logie, 11 December 1937. Logie Collection.

430. Letter of Marion Jack to Shoghi Effendi, 12 February 1938. Marion Jack Collection, Bahá'í World Centre Archives.

431. Letter of Marion Jack to Emogene Hoagg, 17 October 1938. United States National Bahá'í Archives.

432. Letter of Marion Jack to friends resident in Green Acre, 15 August 1938. Marion Jack Collection, Bahá'í World Centre Archives.

433. Letter of Marion Jack to Louise Hubbard, 21 March 1939. Marion Jack Collection, Bahá'í World Centre Archives.

434. Letter of Marion Jack to Ella (Robarts?), 22 June 1939. Marion Jack Collection, Bahá'í World Centre Archives.

435. Letter of Marion Jack to Rúḥíyyih Khánum, 4 November 1939. Marion Jack Collection, Bahá'í World Centre Archives.

436. Letter of Marion Jack to Marie (Hopper?), July–August 1939. Marion Jack Collection, Bahá'í World Centre Archives.

437. Unfinished note of Marion Jack, Friday, 10 November 1939. Marion Jack Collection, Bahá'í World Centre Archives.

438. Letter of Marion Jack to Shoghi Effendi, 1 July 1939. Marion Jack Collection, Bahá'í World Centre Archives.

439. Letter of Marion Jack to Marion Logie, 23 November 1939. Logie Collection.

440. Gustave Lowe quoted in Jasion, *Marion Jack – Immortal Heroine*, pp. 4–5.

441. Letter of Marion Jack to 'Très Chères Amies', 3 Septembre 1940. Marion Jack Collection, Bahá'í World Centre Archives.

442. Letter of Marion Jack to Louise Hubbard July 28 1941. Marion Jack Collection, Bahá'í World Centre Archives.

443. From a letter written on behalf of Shoghi Effendi to an individual believer, 9 November 1931. 'Eastern Europe and the Soviet Union', in *Bahá'í Studies Review*, vol. 3, no. 1 (1993), p. 104.

444. From a letter written on behalf of Shoghi Effendi to Marion Jack, 19 November 1931. Marion Jack Collection, Bahá'í World Centre Archives.

445. Shoghi Effendi's personal postscript to ibid. Quoted in *Quickeners of Mankind*, p. 154.

446. From a letter written on behalf of Shoghi Effendi to an individual believer, 11 November 1931. 'Eastern Europe and the Soviet Union', in *Bahá'í Studies Review*, vol. 3, no. 1 (1993), p. 104.

447. 'Say,' Bahá'u'lláh Himself declares in the Súriy-i-Ra'ís, 'this Youth hath departed out of this country and deposited beneath every tree and every stone a trust, which God will erelong bring forth through the power of truth.' Quoted in Shoghi Effendi, *God Passes By*, p. 181.

448. From a letter written on behalf of Shoghi Effendi to the Bahá'ís of Sofia, 11 November 1931. 'Eastern Europe and the Soviet Union', in *Bahá'í Studies Review*, vol. 3, no. 1 (1993), p. 105.

449. From a letter written on behalf of Shoghi Effendi to Marion Jack, 30 July 1932, in *Quickeners of Mankind*, p. 153.

450. Letter of Shoghi Effendi to Marion Jack, 30 July 1932. Marion Jack Collection, Bahá'í World Centre Archives.

451. Letter of Shoghi Effendi to Marion Jack, 30 July 1932. Marion Jack Collection, Bahá'í World Centre Archives.

452. Esslemont, *Bahá'u'lláh and the New Era*, translated into Bulgarian and published in 1932 by the International Bahá'í Bureau in Geneva.

453. From a letter written on behalf of Shoghi Effendi to an individual believer, 31 October 1932. 'Eastern Europe and the Soviet Union', in *Bahá'í Studies Review*, vol. 3, no. 1 (1993), p. 105.

454. The 6th Jugoslavia Esperanto-Kongress, 4–5 June 1933.

455. From a letter written on behalf of Shoghi Effendi to Marion Jack, 14 March 1933. Marion Jack Collection, Bahá'í World Centre Archives.

456. Shoghi Effendi's postscript to the above letter.

457. Louisa Gregory, Marion Jack and Martha Root

458. From a letter written on behalf of Shoghi Effendi to an individual believer, 30 April 1933. 'Eastern Europe and the Soviet Union', in *Bahá'í Studies Review*, vol. 3, no. 1 (1993), pp. 102–3.

459. From a letter written on behalf of Shoghi Effendi to an individual believer, 17 September 1933. ibid. pp. 105–6.

460. From a letter written on behalf of Shoghi Effendi to the Summer School in Esslingen, 1 October 1933. In Shoghi Effendi, *Light of Divine Guidance*, vol. pp. 52–3.

461. From a letter written on behalf of Shoghi Effendi to an individual believer, 5 October 1933. 'Eastern Europe and the Soviet Union', in *Bahá'í Studies Review*, vol. 3, no. 1 (1993), p. 106.

462. From a letter written on behalf of Shoghi Effendi to Marion Jack, 17 November 1933. Marion Jack Collection, Bahá'í World Centre Archives.

463. Shoghi Effendi's postscript to the above letter.

464. From a letter written on behalf of Shoghi Effendi to the Bahá'ís of Sofia, 1 December 1933. Bahá'í World Centre Archives.

465. Shoghi Effendi's postscript to the above letter.

466. From a letter written on behalf of Shoghi Effendi to Marion Jack, 6 June 1934. Marion Jack Collection, Bahá'í World Centre Archives.

467. Shoghi Effendi's postscript to the above letter.

468. From a letter written on behalf of Shoghi Effendi to Marion Jack, 4 October 1934. Marion Jack Collection, Bahá'í World Centre Archives.

469. Shoghi Effendi's postscript to the above letter.

470. From a letter written on behalf of Shoghi Effendi to Marion Jack, 29 May 1937. Marion Jack Collection, Bahá'í World Centre Archives.

471. Shoghi Effendi's postscript to the above letter.
472. Rabbaní, *Priceless Pearl*, pp. 126–7.
473. From a letter written on behalf of Shoghi Effendi to Marion Jack, 18 November 1939. Marion Jack Collection, Bahá'í World Centre Archives.
474. Shoghi Effendi's postscript to the above letter.
475. Rachev, *Anglo-Bulgarian Relations during the Second World War (1939–1944)*, p. 151.
476. Marion Jack, 'Diary'. Marion Jack Collection, Bahá'í World Centre Archives.
477. Letter of Marion Jack to Neneva Rozeva, 15 and 26 April [1944]. Pordim. Marion Jack Collection, Bahá'í World Centre Archives.
478. Rachev, *Anglo-Bulgarian Relations during the Second World War (1939–1944)*, pp. 153–4.
479. English-Speaking League (E.S.L.), an association established to promote international understanding and human achievement through the use of English.
480. Refers to two patriotic songs, the first American, the second Canadian. Letter of Marion Jack to Marion Logie, 16 May 1945. Logie Collection.
481. Letter of Marion Jack to Neneva Rozeva, 20 March [1944]. Pordim. Marion Jack Collection, Bahá'í World Centre Archives.
482. Letter of Marion Jack to her niece, 16 May 1945. Logie Collection. Quoted in *Quickeners of Mankind*, p. 126.
483. Letter of Marion Jack to Marion Logie, 16 May 1945. Logie Collection.
484. ibid.
485. Letter of Marion Jack to Louisa Gregory, 20–1 November 1948. Marion Jack Collection, Bahá'í World Centre Archives.
486. Letter of Marion Jack to Victoria Bedekian, 4 May 1949. Marion Jack Collection, Bahá'í World Centre Archives.
487. Letter of Marion Jack to Mrs Leslie [n.d., c. 1945]. Marion Jack Collection, Bahá'í World Centre Archives.

488. Letter of Rúḥíyyih Khánum to Marion Jack, 20 July 1946. Marion Jack Collection, Bahá'í World Centre Archives.
489. Letter of Rúḥíyyih Khánum to Marion Jack, 25 June 1947. Marion Jack Collection, Bahá'í World Centre Archives.
490. ibid.
491. Louise Hubbard, sister of Marion Jack.
492. Letter of Marion Jack to [Florence] Lorol Schopflocher, 21 August 1947. Marion Jack Collection, Bahá'í World Centre Archives.
493. Marion Jack, quoted in Jasion, *Marion Jack: Immortal Pioneer*, p. 11.
494. Letter of Marion Jack to Rúḥíyyih Khánum, [1950s]. Marion Jack Collection, Bahá'í World Centre Archives.
495. Letter of Marion Jack to Marion Logie, 24 April 1947. Logie Collection.
496. Letter of Marion Jack to Marion Logie, 24 April 1947. Logie Collection.
497. Quoted in a letter of Marion Jack to the National Spiritual Assembly of the Bahá'ís of the United States and Canada, 31 August 1947. Marion Jack Collection, Bahá'í World Centre Archives.
498. Letter of Marion Jack to Miss Voelz [late 1947 or early 1948]. Marion Jack Collection, Bahá'í World Centre Archives.
499. Letter of Marion Jack to Philip Sprague, 18 October 1948. Marion Jack Collection, Bahá'í World Centre Archives.
500. Letter of Marion Jack to Marion Logie, May 1950. Logie Collection.
501. Letter of Marion Jack to Louise Hubbard, 19 March 1951. Logie Collection.
502. Letter of Marion Jack to Marion Logie, 17 July 1951. Logie Collection.
503. Letter of Marion Jack to 'My dearest sister in El Abha (in Scotland)', 1 April 1948. Marion Jack Collection, Bahá'í World Centre Archives.
504. Letter of Marion Jack to Marion Logie [195?]. Marion Jack Collection, Bahá'í World Centre Archives.

505. Edward Beadle 'Saffa' Kinney
506. Letter of Marion Jack to Rúḥíyyih Khánum [late 1940s?]. Marion Jack Collection, Bahá'í World Centre Archives.
507. Letter of Marion Jack to Marion Logie, 25 September 1951. Logie Collection.
508. Letter of Marion Jack to Marion Logie, 25 May 1953. Logie Collection.
509. Drew Edwards; Louisa and Louis Gregory; Emma and Louise Thompson; Edith ___; Dorothy ___; Marie Hopper; Grace Robarts Ober.
510. Letter of Marion Jack to Ella Robarts, 31 May 1949. Ella Robarts Papers, United States National Bahá'í Archives.
511. Letter of Marion Jack to Marion Logie, 16 May 1945. Logie Collection. Quoted in *Quickeners of Mankind*, p. 126.
512. Letter of Marion Jack to Ella Robarts, 2 January 1946. Ella Robarts Papers, United States National Bahá'í Archives.
513. CARE = Cooperative for American Relief Everywhere, Inc.; a federation of United States charities giving financial and technical assistance to many regions of the world.
514. Letter of Marion Jack to Louisa Gregory, 20–1 November 1948. Marion Jack Collection, Bahá'í World Centre Archives.
515. Letter of Marion Jack to unknown Bahá'í, 22 September 1947. Marion Jack Collection, Bahá'í World Centre Archives.
516. Letter of Marion Jack to Alma Woodruff, n.d. [c. 1946]. Marion Jack Collection, Bahá'í World Centre Archives.
517. Letter of Marion Jack to Louise Hubbard, August 1947. Marion Jack Collection, Bahá'í World Centre Archives.
518. Letter of Marion Jack to Lauretta E. Voelz, 9 March 1949. Marion Jack Collection, Bahá'í World Centre Archives.
519. Letter of Marion Jack to Miss Rozeva, 2–7 September [1944], Pordim. Marion Jack Collection, Bahá'í World Centre Archives.
520. Letter of Marion Jack to Marion Logie, 14 December 1948. Logie Collection.

521. Letter of Marion Jack to Ella Robarts, 2 January 1946. United States National Bahá'í Archives.

522. Letter of Marion Jack to Marion Logie, 25 February [194?]. Logie Collection.

523. Letter of Marion Jack to Marion Logie, 5 May [194?]. Logie Collection.

524. Letter of Marion Jack to Ella Robarts, 2 December 1945. Ella Robarts Papers, United States National Bahá'í Archives.

525. Letter of Marion Jack to Margaret Lentz, September 1946. Marion Jack Collection, Bahá'í World Centre Archives.

526. Anne Lynch

527. Second Seven Year Plan of the United States and Canada (1946–53)

528. Rúḥíyyih Khánum to Marion Jack, 20 July 1946. Marion Jack Collection, Bahá'í World Centre Archives.

529. Early Bulgarian believer. In other documents spelled Züssman.

530. Trojan = Troyan. City in central Bulgaria, east of Sofia.

531. 'Bulgaria', *Geneva Bureau News Exchange* (March 1947), pp. 1–2.

532. Stanwood Cobb. *Security for a Failing World.*

533. 'Bulgaria', *Geneva Bureau News Exchange* (June 1947), p. 2.

534. 'Bulgaria', *Geneva Bureau News Exchange* (November 1947–March 1948), p. 1.

535. Letter of Marion Jack to Marion Logie, 17 July 1951. Logie Collection.

536. Letter of Marion Jack to Anna Lynch, June–July 1947. Marion Jack Collection, Bahá'í World Centre Archives.

537. Letter of Marion Jack to Louisa Gregory, 20–1 November 1948. Marion Jack Collection, Bahá'í World Centre Archives.

538. Letter of Marion Jack to Jessie Revell, 20 June 1953. Marion Jack Collection, Bahá'í World Centre Archives.

539. Letter of Marion Jack to Fred Hubbard, 13 July 1952. Marion Jack Collection, Bahá'í World Centre Archives.

540. Letter of Marion Jack to Marion Logie, 16(?) September 1948. Logie Collection.

541. Letter of Marion Jack to Ella Robarts, 2 January 1946. United States National Bahá'í Archives.

542. Remark of Shoghi Effendi, 22 January 1940, quoted in Rabbani, *Priceless Pearl*, p. 161.

543. Cable of Shoghi Effendi to the National Spiritual Assembly of the United States and Canada, 16 April 1941, in 'Messages to the National Spiritual Assembly', *Bahá'í News*, no. 143 (May 1941), p. 1.

544. Letter written on behalf of Shoghi Effendi to Marion Jack, 23 January 1945. Marion Jack Collection, Bahá'í World Centre Archives.

545. Shoghi Effendi, postscript to the above letter.

546. Letter of Shoghi Effendi to Marion Jack, 10 April 1947. Marion Jack Collection, Bahá'í World Centre Archives [copy].

547. Shoghi Effendi, quoted in Jasion, *Marion Jack: Immortal Heroine* [1975], p. 7.

548. From a letter written on behalf of Shoghi Effendi to the National Assembly, 8 November 1948, in 'Marion Jack', *Bahá'í News*, no. 216 (February 1949), p. 1.

549. Shoghi Effendi, *Messages to Canada*, p. 22.

550. Cable of Shoghi Effendi to the National Spiritual Assembly of the United States, 8 October 1952. United States National Bahá'í Archives.

551. Marguerite Sears, 'Marguerite Sears' Pilgrim Notes Taken during March 1953 at Haifa.' Photocopy of typescript. Author's papers.

552. Refers to a line from 'O Canada', the Canadian national anthem.

553. Letter of Marion Jack to N. Rozeva, 11 October 1944, Pordim. Marion Jack Collection, Bahá'í World Centre Archives.

554. Letter of Marion Jack to Marion Logie, 16 May 1945. Logie Collection.

555. Letter of Marion Jack to Marion Logie, 5 March 1947. Logie Collection. Quoted in *Quickeners of Mankind*, p. 127.

556. Letter of Marion Jack to Marion Logie, 24 April 1947. Logie Collection.

557. Letter of Marion Jack to Fred Schopflocher, 28 October 1951. Marion Jack Collection, Bahá'í World Centre Archives.

558. Second Bahá'í European Teaching Conference, Brussels, 5–7 August 1949.

559. Letter of Marion Jack to Ella Robarts, 31 May 1949. United States National Bahá'í Archives.

560. Letter of Marion Jack to her niece, 25 September 1951. Quoted in *Quickeners of Mankind*, p. 128.

561. Bahá'í Intercontinental Conference, Stockholm, Sweden, July 1953.

562. Letter of Marion Jack to Shoghi Effendi, [n.d., probably 1952]. Marion Jack Collection, Bahá'í World Centre Archives.

563. Letter of Marion Jack to Marion Logie, 7 May 1951. Logie Collection.

564. Grace Fernyhough, 'Statement by Mrs Grace Fernyhough, who knew Miss Marion Jack in Bulgaria', Stanley, Falkland Islands, 1986. Copy in author's collection.

565. ibid.

566. Quoted in Jasion, *Marion Jack: Immortal Heroine* [1985], p. 12.

567. Reprinted in Jasion, *Marion Jack: Immortal Heroine*, p. 13. It was published first as Shoghi Effendi, 'Immortal Heroine', *Bahá'í News*, no. 278 (April 1954), pp. 1–2.

568. From a letter written on behalf of Shoghi Effendi to the European Teaching Committee, 24 May 1954, in Jasion, *Marion Jack: Immortal Heroine* [1975], pp. 5–6.

569. From a letter written on behalf of Shoghi Effendi, 17 June 1954, in *Unfolding Destiny*, p. 336.

570. From a letter written on behalf of Shoghi Effendi, 25 June 1954, in *Light of Divine Guidance*, p. 217.

571. Shoghi Effendi, *Messages to Canada*, p. 58.

572. 'Monument Erected in Sofia to Immortal Bahá'í Heroine', *Bahá'í News*, no. 324 (February 1958), p. 6.

573. Bahá'u'lláh, *Gleanings*, p. 280.

574. Bahá'u'lláh, *Seven Valleys*, p. 34.

575. *'Abdu'l-Bahá in London*, pp. 48–9.

576. 'Abdu'l-Bahá, in 'Marion Jack', *Star of the West*, vol. 10, no. 1 (21 March 1919), pp. 7–8.

577. Mrs Catherine Burke (b. 1851). See Armstrong-Ingram, 'Early Irish Bahá'ís', *Research Notes in Shaykhí, Bábi and Bahá'í Studies*, vol. 2, no. 4 (July 1998), p. 5. Internet document: http://h-net.msu.edu/-bahai/notes/vol2/irish.htm

578. Addressed c/o Mrs Lundberg, 3937 Clarendon Ave., Chicago; copy in Ella Robarts Papers, United States National Bahá'í Archives.

579. Bahá'u'lláh, *Gleanings*, p. 139.

580. 'Abdu'l-Bahá, *Selections*, pp. 270–4.

581. Morgan, *Dominion Annual Register and Review*, p. 194.

582. Birmingham Royal Society of Artists. *Autumn Exhibition Catalogue*, 1898, pp. 49, 51, 56.

583. Birmingham Royal Society of Artists. *Autumn Exhibition Catalogue*, 1899, pp. 41, 50, 58, 64.

584. Birmingham Royal Society of Artists. *Autumn Exhibition Catalogue*, 1901, pp. 40–1.

585. Birmingham Royal Society of Artists. *Autumn Exhibition Catalogue*, 1902, pp. 28, 43, 81.

586. Allaire, 'Les Artistes Canadiens', p. 101, in Afnan, 'Introduction to the Life and Work', p. 34.

587. ibid.

588. ibid.

589. Morgan, *Canadian Men and Women of the Times*, p. 572.

590. ibid.

591. Royal Canadian Academy of Arts, *Catalogue 1908: Twenty-ninth Annual Exhibition*.

592. McMann, *Montreal Museum of Fine Arts*, p. 188.

593. Dominion Exhibition, *Catalogue*.

594. The Art Association of Montreal, *Catalogue of the Thirtieth Spring Exhibition, 1913*.

595. Royal Canadian Academy of Arts, *Catalogue of the Thirty-sixth Annual Exhibition.*

596. The Art Association of Montreal, *Catalogue of the Thirty-first Spring Exhibition, 1914.*

597. Provincial Exhibition, St. John, N.B., September 5 to 12, 1914.

598. The Art Association of Montreal, *Catalogue of the Thirty-second Spring Exhibition, 1915.*

599. The Art Association of Montreal, *Catalogue of the Thirty-third Spring Exhibition, 1916.*

600. Saint John Art Club, *Programme 1917–1918.*

601. Aidun, 'Let Us Turn Our Gaze to General Jack – The Immortal Heroine and Artist,' Conference paper, Association for Bahá'í Studies, 1986, p. 6, in Afnan, 'Introduction to the Life and Work', p. 31.

602. Hoagg, '1919 Alaska', Ella Robarts Papers, United States National Bahá'í Archives.

603. British Columbia Society of Fine Arts, *Annual Exhibition . . . September 18th to 25th, 1920.*

604. 'Vancouver Sketch Club Takes Part in Exhibit', *Western Women's Weekly*, vol. 3, no. 41 (18 September 1920), p. 3.

605. 'Vancouver Sketch Club', *Western Women's Weekly*, vol. 3, no. 44 (9 October 1920), p. 7.

606. 'Fine Art Exhibition Shown in Y.W.C.A. Home: Miss Marion Jack's Work Compares with that of Noted Painters', *Transcript* (9 November 1922).

607. Kessler, *Century on Spring Street*, p. 189–90.

608. 'An Artist's Trip Through Alaska', *The Standard*, 26 April 1923.

609. Saint John Art Club, *Saint John Art Club 50th Anniversary.*

610. G. Pelletier, to the author, 26 May 1983.

611. Parts I-VI of this list are reproduced with slight modifications with the kind permission of Nooshfar Afnan. 'An Introduction to the Life and Work of Marion Elizabeth Jack 1866–1954', pp. 37–42.

Index